# IT ALL COUNTS

## Carol Vorderman

**WINDSOR**

**PARAGON**

First published 2010
by Headline Review
This Large Print edition published 2011
by AudioGO Ltd
by arrangement with
Headline Publishing Group

Hardcover  ISBN: 978 1 408 46020 7
Softcover   ISBN: 978 1 408 46021 4

**British Library Cataloguing in Publication Data available**

Printed and bound in Great Britain by
CPI Antony Rowe, Chippenham and Eastbourne

# IT ALL COUNTS

# CONTENTS

# ACKNOWLEDGEMENTS

I didn't realize just how much work it would take to put this book together.

Write your autobiography? Well, it can't be that difficult surely? Remember some stories and put them down on paper? Not so.

It's taken many months and many attempts, a swimming pool of tea, and a lot of tears at times. One chapter still breaks me no matter how often I read it. So thanks to everyone who's assisted.

Special thanks to Amanda Cable, who helped to write the book, and listened to me droning on for hours about things that never made the final cut. Also to Amanda's children Ruby, Charlie and Archie for not interrupting when we were deep in conversation. I'd still be writing Chapter Three if it wasn't for Amanda. Thank you.

Thanks also to Carly Cook, my editor, for working her socks off and for her support.

I really have to thank my family for reminding me of some of the bits that had slipped from my memory banks. To my Mum, my sister Trixie, and my brother Anton. To Trixie's husband Meirion for not minding all the early morning emails to my sis (usually before 6am).

To my children—Cameron who was the 'tea slave' for months and to Katie, who is the best cook in our house.

To my former husband Paddy who has been most gracious.

To John Miles as ever, and to Mandy Berry, his ace PA and to Viv in the office, for searching through endless contracts in the archives and notes and records. To Lyn, John's wife, for taking pity on me and feeding me when my head was too buzzy.

To Des Kelly for helping me through some tough bits.

My stepbrother Arthur Rizzi and his wife Elaine for enjoying the stories about Gabriel (Dad). Elinor Pritchard and her mum Aunty Dorothy for those times too.

Thanks to Mr Jemmett and his wife Joan and Mr Ashworth for checking it all out.

To Rick Vanes for laughing about the early years of *Countdown*, of which he was such a big part.

To Kathy Apanowicz, Richard Whiteley's partner, for reading through all of it twice and loving the bits about Richard. It can't have been easy.

To Clare Pizey who has been a great friend and boss for many years. Top woman.

For Will Hanrahan for reminding me of all the funny times we shared on a hundred shows together. He's from Liverpool, but I forgive him for that on a regular basis. And thanks to Gillian Mary, "the woman he married", for making him find the photos.

To Peter Willis, Mr Pride of Britain.

To Grant Mansfield who has always been supportive.

To Karen Cleverley, my PA, who makes me laugh daily and is one of the most patient people I know. Thanks, Karen.

To Amanda Bell who runs The Maths Factor for

allowing me all the time off work to write the book.

To my friend Mandy Prowse, who constantly told me how c**p I was, and then fed me cakes and coffee. You're funny and obviously a nightmare too!!

To Simon Smith who has checked the manuscript thoroughly quite a few times over.

For all those I haven't been in contact with for a long time who leapt to help and remind me of my more embarrassing moments!!

For Katie and Cameron,
who own my heart.
I love you.
X

# JUST THE FOUR OF US

I was born on Christmas Eve, 1960—and my mother's life fell apart just 21 days later. It would be 20 years before I made her burn with pride and a further 20 years before I met my father.

The shattering of my mother's life happened one evening, once I had been fed and settled and my older brother Anton and sister Trixie lay sleeping peacefully in their beds.

How contented my mum must have felt as she kissed everyone goodnight. She was desperately proud of her tidy three-bedroom home on a new-build estate in Bedford, where her life revolved around her family. A surprise third baby, me, had been a delightful if unplanned addition, and life seemed very sweet indeed.

Mum was lying in bed next to my father, Tony Vorderman, when he turned and told her that he had some news. And then, in three short phrases, he tore her life, and our lives, apart. 'I've met someone. I love her and I want to be with her.'

The affair—the betrayal—had been going on as I was growing in my mother's womb. To add to her pain, she later realised that she had even been conned into meeting the mother of the girl who was destroying her family. My father was 40 at the time, and the girl with whom he was having the affair was 16.

The girl's mother, who had cooked for my father while Mum was in hospital, knew of the affair and approved of it, and so when my mum came home a week after giving birth to me, Tony begged her to

1

come and meet the 'kindly' neighbour who he claimed had been looking after him so well. My brother and sister were back in North Wales being cared for by our grandparents so my father had been free to do as he pleased.

This 'wonderful' lady had made him meals every day, he enthused. It was only right and proper that my mum should thank the woman for her kindness.

It seemed so important to him that Mum even went out and had her hair done so she looked nice. She went with my father and ate tinned salmon and cucumber sandwiches, drank tea and passed the time of day.

Always polite, my mother thanked the lady for everything she had done. She never thought for one second that the hospitality had extended to a full-blown affair with the woman's teenage daughter.

So when she lay in bed—so stunned by my father's news that she could hardly speak—the full impact of his cheating hit her. She determined in that instant that family life as she knew it was over. There was no going back. He had played around and caused traumas before.

For years, my mother felt too distressed to tell anyone the details of what happened, and she didn't tell me about the affair until I was 15. She never spoke badly of my father while I was growing up, but she didn't need to. His actions since that day, or lack of them, spoke louder than any words could. In turn, I have only told those closest to me until now, but it is impossible to tell my story without sharing my beginning.

My father's total rejection of me, which continued for decades, has had an impact throughout my life. I never told my mother how I felt, because it might have made her wonder if she wasn't enough, and so those feelings remained unspoken. But it has driven me to try to prove myself time after time, to be better, to do more, to work harder, to give my mum back the self-respect she felt she had lost. Mum and I have lived together all my life; she is a huge part of my everyday and I would do anything for her.

*     *     *

Back in January 1961, when my father dropped his bombshell, Mum could only think of getting back to her own parents as fast as she could, for comfort.

The following morning, once she had fed all the children and changed me, she rang the farm in Prestatyn, in North Wales, where my grandparents lived, and told her mother what had happened.

Two days later, on a grey and miserable day, Tony Vorderman drove his whole family to the nearest station to dump them. Nothing was said, no tearful, long-drawn-out goodbyes exchanged. Trixie and Anton, who were then aged nine and seven, were told that they were being taken on a trip. My mother remembers that my father seemed utterly relieved that we were all going. As the train pulled away, he turned abruptly and left. It was the last time my father and I had anything to do with each other until I was in my 40s.

During the next couple of years, Tony Vorderman would occasionally drive up to North Wales to see my brother and sister. But on these visits he refused to have anything to do with me.

He wouldn't hold me. He never cuddled me or kissed me or stroked my head. It was as if I didn't exist.

My mother clearly remembers one instance when Trixie and Anton were being driven off in the back of Tony's big, posh Jaguar, waving out of the window, both clearly puzzled why their baby sister wasn't coming too. He'd come to collect them from school to take them out for tea. Mum was there for the handover and I was in a big, old-fashioned pushchair. She needed to get home to feed me, but he wouldn't give us a lift, so she pushed me back up the street to the bus stop and felt, in that instant, a crashing sense of loneliness. I was a happy baby and was kicking and laughing, obviously far too young then to understand. But many times since then I've thought that, to my father, I was the child who should never have been born.

How different life had been back in 1946, when timid little Jean Davies met the charming and affable Anton Vorderman, known as Tony, who was 25, courteous and flirtatious. He had been a member of the Dutch Resistance during the war, and after the liberation of Holland he joined the Royal Netherlands Army and was posted to North Wales. Meanwhile, my mum, Jean, was a naïve and unworldly young girl who had been raised on a farm in Prestatyn, a genteel seaside resort. The middle one of three daughters born to David Davies, a tenant farmer, and his wife, Jane, she was bright and won a scholarship to the local grammar school.

She left school at the age of 15, as most girls did in those days, and went on to 'business college' to learn shorthand and typing. By the age of 17, she had found a job with the War Department in nearby Rhyl. It was there, at the popular British Restaurant tucked behind the town hall, that she first met and fell in love with my father.

They married within 18 months. My mother—who had never been outside Wales before—set off for her wedding in Holland. This was a huge adventure and her sister Megan travelled with her to be a witness at the wedding.

Where my mother and father lived in Holland, few people spoke English and most teenage brides would have been daunted and isolated by this strange new post-war world. But my capable mother simply rolled up her sleeves and got on with life. She quickly learned the language and made new friends.

When Tony was demobbed from the Army a couple of years later, my parents returned to Prestatyn, where they started a business with just £20 of savings. Tony was very good at mending bikes and quickly earned a good reputation for his work. Eventually they had a thriving enterprise, with two shops which sold bicycles, prams, toys and motorbikes.

Mum was delighted when she became pregnant with their first child but, tragically, she miscarried. Soon after she became pregnant again, and was thrilled to carry the baby to full term. This was 1950, when there were no scans during pregnancy, so when this small framed five-foot-three girl went almost four weeks overdue with her baby, nothing was done to hasten labour.

When it was finally time to give birth, she went to a local 'cottage hospital', as they were known.

But the damage had already been done and after the joy of discovering she was the mother of a boy who weighed 9lbs 6oz, a huge baby for a girl so small, she realised her son was dying.

The birth had been so physically traumatic that the baby, hastily named John, lived for just one hour. My mother was 21 years old when she held her dead baby in her arms—and she came out of hospital alone.

My older sister Beatrix, or Trixie as we know her, was born in 1951, to be followed a couple of years later by Anton.

Anton, my bright, loving and charismatic big brother, was born four weeks early with a double-cleft palate and a double-cleft lip. His deformity was so bad that the midwife ran from the room with the baby in her arms so that my mum couldn't see his face. He developed severe breathing problems and Mum was warned that he might not survive the night.

He was baptised and confirmed by the dean of our Catholic church, but incredibly my mother still wasn't allowed to see him. It would be another five days before she saw her son. Mum told me later: 'It was such a shock to see his poor little face.' His upper lip was split and tissue was bunched up in a large lump under his single nostril. His nose was twisted to the side of his face and his lower lip pulled down.

She wasn't allowed to hold him and visits were restricted to an hour a day in the nursery where he lay among the other babies. All she could do was sit by the side of his cot, look at the son for whom she had unconditional love and pray.

It was a full month before Mum was asked to

bring Anton home. The reality was that looking after this baby was a full-time job and there just weren't enough hospital staff to cope. She was told that Anton would be better off being cared for by his family. So he came home. But because of his medical condition, he couldn't breastfeed or accept a bottle. The only way Mum could feed him was by carefully tipping milk from a medicine glass into his mouth—a process which would take hours and leave both of them exhausted. But Mum was determined.

Anton's first operation at Alder Hey Hospital in Liverpool, at the age of just five months, was to lift and centre the bone in his nose. Three weeks later, he had his second operation, to re-shape the bubble of tissue under his nostril into a functional upper lip and make a second nostril.

For the first time, at the age of six months, Anton had something resembling a mouth. It made his torturous feeding routine much easier, and he repaid my mum with the first of his endless smiles. He went on to beam his way through 24 operations, as his face was slowly and painfully reconstructed. He smiles a lot, my brother. But, after losing two babies, none of this was easy for Mum.

Anton's operations continued when we went back to live in Prestatyn, and when I was just 18 months old, she worried about me too as I was rushed by ambulance to hospital for an emergency operation on my twisted bowel. She was told I had just hours to live.

\*       \*       \*

When I was a very young child, all I knew of my real father stared out at me from a black and white photograph. There were no pictures of him on display in our little flat in Prestatyn, but at some time I must have seen one surviving snapshot. It was a head-and-shoulders photograph of a man wearing a soldier's cap and it became the only hazy image I harboured of him. I remembered that our eyes were the same, with huge eyelids. And he had an enigmatic smile.

We never mentioned my father's name, and I didn't ask my mother any questions about him. Unlike Trixie and Anton, who had spent their formative years with him, to me he was nothing more than a mythical construct, like a character out of a piece of fiction or a historical figure.

If, as they say, ignorance is bliss, then my situation in these early years was preferable to that of my brother and sister, who must have been scarred by the sudden separation. I know that they both missed him at times—particularly Trixie.

Birthdays and Christmas were always sad for them because we never heard from our father—we used to call him 'Our Father who art in Bedford', a sarcastic twist on the Lord's Prayer. He never sent cards or presents, but Trixie's godmother, our Aunty Flo, always made sure there was a present for her and my own godparents always managed to find some money for me to have a little party with jellies and cakes.

I suppose I just assumed, when I was very small, that all families were like ours. It wasn't until I was older, around five or six, that I became truly conscious of his absence and it slowly began to dawn on me that I seemed to be the only child in my school whose father wasn't around. In our world, divorce was something of a rarity, all the more so at the Catholic school I went to, and so I started to think about it. Sometimes I would have tea with my friends and see them run into their fathers' arms, or see how their dads helped them with their homework and gave them hugs and little kisses on their heads. At these moments, I would feel a strange pang. Not envy, because Mum, of course, would do all those things, but more a moment of wondering why my father wasn't even around.

The most difficult pill for Trixie, Anton and I to swallow had to be that, before long, our father acted as though we didn't exist and yet was happy to play Dad elsewhere. When my parents divorced many years later, Tony remarried. He and his second wife had two children together, our half-sisters Karen and Alberdina. To them, he was the perfect father and for their sakes, I'm very glad about that. To me, he completely refused to be a father. For a while he would roll up from time to time to see Trixie and Anton, but I was not part of any of that. After just a few years, he stopped contact with my brother and sister too. That was bad enough, but what was unforgiveable was that he refused for very many years to give my mother any money whatsoever to help raise his children, a nine-year-old girl, a seven-year-old boy with a serious medical condition and a baby just weeks old.

\*     \*     \*

After the shock of Tony's words back in 1961,

Mum left her home in Bedford and turned up at her parents' farm in Prestatyn.

Mum quickly found us somewhere to live. Number Three Palmeira Gardens belonged to her father's brother, Uncle Will, who rented the property to her. So, with a little help from her parents, who delved into their pension money, we moved to 'Number Three, Pal Gardens', as we always called it.

The semi-detached house was divided into two flats and the idea was that we would live on the ground floor and Mum would sub-let the top floor for a couple of pounds a week.

It was a street full of family. My mum's older sister Aunty Megan, her husband Uncle Arthur and my cousin Mark lived at Number Seven, and my mum's cousin Aunty Dorothy, her husband Uncle Neville and our cousins Pamela, Peter and Paul lived at Number Nine. Cosy.

Because our ground-floor flat only had two bedrooms, Mum decided that she, Trixie and I should be in one room and Anton, who was seven, in the other. So my big brother slept in the tiny box room down the narrow hallway, and we girls had the bigger room at the front. Our dormitory was a bit cramped but lively (everything was lively in that flat). Trixie had a single bed in the bay window, while Mum and I shared a double bed in the centre of the room. If that wasn't cramped enough, our little bedroom would soon gain another occasional lodger—our cousin Pamela.

Quite why Pam decided to spend so much time with us I shall never really fully understand, as she only lived three doors away. But this was the 60s and Trixie and Pam were becoming glamorous teenagers, and within weeks of getting to know each other properly, the pair of them became inseparable—bonded by their mutual love of mischief.

After months of serving Pam breakfast, lunch and tea, Mum finally tired of having to march her up the street every night at bedtime (that was when Trixie and Pam were actually home by bedtime). She realised it was much easier to squeeze another bed and body into our room, we were squashed but happy. We stayed like that, four to a room, until I was about nine years old.

Life at Number Three, Pal Gardens was never, ever dull. Down the hallway was our main room, where all life seemed to be played out. It was a long, narrow room with an old, battered sofa with a red bri-nylon cover taking centre stage, a new material in the 60s which came in every colour. Its arms had quite a few brown-rimmed holes—cigarette burns from the days when Trixie and Pam started to smoke. Well, no-one knew about cancer in those days; it was glamorous and just a bit naughty, so they had to do it. They had thick and long false eyelashes, very trendy haircuts and wore the shortest skirts with white PVC boots.

There was also room for a table in our main room and with it a long stool which spent most of its time upside down, as it was my 'island'. A big cardboard box served as my boat, in which I'd push myself along for hours on end while bedlam went on around me.

At the other end of the room, through a wobbly sliding door, was what we exaggeratedly used to call the kitchen, but by today's standards it was nothing more than a scullery, with the only fixtures and fittings being an antiquated gas cooker and a sink. The only 'gadget' we owned was our chip pan, which lived permanently on top of the stove.

Mum, bless her, has never been much of a cook, but the one thing she could make was chips and so that was the staple of our diet. My grandfather (we called him Taidie—pronounced Tidy—the Welsh word for grandad) would arrive once a week with my kind and lovely grandmother Nainie (pronounced Niney—Welsh for grandmother) and present Mum with a sack of potatoes and a tray of eggs from the local farm. 'If you've got potatoes, eggs and a tin of beans, then you've got a meal,' Taidie used to say. Eggs, chips and beans: that was the regular but always much appreciated menu in our flat.

The chip pan was black and crusty on the outside from constant use, but bright and shiny inside, and when Mum wasn't looking, I used to entertain myself playing with it because as the lard slowly heated up over the gas flame, the solidified fat would start to melt away and I could make patterns in it by poking the chip basket up and down.

At the back of the flat was the garden. It was no more than a patch of scrub really, and it backed onto the local bakery. There was a rickety old table out there, which Anton decided to jazz up, painting it in 60s psychedelic colours. I thought it was the most glamorous thing we had, even though the paint was peeling as it was left out in the rain. Right at the end of the garden was an old shed with a slanted, corrugated-tin roof, which Trixie used to sunbathe on in the summer months, basting herself in vegetable fat so she could burn as

12

much as possible in what little sunshine there was.

And then there was the bathroom—the dreaded bathroom—a room so cold that even when you ran hot water in the summer months, steam would still come off the windows. Somehow it always had a micro-climate—with a bitter, damp, biting and cutting-right-through-you cold. Bath time, just once a week in those days, was always on a Sunday night before school and it was an uncomfortable ordeal, loathed by all of us, including my mother.

In the winter months, it was a constant battle to stay warm and as a young child I learned to tackle the lack of heat with military precision. To go to bed, I would layer myself up in as many night-clothes and jumpers as I could find, wait for Mum to make my hot water bottle and then dive under the eiderdown and warm my patch. One of the benefits of sharing a bed with Mum as a child was that when she was eventually able to turn in for the night, I could snuggle up close to her for extra warmth. We had no double-glazing or central heating, but we did have one heater in the main room. It was called a Cannon Gas Miser and because it had the word Cannon (the manufacturer) printed over its white Bakelite bars, I always assumed that it must have been a gift from our local priest, Canon Collins. I hadn't spotted the difference in spelling in those days. As a result, I always felt grateful to him and gave him a special mention in my prayers before bed.

While my father continued to refuse to pay a penny towards our upkeep, my mother—working desperately to keep us fed—held down three or more jobs at any one time. During the first part of the day, she was employed as a secretary in a

13

primary school. Then, in the afternoons, she worked for a local accountancy company. She also earned extra bits of cash at home by typing and would sit at the table and crash through mountains of papers, carefully copying every word and column on the sheet. And on two nights a week, she went to the local harness racing or "trotting" track, where she was the track secretary, while Trixie worked there selling programmes at the entrance and Anton looked after me. Sometimes we were allowed down to the track and those evening meetings, with the bright lights and the roar of the crowd and the sulkies (or chariots, as I dreamed they were) and the horses blasting around the track . . . well, it was uncontrolled excitement. And there were people all the way from New Zealand and Australia. Imagine that!

Trixie went out with one of the Australian drivers (they weren't called jockeys) and he was lovely. He smoked, so I used to try out all the cigarette machines in town, tugging at the little silver drawers until one of them opened and I could sell him a packet of ten No. 6 cigarettes for a shilling. What profit that was, it was worth all the weeks of tugging. The trotting track was eventually bought by Mum's schoolfriend Albert Gubay, who had set up the Kwik Save group of supermarkets. Albert later sold the track to Fred Pontin and that's what it has now been for years, Pontins Prestatyn, but in my time it was a place of chariots and Aussie gladiators.

In 1964, when Trixie was 13, Anton was 11 and I was three, Mum bought an old Gestetner duplicator for Anton to start his own business printing pamphlets for local churches and knitting

14

patterns for Aran sweaters. She would come home from work and Anton would stand the duplicator on the table and put the little one, me, on the stool beside it.

My job was to watch the paper while Anton turned the handle and fed the paper through. Mum had typed the stencils, so it was all ready for Anton to print.

If she resented the extra work, she never said. She was utterly determined to make sure that we would be given the chance to work our way out of the poverty trap when we were older. To help towards this, she insisted that the three of us should learn to touch-type when we reached the age of eight—including my brother, which was unusual for a boy at that time—her mantra was, 'You'll never be out of work if you can type.' In those days, typing pools were full of girls copy-typing (no photocopiers or computers or printers then—everything had to be re-typed endlessly). And she was right; there was always work waiting for us because we could type. And we would all have to work when we were older.

Mum had old vinyl 78 records that weighed a ton, with classical tunes like the *William Tell Overture*, and would sit us at her heavy manual typewriter, where we would thump the keys until our little fingers hurt, desperately trying to keep in time with the music. She would only let us stop learning once we had reached forty words per minute, which was fast for an old manual keyboard. Trixie was always the fastest. Speedy fingers.

As a very young girl, I had no idea how hard it was for my mother. It never occurred to me that we were poor. I didn't see my childhood as austere, I just took it for what it was and assumed that most people lived like we did, sleeping four to a room. I never questioned why the three of us qualified for free school meals, why my mother held down many jobs at any one given moment, and why all my clothes were hand-me-downs from a girl who lived in the next street. I never realised that my mother had to sell the family trinkets to buy Anton a school uniform or how difficult it was for her to raise a family of four on the little income she had.

In all those years of struggle and financial hardship, I only ever saw her cry twice. The first time was when she gave me a ten bob note (ten shillings is the equivalent of 50p today) to go to the shops. I must have been about seven years old and I walked happily into town, picked the bits and pieces that were on the shopping list from the shelves and then reached deep into my pocket for the crumpled brown note. Nothing. I fished around in the other pocket, but the note was gone. With a growing sense of panic, I looked around the shop, but there was no note lying on the floor.

Putting back the tins of food, I retraced my steps all the way home, but could find no money lying on the pavement. When I told Mum what had happened, she didn't tell me off, but she quickly pulled on her coat and came outside with me, saying, 'I'm sure it will turn up somewhere, Carol.' But we walked back and forth, searching the roads and gutters for the money, to no avail. It was only when we arrived back home again, empty-handed, with no ten bob note—and no food—that Mum just crumpled. It was a huge amount of money for her, and she just slumped down at the kitchen table and wept.

I felt utterly wretched. I knew that the money was important, but I was still too young to realise the implications of trying to feed a whole family once the weekly income had gone.

Later that day, we had a knock at the door. It was a neighbour, who said he'd found the note lying on the pavement and had heard from the grocery store that we had been hunting for it. Anton and I often wondered if he had really found the money at all; we still think that our neighbour was a good man who claimed he'd come across it just so that Mum would accept his charity.

The second time in my childhood when Mum cried in front of me was over a frozen chicken. These were the days when frozen food had really only just 'arrived' and it was said—in breathless awe—that it was much better for you than fresh food. Caught up in the excitement, we were all desperate to try our first frozen meal. So Mum saved her money, went to the shops and came back triumphantly with a prize chicken that had cost the grand sum of 7s 6d (seven shillings and six old pence).

We all crowded around the frozen chicken in admiration. Never has a Sunday roast lunch been so looked forward to. The night before, with much ceremony, Mum took the frozen chicken out of the fridge, explaining that it needed to 'defrost' overnight. Wow!

The next day, the chicken had done its job and shed the ice. So Mum placed it carefully onto a roasting tray and into the oven. We all sat back, looking forward to a really special meal. But after about an hour, our senses were interrupted by an

17

acrid smell which filled the air. With a dawning horror, we realised that this foul burning odour was coming from the oven.

When Mum opened the oven door, smoke billowed out. She pulled out our frozen chicken and there, spilling from between its legs, were the melted plastic remains of the bag which had contained the giblets. Mum had forgotten to remove it before putting the chicken in the oven.

In other circumstances, it might have been a funny mistake. But this was the chicken that my mum had saved so hard to buy. There was no other food, apart from the vegetables which had been ready to go with our magnificent roast.

Once more, Mum broke down and wept. Later, we all gamely picked at the vegetables on our plates and tried to talk about anything but our ruined meal.

But we did have treats. Every Sunday, my brother Anton would buy one Mars bar and then cut it into perfect, thin slices which he would arrange in an artistic spiral on a small plate. We would all sit and admire his skill and then make the Mars bar last all night. Our other treat was collecting 'fish bits' from the local fish and chip shop. These were the pieces of batter which had broken off in the fryer—no actual bits of fish were involved at all. They were scooped out and given to us for free. It was so tasty.

Each year, in the build-up to Christmas, Anton and I would get a *Burlington Catalogue*, which we would pore over excitedly every night, while Trixie was out and about with Pam. Many pages carried photographs of toys, gadgets and new-fangled inventions, of which there were many in the 60s, and we would carefully tick or draw rings around the ones we wanted.

From September onwards, we would write out our fantasy wishlists, based on the toys in the catalogue. I would go to bed, playing with my list in my head, mentally wondering if I should swap the Monopoly game for a pair of shiny plastic roller skates, which would strap over my shoes. Or perhaps change the brand-new Saturn V rocket model for a nurse's uniform. The rocket always won.

It was, of course, a fantasy and we knew it, but it was harmless. We never asked Mum for anything from the *Burlington Catalogue*, we knew she couldn't afford it and, instead, would wait for Christmas Day and the chance to open what single present our mother had been able to afford for us, and we would holler and whoop with excitement whatever it was.

When I was very young I would sit on the sofa with my Janet and John books and my much-loved teddy bear Bungee, which Mum had bought for me as a joint birthday and Christmas present. Bungee was in a sale for a few shillings, on account of the fact that he only had one ear and nobody else would buy him. I loved Bungee, and over the years he has been stuffed with old pairs of tights and patched with bits of old dresses, but he's still with me, I still love him and he still only has one ear. Bungee is precious.

In the corner of the lounge sat a small black-and-white Bush television with a huge tuning dial, like a radio. From this, twice a week, the *Coronation Street* theme would crackle out, calling us from wherever we were. I was a *Coronation*

19

*Street* baby; I was born on 24 December 1960, and *Coronation Street* aired for the first time just two weeks earlier, on the 9th. I've always watched it and probably always will.

So the instantly recognisable theme tune and the familiar faces who appeared in black and white in front of me became as much a part of my childhood as the smell of frying chips and the static which left my hair sticking up and sparked lightning whenever I took off my acrylic jumper in the dark.

But while we might have lived in relative poverty, Mum enriched our lives and my abiding memory of our time in our tiny flat is one of love and laughter. Mum always used to say: 'We ain't much money, but we do see life!' And how right she was.

Every day, Trixie and Pam and their boyfriends of the time would tear through the flat, screaming with laughter. They would spend hours dancing and singing along to Motown hits on the record player. Their particular favourites were the Crystals' 'Da Doo Ron Ron' and the Foundations' 'Build Me Up Buttercup', still my favourite song to this day. And when they weren't busy experimenting with the latest 60s fashions and the terrible-smelling sample face packs they got from the Avon lady, they would be plotting their next act of mischief. They liked nothing more than a practical joke, whether it was ringing all the doorbells in the street and then running away or making prank calls when we eventually got our first telephone in 1968, a blue Trimphone that made a trilling sound when it rang. I remember the day they roped Anton into printing fraudulent tickets to the school disco and the time they changed Miss Williams' milk order by adding a zero to the number four on a note she had left for the milkman. Luckily, my mother was able to unravel their plot and alter the note again before it was too late and Miss Williams woke to find 40 bottles of Gold Top on her doorstep.

My favourite was a trick they used to do on the phone. I'd sit and watch it happening time and time again quite happily. They'd pick a number from the phone book and dial. When the person answered, one of them would shout, 'Quick, quick, send Fred, my tap's burst!' And before the person had a chance to say that Fred didn't live there, they would put the phone down. Then, five minutes later, they'd ring up again and say, 'Quick, send Fred the plumber, 'cause the water's rising fast and my feet are wet.' They would repeat this about five times, while this supposed water level was rising, and the person on the end of the phone kept saying: "Fred doesn't live here". Until eventually they would force Anton to ring up and in his deepest voice say, 'Hello, Fred the plumber here. Got any messages?' And everyone would squeal with laughter.

Because of his health problems, Anton was very much a homeboy. Though I never saw anything 'different' about him—to me he was just my older brother—other people did. If we walked down the street together I would see people do double-takes as they looked at his face. He would smile, but there is no doubt that his cleft lip and palate dented his confidence and it was only when I was older that I realised he had been crippled with shyness as a result. Of course, he had friends, but

21

unlike Trixie, who was really popular, Anton preferred to keep himself to himself. And so, when I was younger, we spent a great deal of time together.

Anton loved chess and taught me to play when I was very young. We would sit for hours while he showed me another little trick or pattern. In his woodwork lessons in school he made a chess table, which was our most cherished item. It had four triangular wooden flaps that folded over to protect the surface and he kept his chess set in the drawer he'd built within it. We enjoy similar things, my brother and I.

Anton was responsible for one of our 'golden days', when the Camay Soap Princess came to call at our house. He'd seen a poster for a Camay competition where to enter you had to buy three bars of soap, so he nagged Mum to buy them and she gave in to him, as he was always such a good boy and never normally asked for anything. Not long after, Mum had to take him to the doctor. When they got back, there was a knock on the door and the Camay Princess (a young lady in a beautiful dress with a sash) was standing there, with the Camay Princess car behind her, which had a huge golden crown on top of it. She asked if Mum had any Camay products in the house, which of course she did, as she'd just bought Anton's three bars of soap. We all gathered at the front door to witness this sprinkling of glamour and excitement. Then the Princess said that for every general knowledge question Mum answered correctly, she would get £5, as long as she had a bar of soap to go with every question. If she answered three questions correctly, she got a bonus of another £5. That day Mum and Anton won £20, which the Princess presented to them in a golden plastic wallet. Life was full of wonderful surprises. This was wealth beyond our dreams.

Anton and I loved to go 'jumbling'. On a Friday evening, when there was a little bit of money to spare, Mum would take us to the local jumble sales as a treat and give us a couple of shillings each (about 10p today) to spend. Mum would go off in search of clothes, Anton would spend his money on broken toys to fix and I would go rummaging through the bookstalls for my maths books, a subject I had loved from almost the first moment I went to school. Old books with sheets of sums to tackle—they were beautiful things to me.

Saturday mornings were spent at the Scala cinema at the bottom of the hill, loudly banging our feet up and down waiting for the children's film to start, and Saturday afternoons we'd all be found hiding behind our lounge curtains, looking out at the back hedge and trying not to be seen. Our hedge separated us from the garden of the baker's shop and Mrs Jackson, the owner of the bakery, was very kind. Anything she couldn't sell by the end of the week and which wouldn't stay fresh over the weekend would be popped into a cardboard box and put on top of the hedge on a Saturday afternoon. Somehow she always managed to do it when we weren't looking; the box would magically appear. We loved those cakes, a gift from the bakery goddess.

We didn't have holidays as such. In the summer, I would be sent off to stay with Mum's sister, Aunty Dilys, who was married to a wonderful man—my Uncle Glyn—and my two fab cousins Sian and

Robert (both more or less the same age as me). They lived on a dairy farm called Bryngwyn, which was a few miles away.

I loved it there, as it was so free and easy. The men would be working hard in the fields or with the animals and the kitchen window was always open so that Aunt Dilys could hand out cups of tea and snacks as the day went on. I enjoyed helping (well, I thought I was helping) when the hay was being baled, sitting in the fields with the men, my cousins and the Caldicott boys from down the road eating our lunch. Once, when the trailer of hay bales was stacked off centre the whole lot toppled over.

Twice a day the cows were brought into the 'shippon' (the milking shed) where they'd be fed while they were milked. My job, to help Uncle Glyn, was to weigh out the cow nuts from an enormous galvanised trolley. Cows tend to kick a bit, so I'd be very careful when I sidled up beside them to pour the food into their troughs, but I loved those animals. I loved their daft faces and their softness and their pace. I still do. Calves would be born, rats would be found, all manner of things would happen on that farm, stuck up a bumpy lane where no traffic ever went. I'd set up a pretend shop on a big lump of concrete by the gate and accost anyone who ventured past or, if no-one happened my way, I'd have to be the customer *and* the shopkeeper, selling grass and stones. In my child's mind, the stones would act as potatoes and cakes as well as money, which was a bit confusing but kept me busy.

My grandfather Taidie moved to the farm when my grandmother Nainie died and that is where I

24

remember him best. Always smart in his farmer's tweed jacket, flat cap and good walking boots, he would offer us Callard & Bowser butterscotch sweets, which would take ages to suck, and Nuttall's Mintoes. Taidie was a gentle man, strong and handsome and smiling. He still went to market with the animals every week. He died when he had a heart attack at the age of 83 trying to pump up the tyres of his old Morris Minor with a stirrup pump. My grandparents were good people and Mum missed them desperately.

Bryngwyn was geographically as far as we ever seemed to get. Not that we minded, for one of the great things about growing up in Prestatyn was that there was never any need to go away. We had it all on our doorstep.

When the weather was good, we would tear down from the top of the town where we lived, either on bikes or on foot, to the sea, which was about a mile away. There, my friends and I would sit lapping up the sun on the sea wall or venture down onto the long, sandy beach and wile away the day building sandcastles or paddling around in the sea.

On the way down to the beach and next to the big traffic lights (the *only* traffic lights in town) was a bingo hall and, off-season, the manager would let us in free because he wanted to make it look busy. We weren't allowed to win anything, but that didn't matter—just playing the game and flicking the plastic covers over the numbers as fast as they were called was a thrill in itself for me. Numbers, always numbers.

And when Prestatyn became one of the first towns in the United Kingdom to boast a proper supermarket in the mid 60s, we were beside ourselves with excitement. Not because of Kwik Save itself, but because of the rubber mat which activated the automatic doors—the like of which we had never seen before. Many a happy afternoon was spent leaping on and off the rubber mat and watching the magic doors open and shut, much to the annoyance of the shop manager.

The rest of the time was spent playing in our street. Most of the houses had an open-door policy and we were allowed to come and go as we liked, as long as we were always 'back for tea'. Because few people in Palmeira Gardens had cars, there was very little traffic and so we claimed it as our playground. In the winter it was a football pitch (although tricky, as it was on a slope, so you always tried to be on the team heading downhill); come summer it was a cricket field or a tennis court. As long as we had a bat and ball and enough imagination; the possibilities were endless.

Some of my fondest memories of that time revolve around my school days. I just loved being there. Ysgol Mair, which translates from the Welsh as St Mary's School, was a Catholic primary school in the next town of Rhyl. My mother wasn't born a Catholic. She converted to the faith when she married my father, but she took her newly found religious beliefs seriously enough to want us all to have a Catholic education, even if that meant I had to travel by bus to Rhyl every day rather than go to the local primary school in Prestatyn.

It was a small but very happy school run by the truly exceptional headmaster, Mr Jemmett. Fred Jemmett was everything that a great teacher should be. Strict yet funny at the same time, he wouldn't accept low expectations; he knew that for most of us education was our best chance in life and he did everything in his power to help the children he taught. Short in stature, with an incredibly smiley and welcoming face, he was devoted to his school and his pupils and we all wanted to please him and do our best for him.

My formal love affair with numbers and maths began when I was four years old and I was first introduced to proper arithmetic by my Class One teacher, the diminutive nun Sister Zita. I was sitting at the front of the class as the tiny nun, who was not much taller than the children she taught, carefully chalked some numbers on her blackboard and asked us to add them up. To my delight, she gave each of us a pristine new exercise book to work from, and I can still feel the excitement and trembling anticipation I felt as I worked on my first maths exercise. The numbers and sums just seemed to dance off the page and as the other children in my class methodically completed their exercises, I hurriedly and eagerly raced through mine.

One day in Sister Zita's class, I weed my knickers (I was too scared to ask to go to the toilet). We were all painting pictures at the time and not wanting the rest of the class to know what I had done, I knocked the jam jar of dirty water over, so that it splashed across my dress and covered up the mess underneath my chair. A completely wet dress was the lesser of two evils as far as I was concerned.

My best friend in school was called Debbie Cawthray. Her nana was from Gibraltar and was our school cook—she made the best ever millionaire's shortbread. Debbie was so pretty, but I was a tomboy, with a pudding basin haircut and a monobrow. I was so much of a tomboy, in fact, that bus conductors used to think I was a boy whenever I wore trousers.

I'm not sure why, but I just loved to learn and, with the exception of PE, which I never really took to or saw the point of, I was good at all my subjects, so much so that within a year of entering school, I was doing the work of the children two years older than me and I was moved up one year. I tried hard at everything, but it was maths which I loved above all else.

For me, it wasn't just about getting the sums right; it was about getting them right in the shortest amount of time—that's what mattered. Even then, beating the clock was important. I may not have been fastest child in the playground when it came to running, but I was determined to be the fastest child in the classroom when it came to mental arithmetic.

Once Mr Jemmett had moved me up a year, I found my competition in the shape of a fiercely intelligent girl called Francesca Cerefice. Franca, as she was known, was a brilliant all-rounder and she and I would go head to head for top position in most subjects, although it was in maths where we really pitted ourselves against one another. Though I was more than a year younger than her, I wasn't going to use my age as an excuse. I wanted to be as good at maths as Franca was. Indeed, I yearned to be better and so throughout my time at primary school, unbeknownst to her, she spurred me on. I have a lot to thank her for. Franca very sadly died when she was a young woman, but she is a part of my story. God bless you, clever girl.

But it wasn't just my friends, or even Mr Jemmett, who inspired me to do well at school. My main motivation to succeed came from my mother. Far from being pushy, she only ever told the three of us that all she expected was for us to do our best. But I knew it made her happy when I got a good school report. As a child, this was the one gift I could give her. I couldn't buy her things or make things right in her private life, so my school report was my present and I wanted it to be the best present, so that she didn't have to worry about me. I will never forget the proud smile that broke on her face the day she read my end of year report when I was eight years old and had come top of my year in maths again.

It was written by our glamorous class teacher Mrs Wynne-Jones. Across all the subjects, I'd scored 586 out of 600 and the words my teacher wrote were: 'An excellent result in every way. Carol has a masterly hold over mathematical computation, which should prove profitable later on.'

With *Countdown* still 13 years away, never was a school report quite so prophetic, as Mum likes to say.

## I GET A DAD

When I was nine and the hazy, crazy days of the 60s were drawing to a close, I suddenly found myself with a Dad at last, and it was every bit as wonderful as I had dreamed. I didn't know my father, Tony Vorderman, but I really came to love my new 'Dad', Gabriel.

My mother has always been a strikingly pretty woman; beautiful, inside and out. She is the only member of the family to win a beauty contest: 'Prettiest Mother in Prestatyn' in 1952—and, yes, she has made me put that into this book! She always liked to make an effort with her appearance, although she never spent what scant money we had on new dresses or shoes for herself. She always looked ten years younger than her age, but because of us, her social life was non-existent. Exhausted with the effort of having four jobs, she spent every evening in the flat with us. She didn't enter a pub until she was 34 years old!

One day, she was invited out to dinner with friends at a restaurant in Cheshire. Mum going out was such a rarity, I remember how we helped her to get dressed up, do her hair and look beautiful. She went off, full of trepidation, and she found the whole experience so daunting and unnerving that she simply couldn't wait to rush back to see if we were OK. She was home a few hours later.

If there were nights when she sat in our flat and yearned for some adult company, she never once let on. But towards the end of the 60s, that changed when a colourful Italian man came into our lives with all the force of a volcanic eruption.

When he met my mother, Gabriel Rizzi was a widower with two grown-up children of his own, Annette and Arthur. He lived in the Welsh market town of Denbigh, which was 13 miles away from Prestatyn. Gabriel owned a small but successful building company called A & A Rizzi Builders (the first A was for the initial of his first name, Armido, and the second was for his son, Arthur). When he wasn't renovating properties around North Wales, he was a regular at the evening race meetings at the Prestatyn trotting track, which is where he got to know Mum. After their friendship blossomed, they started to court.

Mum was always mindful not to flaunt her relationship in front of us, but it was obvious to everyone that they were becoming increasingly close. On the special nights when we were allowed to go with Mum to the raceway—or the 'trots', as we called it—Gabriel was always there. Sometimes he would come round to our flat to call on her, and whenever my mother needed to take Anton on one of his regular trips to the hospital, he was always on hand to ferry them back and forth to Liverpool in his car. Gabriel was the first person I knew who had a sports car. To me, this elevated him to the same glamorous status as a Hollywood star. A car and a foreign accent—as far as I was concerned, Gabriel was amazing.

Trixie, on the other hand, didn't get on too well with him in the beginning. And I don't think Gabriel's children were very happy about the romance either at that time.

So, for reasons best known to themselves and probably to avoid endless months of family debate, Gabriel and my mother decided to get married in secret in the summer of 1970. I think Mum found it easier to simply slip away and marry the man she loved rather than risk any arguments—she hates confrontation of any sort.

Even though I didn't know that they were to be married, I wasn't surprised when it happened. I was nine years old and had just been upgraded from sharing a bed with Mum in our dormitory downstairs to a bedroom all of my own in the upstairs flat, which had recently been left vacant by the tenants. It was a box room, but there I slept happily, beside the giant duplicator which Anton was still using to churn out knitting patterns every evening.

That morning, Mum came into my bedroom to break the news. She hesitated for a split second before coming over to the bed, where I was reading comics. 'Helloooo,' she trilled in an unusually high voice. 'I've got something to tell you . . .' she added, trying to sound casual.

As I lifted my head from beneath the layers of quilts I was buried under, I took in the figure of my mother standing there above me. She was wearing a smart, knee-length dress, which I hadn't seen before, adorned with embroidered silver flowers. I'd never seen her look quite so lovely, so radiant. Somehow I immediately guessed what had happened earlier that morning, or maybe it was wishful thinking on my part.

'You've got married, haven't you?' I said, smiling.

'Yes, Carol. What would you like for your tea?'

Talk about a terrible way to change the subject! Mind you, I was very happy. Gabriel made me laugh . . . a lot. He was standing in the doorway as Mum broke the news and my heart soared. I had my Dad at last.

Now, Gabriel was not someone you would describe as conventionally good-looking, with his dark skin, curly black hair and strong Roman features. While he may not have possessed the symmetrical looks of a matinee idol, it was easy to see why Mum had fallen for him. He had to be one of the most mischievous and charismatic men I have ever known. He was really tactile and alive and his face told stories. He was utterly unpredictable and I loved him for it.

Everything about him just seemed big, from his deep, booming voice, to his deafening laugh, to his huge hands, always covered in concrete from building sites. He used to slam his hands down on the table when we were having our tea, so whenever he was making a point everything on the dining table jumped up, and I laughed and he roared. He was like a force of nature. He only had to walk into a room and at once everyone else faded into the background. In many respects, he was the polar opposite of my mother, for while she is inwardly strong, she has always been softly spoken and gentle by nature, a true lady in the old-fashioned sense of the word.

Born and bred in Italy, Gabriel had been brought to Wales as a prisoner of war, but unlike most of his fellow Italians, who couldn't wait to return home when peace was declared, Gabriel decided to settle in the area, having fallen in love with a farmer's daughter, who he went on to marry and have a family with.

Yet despite all the years he had spent over here, Gabriel never exactly mastered English. When he and Mum exchanged their vows at the registry office he, unwittingly, took her as his 'awful wedded wife' rather than his lawful one, which probably wasn't the most auspicious start to a marriage. He called baked beans 'bim bims' and when I was going to school he would say, 'Catty [his name for me], can you brush your bloody hairs?' Or, if we were out and about, 'Let's go now to ours house.'

I loved those little phrases; they were part of what made him special. And his language was colourful, to say the least, with men and women often referred to fondly as either 'bloody baastaads' or 'beetches'. When I joined him in a room, his face would light up, he would throw his arms out wide and yell, 'Catty! You beetch you!' and then laugh. The strange thing is that no-one who knew him ever found it offensive, such was his charm. But he was particular about his swearing—I never heard him say any really bad words and whatever he did say, he always said with a huge grin on his face and would follow it with a loud cackle of laughter.

Even Doctor Gwyn Thomas, the local GP and, as such, possibly the most respected man in Denbigh, was referred to as a 'baastaad'. I will never forget the day that Dad and I drove past the good doctor in the pick-up truck. 'Doctor Gweeeeen!' Gabriel bellowed from the window (he always drove through town with his window down) for the whole of Denbigh to hear. 'How da hell are you today? You old baastaad!'

I had never known anyone speak like that before, not least to a doctor! What was he going to say? Well, Doctor Gwyn simply turned round and waved to us with an amused smile. That was the extraordinary thing about Gabriel. You couldn't help but love him.

So I was completely happy with the idea of Mum marrying Gabriel. To me it made perfect sense.

But when two people get married, normally they move into the same home together. Not Mum. She insisted on living 13 miles away from Gabriel, staying in our flat in Prestatyn, as she thought that Anton, at 16, wasn't old enough to look after himself. He was studying for his A levels and Mum didn't want to disturb him by moving him to another town, as he was doing well at school, in spite of his very difficult beginnings. So six months after their wedding, we were still living in Prestatyn and Gabriel was still in Denbigh.

When Mum and Gabriel got married, Trixie was 19. Three years earlier, she had decided to leave school. She had been one of the brightest girls there, but while Mum was working every hour she could to feed us, our father in Bedford had insisted on going back to court to reduce his child payments to £1 a week, as Trixie had reached the age of 16. When Trixie heard him saying in court that he didn't want to help her stay in school by paying even a small sum, she just rebelled, and who can blame her?

Trixie had always harboured an ambition to become a journalist and when a work placement came up on the local paper she leapt at the chance. And then she decided to leave Wales completely to take a job with Billy Smart's Circus. Back in those days, Billy Smart's Circus was a huge phenomenon and the day they came to Rhyl, there was a great parade through the streets with the clowns and the acrobats and the elephants and the horses in their bright headdresses—Trixie went to cover the story. They were so impressed with her secretarial skills that they offered her a job immediately. This was the opportunity of a lifetime and she grabbed it. By 1970, my exciting and glamorous sister was travelling with the circus as Billy Smart Junior's PA and having a ball. In my eyes, at the age of nine, my big sister now lived in a world of showbiz glamour.

While Anton, Mum and I were still living in Prestatyn, Mum had a suspicion that Gabriel had another woman. After the humiliation with Tony, she didn't want to go through it all again and so she decided to leave him. But how do you leave someone if you're not actually living with them?

Trixie was with the circus in another part of the country and so Mum decided that she and I should join her. Well, it seemed the obvious thing to my mum. So we went 'on the run' and joined the circus in Leicester. Being with the circus was jaw-dropping for me, a small girl from a small town. While we were there, I helped to sell candy floss in the intervals with a handsome boy called Lionel who was very kind to me because, unlike every other child there, who seemed to be born gymnasts, I couldn't even do a handstand.

There was no space in any of the circus caravans, so Mum and I had to move into a bed and breakfast offering a single room overlooking the wall of Leicester jail. It was grim. A window pane was smashed near the bed, so a freezing wind blew into the room at night.

There was one bed for us to share, with a damp, stained mattress. We taped newspaper over the broken window to keep out the cold and Mum tried her best to make it feel like some kind of wonderful adventure, but I didn't like it at all.

Tight in my grasp was my old one-eared teddy bear, Bungee, whom I took everywhere with me. I turned to Mum one night at bedtime and said, in the honest way that children have: 'Bungee doesn't

36

have a kingdom anymore.' Mum told me later that it simply broke her heart. We left Leicester and carried on running, down to Windsor. We were now lodging with some kind friends of Trixie's and, in an attempt to settle down, Mum put me into a primary school which I hated. I refused to go back after the first day, which wasn't like me at all. I was only nine years old and I wanted to go home.

So our 'escape' was falling apart and after less than a year of marriage and one separation, Mum decided to go back to Gabriel. Not the most conventional of starts to a marriage, but I was thrilled that we were going back to North Wales and I could see our family and my friends at school once more. I had been rocked when we ran away, even though I was trying hard to like it, for Mum's sake, and now I basked in the warmth of the reconciliation. Mum and I left our flat in Prestatyn and moved to Denbigh to live with Gabriel.

Anton was now even closer to his A levels, so he stayed on in the flat. Mum still says she regrets leaving him alone, but Anton says he had the time of his life. After all, this was 1971 in a small, quiet town in North Wales, with an extended family living in the same street.

Denbigh had an appeal entirely of its own. Based around a steep hill with an old castle on the very top, it boasted commanding views of the Vale of Clwyd, and with its market square, long, winding streets and back alleyways dotted with pubs, it was incredibly picturesque. We lived at the 'bottom of town' in a perfect house—the kind that children draw. It was double-fronted, detached, built from smooth red brick and set in half an acre of land, with its own Italian sunken garden, designed and crafted by Gabriel, with a big monkey puzzle tree in the middle, fringed by a wall of apple trees. The first time I set eyes on the house I couldn't really believe that this was to be my home or that, when we did eventually move there, I would be given my choice of bedrooms. Gabriel showed me round the house and said to me, when I was wide-eyed, "which bedroom you want, Catty?" "I want the smallest one Dad . . . please".

The smallest one was above the back kitchen where Gabriel had fitted an old Aga and I figured that the heat would keep my bedroom warm all year round. I was right. It was so different in every way from our cold flat and I just revelled in it. I loved the noise of the house and the symmetry of the rooms and the big staircase and the front door with pretty leaded glass and all the vans and pick-ups and trucks in the driveway. It was fantastic.

If the front of the house looked like something from a picture book, then I think it would be fair to say that the back had a completely different feel. The back was where Gabriel ran his business and it was a builders' yard. You couldn't move for all the machinery, the stacks of bricks, bags of sand, cement mixers and the extraordinary amount of bric-a-brac that Gabriel loved to collect. Old stoves, car parts, Welsh slates and banister rails were piled high, waiting for Gabriel to work his magic on them. My mum would smile when he dragged yet another of his 'finds' over the threshold. I loved it all and just thinking about it years later still makes me feel warm inside.

Gabriel wasn't just a builder—he was a master builder, and a successful one at that, employing over ten staff at any one time. He loved old buildings with a passion and had he not lost his youth to war, he might have even become a brilliant architect.

It was Gabriel who gave me my love of bricks and mortar, quite literally. During the holidays he would take me on site with him and at weekends he'd set me projects—like making bricks and tiles. He was fanatical about building. At five in the morning, before the larks were even up, I would be woken by the sound of Gabriel modelling his tiles with a little hammer. Tap, tap, tap, tap; followed by a deep, throaty cough, a legacy from his years of unrelenting smoking. It all made a soothing noise.

Aside from building, Gabriel had one other great passion and that, not surprisingly given the fact he was Italian, was food. He was a great cook. Every Friday, to mark the end of the working week, he would come home and we would have our Italian night.

Men didn't cook at home in the 70s—it was considered women's work—but not for Gabriel. Steaks would be battered, tomatoes pureed and made into sauce and bread pummelled into the finest of crumbs, while large pots of boiling water sat on the stove, bubbling away in wait for his fistfuls of pasta. After years of eating a diet of egg or fish with chips, and in an age when olive oil was something you bought from the chemist to clear a blocked ear, this was a total revelation to me. Up until this point, food, with the exception of the free pastries and cakes we were given from the bakery, was little more than fuel. You'd sit down for your tea, you'd wolf it down and then you'd be out of the door again. But here in our new household we looked forward to our tea.

As for all Northerners, we didn't have 'lunch' in the middle of the day, we had our 'dinner' and our main meal at about 5 o'clock was our 'tea'. I didn't know what an evening 'dinner' was until ten years later. But whatever it was called, there was a ritualistic element to each meal. It was not to be rushed, but enjoyed. I remember Gabriel's large, concrete-caked hand reaching out for his trusty cheese grater at every meal, which took prime position on the kitchen table, and adding shavings of fresh parmesan cheese onto his steaming plate, while scattering a light dusting of concrete dust from his arms over the table at the same time.

My mother, on the other hand, was anything but a cook. In all those years of raising us alone, she had relied heavily on chips. But now she was married to a man who came home from work every night at 5.45 and expected a meal on the table. She was horribly exposed. To help her, as she was still working, I would come straight home from school by 4.30 and while I was cooking the tea I'd be trying to do my homework simultaneously. I'd slice bread and butter so thinly it was like lace doilies. I'd put it on a pretty plate and I always laid the table so it looked nice for Mum and Dad when they got home from work. Mum would get in at about 5.30 and Gabriel always and precisely at 5.45. I liked that routine. We had a set menu, with the same thing every Monday—stew, using the leftover bones from the roast on Sunday—and then on Tuesday it was always liver and onions and potatoes, and so on.

At weekends Mum was on her own as far as cooking was concerned. Or so we thought. With a deviousness and innate cunning, she would go to

Marks and Spencer (they'd just started selling food) during the week and buy tins of stuffed green peppers, which were then hidden at the back of our little larder. My mother would smile sweetly and serve them up on plates for Saturday tea, and whenever Gabriel asked when she had made them, she would reply innocently, 'Oh, I made them yesterday, Gabriel. I know how much you like them.'

Gabriel adored his stuffed green peppers and used to boast happily to anyone who would listen: 'My wife is such a good cook. Her green peppers are the best!' My mother would happily bask in the plaudits, making sure that she never caught my eye. This went on for years!

Life under Gabriel's roof was always entertaining and although it was mainly just the three of us living there, the house was always filled to the brim with people and noise. First there was Gabriel's gang of builders, who would come and go during the day, including lovely Paul and Hughie the plumber, who once said, after watching some political show or other: 'I'm sure that David Pimpleby's father must be very proud of him.' A steady line of cars and vans would arrive in the driveway just before seven in the morning, making getting out of the house to go to school a lively old obstacle course.

At weekends Anton would visit and Trixie, when she was on her breaks from the circus, would often come and stay. Gabriel's daughter Annette was married and lived on a farm nearby with her husband and three sons. My stepbrother Arthur worked for Gabriel and I saw him every day. Arthur must have got his looks from his mother, as

41

he is drop-dead handsome and always smiling. When Arthur was building his amazing new house in a village nearby, he and his first wife Jacqui and his children Tino and Faye came to live with us in Denbigh for a bit and we all became very close. Proper family.

Gabriel was not without his foibles. As generous as he was to us, he absolutely hated to part with money. He wasn't beyond a few tricks. I will never forget the time when a man from the Inland Revenue called round to question him about his tax return and a furious Gabriel—purple with rage—threatened to kill him.

'I tell you, I'm not paying you any more money, you baastaad!' he shouted furiously at the taxman, madly gesticulating away. 'Ask me one more time and I swear I get my gun on you and I shoot you!'

Needless to say, even though he was always threatening people with it, Gabriel didn't actually own a shotgun, and Mum would say, 'Gabriel, stop being silly.' But it was enough of a threat to send the poor taxman scuttling away, never to return. Coming from genteel Denbigh, I don't think he had enjoyed much contact with Italians in the past—particularly not ones who threatened him with a shooting. He probably thought Gabriel belonged to 'the mob', and our last view of the poor man was the dust on the drive as he disappeared into the distance.

I couldn't help but love Gabriel. Once you had the measure of him, he was hugely lovable and I know that my feelings for him were reciprocated. He called me "Catty" and when I didn't call him 'the old bugger', which always made him laugh, then he was always 'Dad'. As protective as a lion,

Gabriel's Latin blood meant that, as I entered my teens, even the most innocent mention of a boy's name in a conversation would cause him to erupt. Immediately, he would threaten to whip out his imaginary gun and turn it on whatever hapless youth had been discussed. 'Tell me who he is and I shoot the baastaad!' he would roar, much to my amusement.

*      *      *

I was ten years old and living in Denbigh when I moved on to secondary school, following my brother Anton to Blessed Edward Jones High School in Rhyl, or 'Blessed Teds', as we called it. I used to get the bus every morning, travelling the 12 miles there and then back again after lessons had finished.

Here, in secondary school, I finally had the chance to tackle what I regarded as 'proper' maths. My very strict and wonderfully unconventional maths teacher, Mr Parry, introduced me to the world of calculus, which filled me with awe and excitement. He would drill stuff into us, so that every process came naturally. And the beauty of patterns and shape came alive.

When I was 14, Mr Parry had a year's sabbatical and without him I was bereft and bored and started causing a bit of trouble. I went through endless past papers for O level maths, to see if I could get 96 per cent or more in a third of the time allowed. I would have had no trouble taking my O level when I was 14, but we weren't allowed to do it. I learned the incredible power a single inspirational teacher can have over a child's life, and for me, Mr Parry was that teacher. Luckily, he came back to us after a year or so and school life was good again. He knows I was very fond of him, as he appeared on my *This is Your Life* programme decades later, but he probably still doesn't know that he is one of my heroes.

Because Blessed Edward Jones was a Catholic comprehensive school and there were only two of them in the whole of North Wales, lots of us had to be bussed into school. I had many friends, including Debbie Cawthray from my primary school and Sandy Owen. Sandy lived halfway between Denbigh and Rhyl and I'd keep a seat for her on the bus, where we would do our homework on our knees.

I had to make friends from scratch in my new home town of Denbigh, as most of the children went to the local High School, where my mum got a job as school secretary. Three doors away lived a girl called Elinor Pritchard, her two brothers and her mum and dad—Aunty Dorothy and Uncle Huw. We called everyone Aunty and Uncle in those days, even if they weren't relations.

Every Friday, once we had bolted down our tea, we would go 'up town' to the youth club, which usually had a disco on a Friday night. In the years before we were old enough to go inside, we'd stand on the bench outside and peer in through the window longing for the day we'd be old enough to get in ourselves. This was the time of the Rubettes, the Bay City Rollers and Donny Osmond (I was never a David Cassidy girl). It was the early 70s and I was not yet a teenager, but I was starting to go out and about. The youth club disco was the highlight of our week, and I would spend happy hours carefully choosing which outfit to wear. As I only owned two outfits, the choice wasn't hard.

Outfit number one was a black, slightly flared nylon skirt with tiny white flowers on it, which I would team with a navy blue, woolly tank top (very big in the 70s) and a black shirt with long, sharply pointed collars. Outfit number two was actually pretty much the same, but in a shade of deep 70s brown. Whichever outfit I picked would be complemented by the pride of my wardrobe—a pair of high, black, shiny platform shoes which would send me tottering along the street like a gawky colt.

On a Saturday night the youth club was closed and we would head off to Leno's café for coffee. Leno's was nothing more than a glorified chip shop with a few Formica tables, but it did have a jukebox in the back room and so we'd sit there, making cups of milky coffee last an hour. Sometimes boys would come on the bus from other towns, so we'd have something new to talk about and giggle over. Elinor always wore make-up, but I couldn't see the point. Those days were still to come.

On Sundays we'd be in Elinor's bedroom, where she would try to smoke hanging out of her window so her dad couldn't smell what she'd been up to, and we'd chat for hours as we listened to Radio Luxembourg or annoy her older brothers, who were always playing Genesis or the Who or Yes or Deep Purple or Led Zeppelin. I loved the Who, Free and Be-Bop Deluxe's album, Axe Victim. It's a bit weird now when I meet those musical heroes of my young, impressionable days. What I wouldn't have done for a night talking to Roger Daltrey in 1973!

Elinor used to write me fake sick notes so I didn't have to take part in the lesson I loathed the most—PE. I used to have a posh pad of notepaper full of letters, supposedly written by my mum, that all started: 'I'm sorry, but Carol can't do PE today because . . .' Elinor used to have great fun drafting those jottings and would happily write them out for me. As she was in a different school, my PE teacher didn't recognise her handwriting, and generally let me off.

As we got a little older, we swapped the youth club for nightclubs—our favourite being one called the Stables, which was in the neighbouring town of St Asaph. It was owned by a man called Louis Parker and it was *the* place to be seen, not just for locals like us, but lots of the stars from Manchester and BBC Radio One would be there too. I was only 15, but now that I had started wearing make-up I looked a lot older. Our nights there were happily spent dancing away to Motown tracks or to the beat of northern soul until it was time to cadge a lift home with someone we knew.

By the time I was seventeen and on a girls night out, we would spend hours getting ready, complete with Carmen rollers, the shortest of shorts just skimming our bottoms and shimmering make-up on our faces. We would then totter outside on our highest heels and clamber into one of Gabriel's pick-up trucks. There would be a single long seat across the front and while I would sit behind the steering wheel, another would straddle the gear stick—with legs either side—while Elinor would sit on the passenger side.

The pick-ups sometimes had concrete mixers strapped down in the back, so I'd have to take the corners very carefully because of the extra weight, but eventually we would screech to a halt outside the nightclub and jump down from the cab as if we were getting out of any normal car. Carefully, we would wipe off the newly settled layer of builders' dust from our clothes and our bodies and then crash into the nightclub. I suppose we didn't know what 'being cool' was. We just wanted to have a good time.

My ever-protective stepfather would have exploded had he known that I was sneaking out on Friday nights, particularly if it was to see a young man, so each 'going out' evening began in the same way. I would excuse myself from the tea table and tiredly suggest that I was off to do my homework. I'd go up to my room, switch my radio on and quickly get my clothes ready. Gabriel, meanwhile, would get up from the table and sit down in front of the television, inevitably falling asleep.

I would listen out, and once I'd heard the familiar loud snoring coming from his leatherette swivel chair, I knew the coast was clear. I would creep down the stairs like a cat burglar, nick the keys to the pick-up and silently slip out of the back door.

Just after the *News at Ten*, Mum would wake Gabriel from his slumber and insist that they went up to bed. 'I'll just go and check on Carol,' she would say as she passed my bedroom door. She'd go into the room and bid my empty bed goodnight before saying, 'Don't forget to turn your radio off, Carol.' And with that she would flick the switch herself, before turning off the light and shutting the bedroom door behind her. For all those years, Gabriel was none the wiser. My mother had this weekly ritual down to a fine art.

Only once did I come close to making Gabriel properly cross with me. Not for sneaking out to a nightclub, but for borrowing an old Escort estate. I wanted to drive it into town—up the hill to the shops at the top. But as I came to the end of our drive to turn into the main road, I misjudged the distance and scraped the side of the car on the stone wall (well, I hadn't been driving that long and this was a bit of an experiment).

When I got into town, I jumped out to look at the damage. It was even worse than I feared— scrapes and a large dent down the side. My heart was in my mouth and I panicked. Then, suddenly, I had a brainwave. I found some mud and caked it carefully down the side of the Escort, totally hiding the damage that had been done. I thought, 'Whichever of Gabriel's builders takes the car out on Monday won't notice and by the time the damage is found, so many people will have driven it that no-one will know who had actually done it.' It was, seemingly, the perfect plan.

Late that afternoon, I got home without him noticing anything. Sitting in the kitchen, enjoying a cup of tea with Mum, I heard the door slam and Gabriel's footsteps. 'Gina!' he called out joyously (that was what he called Mum). 'I have some good news! I sold that bloody estate car to Dai Ginge [a joiner who worked with him] and he's on his way to fetch it.'

I froze in my seat. 'Aargh, he's sold the bloody car! Today of all days! What's going to happen when Dai finds the damage?' Dai Ginge (so called because he had red hair), arrived and so I sat, frozen, in my chair waiting for the furious Italian to come striding in and make me pay for my mistake. But no, Dai Ginge was in a big rush and simply slapped the money into Gabriel's hands and drove off with the car, without stopping to inspect it.

Once he was gone, I steeled myself to tell Gabriel the truth. I thought he'd go nuts, but with the money in his hands, he thought it was hysterically funny. 'Catty, you beetch!' he roared with heartfelt appreciation.

That was my Dad.


## GETTING A VORDERMAN ... OOPS

Mum and Gabriel's on-off relationship continued—so that by the time I reached my late teens, she had left Gabriel twice more. It became a pattern. Everything would be fantastic for a couple of years, then he would misbehave and rather than face any angry confrontation, she would simply scoop me up and steal away from Denbigh, normally leaving a little note for him next to the kettle in the kitchen.

My mother always tried be low key about the leaving, so that she wouldn't worry me. Mum has never been into huffing and puffing and 'scenes'. She used to wake me up in the morning and say, 'We're off,' very casually. And so it was that as swiftly as she had once married him, she would leave him and I would always go with her. I never complained because she was my mum and the most important person in my universe.

Gabriel wasn't my father, but each time we left,

I missed him and I missed our life with him. Losing my own little bedroom, the room where I felt warm and safe and secure, was difficult. I was settled in Denbigh—I had friends I liked to go out with and I had a job in a sweet shop which gave me a bit of extra money.

I found myself floundering with the upheaval. I loved my mother with all my heart and I wouldn't ever dream of questioning her, or saying anything which made her feel bad. I never begged her to go back to Gabriel, even though I really wanted to. I did understand that it was about things that go on between a man and a woman which I didn't yet comprehend, but it still hurt. I tucked away the pain I felt in a secret place, just as I had before with my father, and kept a lid on it. No-one at school talked about it, as far as I remember, and I learned the lesson: 'Least said, soonest mended.'

But it was during these years that I started to think about what I wanted from life. In the 70s in North Wales, most girls thought about who they'd settle down with. 'Marry a rich boy and you will be taken care of' was how some girls thought, but not me.

I wasn't after riches and, anyway, if I did get married, as my mum's history had proved, it was absolutely no guarantee of anything. My friends were starting to become engaged, but marrying young didn't interest me.

I determined, really deep down, after all the upheavals in my young life, I needed to be independent and I could do that through work, I needed to stand alone. That has largely shaped the person that I am now, for better or for worse. It has been a fundamental force, propelling me forward my entire adult life. Based on this, my mantra has always been: 'The harder you work, the luckier you get.'

I was 14 years old when I started to contemplate my future career. I knew I wanted to buy a home of my own eventually, but I was also determined to leave North Wales to see what else was on offer in the big, wide world. I wanted and liked adventure. After much thought, I decided I would either become the first female prime minister or, failing that, an airline pilot! Ridiculous maybe, but to me it was a plan and I needed a plan to latch on to.

As I considered both of these options, it dawned on me that I would need an excellent university degree if I was ever going to stand a serious chance of getting either job.

I was lucky, as I'd always found schoolwork easy. Homework and revision for me was sitting in front of the telly watching *Crossroads* or *The Golden Shot* with a book on my lap, or reading on the bus on the way to school. I could absorb information very easily and quickly, and had an almost photographic memory. I wasn't a swot in the traditional sense, but after-school clubs and all the things that were available to those in private schools weren't available to us, so, as kids, you did what you could. In my case, I knew how to work when the pressure was on.

So, in the blisteringly hot summer of 1976, I cleared a space among the cement mixers in the back yard for my rusting sun lounger, got out my bikini (although Mum said I had to run inside if I saw a van full of builders coming back) and studied for my O levels in the sunshine.

I was taking them a year early, at the age of 15,

51

and I got ten of them, including a special O level in additional maths, which was a beautiful calculus paper. A year later, I added another two O levels to the list, so by the age of 16, I had 12 O levels with excellent grades. A good start to the master plan.

That summer we went on a fantastic holiday to Gabriel's hometown in Italy. Gabriel was the youngest of 13 children and all the family except for him still lived in the small town of Castelnovo di Sotto, not far from the city of Parma, in northern Italy. The men worked hard in the fields and the businesses, and the women spent the day cooking meals for them. When the men came home from work, the food would be served by the women of the house, while the men sat at the table and ate and drank their home-made wine. As guests, we were allowed to eat at the table. The first time I enjoyed one of these meals, I stuffed my face when the pasta was served, thinking it was the main course, as it would be at home. So when courses two, three, four, five and six followed, I was desperate to say, 'No thank you, I'm full.' But Dad had a face like thunder because to refuse the food was unforgivable, so it turned into the biggest meal I'd ever eaten, as I stuffed plate after plate of what was beautiful food into my mouth and my stomach swelled fit to bursting. I didn't dare let Dad down.

I used to love walking into the little town in the evening, a ritual known as 'la passeggiata', the Italian experience of ambling around town in your best clothes to show off to the people sitting outside the cafés. In the 70s, I don't think I saw a single grown man who wasn't wearing what I called a Mafia hat: a trilby. The little town was full of hat shops for men and shoe shops for women. The gelato (ice cream) was to die for. They were happy days.

This year Dad had found an heavy old bacon slicer on a building site back home and had polished it up to take over to Italy. The family used to cure their own Parma-style ham and this was going to make slicing it so much easier than with a knife. We ended up swinging around various looped passes in the Alps with this horrendously heavy slicer on the roof rack of a Datsun sports car, while Dad refused to stop because obviously he was Italian and Italian men in sports cars didn't stop for anything except pretty women. Mum and I thought we'd never get there in one piece—she worried constantly, while I sat in the back screaming with laughter. I love all that stuff. Anything a bit dangerous or nuts, I just love it, and Dad did too.

School began again and I was called in to see the headmaster, Mr Ashworth. He was a good headmaster and he was very pleased with my results. I had already settled on my A level choices, choosing maths and physics and a 'special paper' in further maths. I wanted to do what was known as double maths, which was two separate maths A levels (much more intensive), but our school was so small that the timetable simply wouldn't allow it and that, I believe, changed my academic life. Instead I did an A level in economics, making three A levels and a special paper altogether. I was astonished to find that an economics A level could not begin to compare in rigour to maths or physics; it came a very poor third in terms of difficulty.

'And what do you plan to do later on?' Mr Ashworth asked that afternoon.

'Well, I'd like to go to university,' I replied. 'Ideally, I would like to read maths.'

'Of course. And where are you thinking of applying to?'

'I'd like to try for Cambridge, sir.'

Mr Ashworth looked at me, as a gentle smile broke across his face. 'You do realise, Carol, that no-one in this school has ever won a place at Oxford or Cambridge before?'

I nodded.

'In fact, Carol, no-one from this school has ever even applied to Oxford or Cambridge before.'

'I know, but if you never ask, you never get, do you, Mr Ashworth?'

'No, not at all. And, unfortunately, we won't be able to prepare you for the special Oxbridge exam either, Carol.'

Almost all students who wanted to go to Oxford or Cambridge in the 70s had to sit the Oxbridge exam, which most private and grammar schools were geared up for. So if I was to go, then I would have to be one of the very few students each year who were given an offer conditional on the results of their A levels. Of the 3,000 places offered, I was told that fewer than 100 were conditional offers in those days, and they were reserved for kids like me, kids who weren't in a school where they could take the other exam. Gulp. These were bad odds.

'But if that's what you want to do, Carol,' said Mr Ashworth, 'you must go ahead with it. We'll help in any way we can.'

So why had I chosen to aim for Cambridge? I knew next to nothing about it, had never met anyone who'd been there other than as a tourist, and, before the days of the internet, information was scarce. But, and there's always a 'but', I'd read somewhere that it was the best university in the world for science-related subjects, so I thought, 'Best foot forward, Carol.' Not for one moment did I think I would actually get in.

So although I really wanted to study maths, I simply hadn't been able to take the right A levels for that to happen. Instead, I chose to apply to Sidney Sussex College, Cambridge, to read engineering, as it brought together my love of maths and physics and my practical building-site experience (all those years of growing up with Gabriel). I figured that engineering would come in useful if I was ever to take to the skies as an airline pilot.

I was called for an interview when I was 16 years old, and because we faced such a long journey, Gabriel offered to take me. However, the thought of him turning up in Cambridge and saying to the senior tutor, 'Hello, how are you, you baastaad?'— well, the game would have been up before it had begun.

So Mum and I travelled down to Windsor Safari Park the day before my interview, to stay with my sister Trixie. By then, the Billy Smart family had closed the circus and set up the safari park. Trixie was now married to Francis, who was in charge of the animals in the park, and together with my nephew Jim, who was a toddler with the longest eyelashes in the world, they lived in a topsy-turvy house within the grounds.

One summer I'd stayed with Trixie and worked in the gift shop. Now I was reunited with the menagerie of animals in Trixie and Francis's house. There was a cheetah with cataracts called Poppy, who would sit happily beside us as we watched television, and there were baby penguins in the bath. When you stood next to the sink in the kitchen, you could watch the giraffes and zebras gambol in their paddock. Francis was an expert with dolphins and killer whales. He was once attacked in the water by a killer whale, but recovered well. I loved to go up to the pool once all the visitors had gone home and sit on the platform, watching the trainers and the animals. It was a special place, full of magic and promise. The safari park was eventually sold and turned into Legoland, which isn't quite the same.

Francis would often bring home the runts of a litter to nurture to health. On the night before my interview, I shared a bed with an orphaned lion cub called Mumfie. I'd slept with Mumfie in the bed before, unknown to Mum. Through the night, Mumfie would wedge her bum in my face and then she would wake me up in the morning by licking me, to say that it was time for her breakfast.

The next morning, the door opened and Mum walked in. She took one look at the lion cub, another at me and screamed her head off, convinced that I was about to be savaged by a wild animal. I suppose she had a point.

Once the fuss had died down, I dressed in my best outfit—a beautiful 40s-style jacket and dress (a very Roland Mouret look), high heels and a handbag, which I hoped would make me look older than my 16 years and far more sophisticated than I felt. And I might have even managed to look a little bit glamorous if I hadn't been hitching a lift to Cambridge in a Windsor Safari Park Range Rover, painted in zebra-striped camouflage.

Scattering straw behind us at every corner, we drove into Cambridge for our first sight of the beautiful city. Ancient colleges, manicured courts and serene cloisters, just as I had seen in the university prospectus, but bigger and so much more imposing in reality. I had never in my young life seen buildings as wonderful and instantly enchanting as these.

Our zebra-mobile juddered to a halt outside Sidney Sussex College and Mum and I jumped down, plucked the last few stray pieces of straw from our clothes and walked in for my interview. We hadn't a clue what to expect and didn't have anyone to consult beforehand, so it was 'make it up as you go along' time.

The porter ushered us through a beautiful courtyard and into the college building. There, I was led into an imposing oak-panelled room for my interview with Mr Donald Green, Director of Studies for Engineering, and Doctor Keith Glover, then a research fellow at the college.

I was immediately taken aback by Mr Green's ordered speech; every word breathed discipline. Never before in my life had I met anyone who actually said 'graaass' (rhyming with a**e) instead of 'grass' (rhyming with ass). I'd only heard it on the BBC.

My hands were trembling slightly and I felt hot, but I hoped they didn't notice. In fact, they couldn't have been nicer. They asked me about school and my interests (I avoided telling them about the nightclubs) and talked a bit about how young I was to apply at 16.

Next, they began to ask me about engineering. Everything was fine until they asked me what a pitot tube was. I didn't have the faintest idea. They started to drop hints. Something at the front of planes, an aeronautical instrument for measuring something. The blood started to rise to my face and I blushed as I tried to bluff my way through.

At the end of the interview, they invited my mother in for a sherry. She was utterly terrified, but, speaking in her very best telephone voice and sitting elegantly, she managed to share pleasantries. As soon as we left, she turned and asked, 'So, how did it go?'

'It was a disaster. I blew it, Mum.'

'I'm sure you didn't. They seemed very nice . . .'

'They were. But they asked me about pitot tubes.'

'And?'

'I didn't know what they were!'

'What's so wrong with that?'

'Only that pitot tubes are on every single plane in the sky. And I told them I wanted to be an airline pilot . . .'

As far as I was concerned, I had blown it.

\*　　　\*　　　\*

In the winter of 1977, Mum had left Gabriel once more and we were living back at Anton's flat. Yet again, I had left my cosy bedroom at home for a small bed next to the duplicating machine.

Anton had a new money-making scheme and I was his willing accomplice. His latest cutting-edge business idea was to sell Christmas tinsel at the markets. It was December and Anton was busily buying offcuts from the tinsel factory, re-bagging it and then driving up to Edinburgh, ready to sell it at the open-air market at Ingliston.

I had spent the previous few weeks painstakingly separating blue, gold, red and green tinsel into different corners of the front room, then measuring the lengths and putting them into bags, ready to be sold. The front room was more glittery than Santa's grotto. Meanwhile, my eyes flashed with sparkling tinsel wherever I looked.

But right now, a letter from Cambridge was sitting under my nose. Mum and Anton had both gone to work and I was on my own. I reached out—and then hesitated. After a pause, I forced myself to pick up the letter, carefully open the envelope and read the first few lines.

I remember seeing 'Dear Miss Vorderman' and then something about a place in Michaelmas Term 1978 (winter term, to you and me). The words literally danced in front of my eyes. My heart lifted inside my chest. I simply couldn't believe the letter that I was reading. I couldn't believe I had got into Cambridge! I knew in that instant that my life had changed. Having convinced myself that I wasn't going to get a place, I was now totally beside myself with joy.

I walked down Anton's road without actually feeling the pavement beneath my feet. My head was light, but my feet were lighter still. I felt as if I were floating, in a dream. I, yes me, had been given a conditional offer, one of a handful given that year. I needed two grade As and a B in my A levels and that letter was my spur. I knuckled down to work far harder than I had ever done before.

Mum decided that I needed stability again and

went back to Gabriel. It was the equivalent of the separation hokey cokey.

*       *       *

I took my A levels, got the grades I needed and celebrated. For the formal do, Mum and Gabriel took us all out for prawn cocktail, chicken in a basket and Black Forest gâteau, all washed down with Lambrusco (we didn't do Champagne in those days) and a few bottles of Chianti. We drank Chianti at home and kept the chunky bottles wrapped in raffia and put candles in them, just like they did in restaurants. I liked them once the wax had dribbled its way down the sides, as they remained the witnesses to laughter and good times.

I 'went up' to Cambridge in October 1978 (you 'go up' to Cambridge, apparently, which confused me, as I was going down from north to south, and I couldn't ever quite get used to saying it). I was only 17 and most of the other students were a couple of years older, but it made no odds.

In my first year I shared a room, on Y staircase, with my friend Sue Thomas, who was reading what's known as 'natural sciences' (chemistry was her thing) and we soon found we had a lot in common. Like me, Sue was just 17, she hailed from Blackburn, so we shared a northern bond, and she had been educated at a state school. We became good friends, which was a relief, seeing as our quarters were pretty cramped. We slept in a tiny room in two metal beds and shared a small sitting room where we entertained and studied.

Sue bounded with energy. She would buy one

loaf of granary bread each day, which she would eat in front of me, despite my protests, as I picked away at a salad. We were both size 8, but Sue—who could pile any amount of food into her mouth each day on top of her requisite granary loaf—maintained her perfect figure with absolutely no effort at all, while I had to work hard to stay slim.

Sue is now a Professor of Chemistry at Imperial College, London, and is one of the finest female scientists of our age. She has won countless scientific awards, including the inaugural Rosalind Franklin award in 2003, a significant prize in the scientific world.

When Sue married the young and handsome Professor Vernon Gibson, now a fellow of the Royal Society, in our chapel at Sidney Sussex College many years later, she was bursting with happiness as she is a beautiful and kind person. We'd never have been able to predict our future paths back then—it's funny where life takes you.

I threw myself into college life. I got a bike like everybody else, but my riding style was a bit hampered by my dress sense. Standard uniform for all students at Cambridge in those days was a pair of jeans, a college scarf and trainers. I was absolutely determined not to change what I would normally wear just to look like everyone else. In those days, I loved to dress in a 70s glam rock style. Abba were at their height, and there were definite shades of Agnetha in my day-to-day outfits.

Pride of my wardrobe was a pair of thigh-length leather boots. Years later, I wore those same boots when I was Cher in *Celebrity Stars in Their Eyes*, proving that a good pair of boots never dies! I wore these boots virtually every single day, teamed with the tightest red velveteen trousers, a white shirt and a matching bow tie. That's how I got my college nickname of 'Boots Vorderman'. Not very original, I suppose, but that's what it was.

If I had worn normal jeans and trainers, I would have reached my lectures at least four times faster than I did. But instead, I would attempt to cycle to the engineering department with my thigh-length boots on, which made each turn of the pedals difficult. The tightly hugging trousers didn't help much either, but I refused to be beaten. I raised the seat of my bike really high, so that I didn't have to flex my leather-clad knees quite so much, which meant my bottom was so high from the ground that my bike resembled a penny-farthing. But I didn't care. I simply set out with plenty of time to spare— and wobbled my way to lectures.

I was on a full maintenance grant, but once I'd paid for my rent and food, there was very little money left over for clothes. So I happily set about making my own. I had the college sewing machine in my room almost all of the time and I would buy cheap material and then fashion myself shirts and dresses. Once I had made my outfits for the term, I would sometimes buy one pot of Dylon dye, pour it into the bath and then dye all my clothes the same colour, as I didn't have the time or money for any variation. So it was that I had a 'green' term, thanks to a green pot, a 'red' term, thanks to a red pot, and so on.

We engineering students had a lot of work to do; we had to go to lectures six days a week, including Saturdays, and we worked 12-hour days. There were around 300 students in each academic year in the engineering department, and just ten of us were girls.

I loved the engineering jocks. We would all cram into the lecture halls together, jostling to sit in the back few rows so we didn't have to put our hands up and answer any questions. Before each lecture started, the boys would happily show me their rugby bruises and tell me, in full, colourful detail, how many times they had thrown up the night before.

I had been brought up on all that stuff, with builders around all day and night, so it was like a home from home. There were a lot of fiercely bright young people: Geoff, who was a genius with electronics; Grant Philpott, one of my big buddies, who was in the army; Kevin, who was a right laugh; Tim and Dave Webber; Pete and all the others. We were a nice gang.

Right at the back of the hall, with our seats raised so that we could look down at the fifteen or so rows of seats ahead of us, we were in prime position for note-passing. One particular morning, I remember seeing something being passed all the way along the first and second rows. I could see shoulders shaking with laughter, and then I noticed that people were looking towards the back and pointing at me.

Slowly but surely, this note was passed along each row, and as it gradually grew closer, I could hear the guffaws of all the male engineers. It reached our row at the back, and now I could see that all the excitement was over a particular kind of magazine. The boys in my row gazed at the open page, looked at me and broke down laughing. I held my hand out and said, 'Give,' and the article reached me at last. My jaw dropped open. There, right in front of me, in a top-shelf lads' mag, was a model who was my absolute doppelganger.

For a split second, I thought I was actually looking at a photograph of myself. Then I realised three things. Her name was Roxy. She wasn't wearing very much at all. And she definitely didn't have her legs crossed. I must have looked utterly horrified, because the entire lecture hall, filled with hundreds of male students, now collapsed in hysterics. I opened my mouth to protest that, no, this wasn't me. But there was no point in trying to insist that this was merely a lookalike; Roxy was my mirror image. I hope she's had a nice life.

It was a privilege to be at Cambridge. I didn't go out with any other student while I was there, as I had boyfriends at home, but I had some great friends. Kumu Ratnatunga was one of my dearest female friends. Kumu's parents were from Sri Lanka and she could halt a party in its tracks when someone asked her what her father did for a living (they asked you questions like that at Cambridge). Gorgeous, sweet, softly spoken Kumu would say, 'Oh, he's a leading venereologist. In other words, he knows everything there is to know about sexually transmitted diseases.' It would make me laugh so much.

And then there was Jon Stoodley, the most handsome man in Cambridge, in my view. Stoodley was doing his Ph.D. in international law, but he could have been studying ancient animal droppings for all I cared. A good friend he was part of the gang as well.

I had friends in other colleges too. In Magdalene was the lovely Luca, an Italian charmer with the most ready smile and soft voice. Clever too, but I guess that went with the territory.

Another of my best friends was Graham Goddard, the president of the university athletics club. Tall and slim, with mountains of bushy hair, his purpose in life was to make people laugh, and he made us laugh all the time. Some years after we left Cambridge, when he was a young teacher and married with a child, he lapsed into a diabetic coma from which he never recovered. Graham was special and I still miss him.

I liked hanging out with my bedder, Vera. If you stayed in the halls of residence, you got your room tidied and your bed made every day and that person was called your 'bedder'. Vera and I, on the days I couldn't quite make it to lectures, would drink tea together and have a chat while I did a bit of sewing. I sometimes used to cycle out to her house on a council estate, where she put up foreign students for a bit of extra cash. I liked Vera very much; she was a kind lady.

At Cambridge I became very quickly aware, for the first time ever, of the class system. Up until I went to university I had never met anyone who had gone to public school, let alone somewhere like Eton. In the first week, a girl invited me to take tea in her room and when I turned up, she asked me what type of tea I wanted. I replied, 'Weak, with milk,' but she said, 'I meant, do you want Assam, Darjeeling or Lapsang Souchong?' Until that moment, I'd thought that the only variety of tea available was tea with milk or without milk. But the class system didn't bother me; I just found it interesting. I had posh friends and not-so-posh friends.

I learned how that just because someone 'spoke

posh' as we said back home, it didn't necessarily mean they were snobs and, equally, how dreadful some snobs could be. I learned about academia, and the joy of knowledge. Cambridge unquestionably taught me many things and not just engineering formulae.

Our holidays were always spent on work placements. 'Oh darling, I spent the summer travelling' was not something you'd hear from an engineering student. My first summer was spent learning how to use a lathe and a blow torch, and during the second summer I spent ten weeks working in Snowdonia at the Dinorwig Power Station, on their pumped-storage hydroelectric scheme.

The construction site was like something from a James Bond movie. The power station was being built deep inside the beautiful Elidir Fawr Mountain and had 16 kilometres of tunnels and an enormous, high central cavern. Out of the 3,000 people who worked there underground, I was the only girl. They were a bit sceptical as to whether or not I could take the heat and the ribbing, but that was water off a duck's back for me, as I'd had it for years on building sites with Gabriel. There wasn't anything I hadn't heard shouted on building sites, and I wasn't fazed at all.

I had three sets of overalls—khaki, orange and white—and every day I would co-ordinate my hard hat with whichever one I'd chosen to wear. A girl still had to be a girl, even if I was hundreds of feet underground!

By the time my third year arrived, I had thoroughly thrown myself into the amazing social life that Cambridge had to offer, but I didn't make quite the same effort when it came to my studies. I had scored a third—the lowest grade—on both my end of year papers, and now, with my final year stretching ahead of me, I decided it was time to get to grips with work. At school, this tactic had always worked, so I assumed that it would work again.

In fact, I worked so hard in those months leading up to the third-year exams that I was quite convinced that I had managed to haul my grade up to a 2:1, or Upper Second, as they were also known. On the day of our final results, the list of grades was put up on a board in the centre of the city and jostling with the others to see the board I checked the 2:1s, 2:2s and firsts and couldn't find my name. I was starting to think that maybe there had been some clerical error, and then my eyes wandered over to the list of Thirds. There it was. I couldn't have missed it because there weren't very many of us on the list. Engineering: Third Class Honours: Vorderman, Carol.

I had got a Third, a gentleman's degree. I was disappointed, obviously, but after a few minutes, my thoughts changed completely.

To hell with it! I had a degree from Cambridge—and I'd had a blast. No-one could take that away from me. With that, I left with my fellow engineers to go and celebrate. Loudly.

I have since been told many times that getting a Third from Cambridge is now known as 'Getting a Vorderman'! So I've been left with an accolade I'm proud of, and I ignore others who can get a bit sniffy about it.

Years later, when Richard Whiteley and I were talking about Cambridge, we realised that we had both scored Thirds in every one of our three years at Cambridge. 'So, Whiters,' I said to him one night in a restaurant, 'three times three is nine. Let's set up the Nines Club and we can be the first members.' He thought that was yet more proof of why we should be together and was so proud of the under-achievement that we both shared. He sat there looking extremely pleased and said, 'It is very difficult to get three Thirds, Vorders—it takes an awful lot of skill. Let's have another bottle to celebrate.'

## HOUSE MATES

My graduation from Cambridge in June 1981 was a 'golden day'. In our family, when things are so good that calling them great doesn't do them justice, we call them golden days, and when they come along they are perfect and filled with love and laughter.

And so it was on my graduation day. Mum was there and she was so proud. I was the first person from our family to get any kind of degree and it was a degree from the University of Cambridge, something we could only have dreamed of all those years before, sharing a bed in our little flat in Prestatyn. Anton had come to see his little sis graduate too. And so had Trixie, Francis and my cousin Pamela. Gabriel couldn't come, as he had a huge building job to finish on a very tight deadline. I don't think my father, Tony Vorderman, was even aware I was at university.

It was such a special occasion that I had my straight brown hair permed. Big mistake. It sprang up, in the style of Ronald McDonald, with my mortarboard bouncing helplessly on top. To this day, Mum has that picture from my graduation on her mantelpiece and everyone who sees it does a double take and says, 'Is that really you . . . with the hair?' Yep. And the cold sore to go with it.

After the graduation ceremony in the Senate House, we all walked back to Sidney Sussex College (famed in Cambridge for having former student Oliver Cromwell's head buried somewhere in the grounds and for being opposite Sainsbury's). There was a huge and happy graduation party in the Master's garden and I've rarely seen my mum look so full of life. Years before, all I could give her was a good school report and now I'd given her the best report of all. She was so proud of me, I nearly exploded with joy. She was walking on air, and so was I.

But the problem with walking on air is that life sometimes brings you down to earth with a bump. And it did just that within a matter of weeks.

*       *       *

Straight after university, I joined a graduate traineeship with a company called Christian Salvesen. I needed to earn money. Years before, I had longed to become a pilot, but by the time I graduated, airlines had hit a rocky economic patch, there was a glut of pilots and British Airways, the only company who could have trained me, had closed down their pilot training school. So what was a girl to do? The only other way to train was to have sponsorship or a huge amount of private money. Needless to say, I had neither, so along with thousands of others, I applied for jobs during what is known as 'the milk round' at Cambridge, when companies come to the city looking for graduates to snap up.

Christian Salvesen was the first job I applied for, and I accepted their offer gratefully. I was just 20 years old and my first assignment in the summer of 1981 was to go to Lowestoft and work in a frozen pea factory.

In Lowestoft, I learned to drive a forklift truck, looking like a Michelin man in the protection outfit we had to wear in the massive cold-storage warehouses, which were held at minus 22 degrees. I was back into engineering and I loved it.

After a few weeks of settling in, I went home to Wales one weekend to see Mum. She was waiting with some devastating news.

She was going to leave Gabriel again. I remember talking to her about it and saying, 'You love him, Mum.' But this was to be the final time. I knew from the look on her face that her mind was made up. She told me that she'd decided to go at least a year earlier, but had kept on with the marriage in case it had upset me and affected my degree result.

I was upset—terribly upset. Gabriel was my dad. He had hugged me, teased me and loved me in a way that Tony Vorderman never had. And now this man, with his booming voice, vast brickie's hands and huge Italian heart, was going to be out of my life for good. I knew now that this was the last time I would say goodbye to my little bedroom which was kept so warm by the Aga in the kitchen.

Mum wanted a clean break and to get as far away from Wales as she could, to start a new life. It was a daunting prospect. She was 53 and she was about to walk out of a marriage, a family home and stability with absolutely nothing—no money, no job and nowhere to live. But there was never any question in my mind that it was my job to support her—and that meant helping her with the getaway.

Much as I hated every moment of it, we both knew that if she was going to make a clean break of it this time, then we had to plan her departure with military-style precision. It was important that Gabriel had no idea that she was leaving, in case he tried to talk her round again. I could see she was in no state for a big scene, so we had to quietly steal away.

We were to leave on a morning when Gabriel was due at the quarry; that way we would have a couple of hours to ourselves to pack up before any other builders were on site at the house. I had passed my driving test when I was 17 and one of the first things Gabriel had done was buy me a clapped-out old Simca. When the Simca gasped its last dying breath from its exhaust, I moved on to a Datsun. It was hardly an upgrade, because the Datsun was literally a rust-bucket on wheels, with a huge hole in the floor, which meant you could actually see the road as you drove. I'd covered the hole with a plank of wood and a bit of carpet, on the principle of 'outta sight, outta mind', and both wing mirrors were taped on with masking tape. But those were our wheels, and they would be our ticket out of Denbigh and out of Mum's marriage.

You could almost set your watch by Gabriel's movements and we knew that he would leave for the quarry just after 5.30 in the morning. Once we heard him start the engine of his truck and head out of the driveway, Mum and I crept downstairs. By the time we had got her few things—and mine—into the car it was 6.30 and we knew we had to leave then because any minute now Gabriel would be coming home for his breakfast.

My heart felt heavy that morning, but we packed quickly. As it was almost impossible to see out of the back of the car for all the boxes and bags we had piled up on the back seat, I inched out of the back yard and down the drive. Now, there were only two ways out of Denbigh. Each route went past a quarry and the last thing I wanted to do was to run into Gabriel on our way out of town. Mum was a nervous wreck by this time.

'Which way?' I asked Mum when we reached the gate.

'What do you mean, which way?' said Mum, looking confused.

'Which quarry did he go to?'

'I have no idea!'

'I can't believe you didn't ask him!' I said.

'I didn't want him to guess what we were up to.'

'Mum! What if we pass him in the road?'

'We'll just have to take our chances, Carol.'

And so, with no other choice, that's what we did. I'd like to say we sped out of town that morning in the style of a grand getaway, but my little Datsun could barely reach 50 miles an hour without leaving clouds of black smoke. So we hopped, belched and juddered our way unseen out of town—and into our new and empty lives. That day, I didn't think about not seeing Gabriel again, as it would have got in the way of the job in hand, and I'd probably have turned back.

Everything we owned was in that car and even if

it did manage to take up most of the back seat and boot, it didn't amount to very much. Just some clothes, toiletries, ornaments, a few photo albums and my books. Mum was adamant that she wouldn't take anything from Gabriel that wasn't hers. She even left all the pots and pans behind. She left Gabriel as she came to him: with little more than the clothes on her back and her youngest daughter, me, in tow. She had virtually nothing in her bank account—maybe a few hundred quid—and I certainly had nothing in mine. I drove, in tears, out of Wales and down the motorway to Windsor.

Mum had decided to move away completely and went to live close to Trixie, who was still at the safari park. Within a short time, she'd found herself a good job as a PA to the gentleman who owned Corby Trouser Presses of Windsor and several other companies. She lived with Trixie for a few months, but when Trixie had her second child, my lovely nephew Chris, she moved into some digs in student land. I helped her move in, and it was a sobering time for both of us.

My mother, who had worked so hard all her life and had put everyone else first, was moving into a little bedsit. Everything we'd had in the back of the Datsun was now in this single room, along with a bed, a wardrobe and a dressing table. While most other 53-year-old women can look forward to winding down and enjoying their home comforts, Mum was facing full-time work and soulless lodgings just to survive.

I found this one of the most distressing times in my life. I was missing my home in Denbigh and the dreams of how the world would be my oyster when

73

I was at Cambridge were fading fast. The reality was that while we were there as students, we were all relatively equal. However, as soon as we'd graduated, money and backgrounds kicked in and the gap widened again dramatically. Cambridge perhaps was the easy bit. It would be work for me from now on, just as I had always suspected.

I was working in Northampton and, while Mum lived in her single room, would drive nearly three hours (before there was an M25) once or twice a week to see her. Sharing a bedroom again, we would have night-time chats in the dark about the things we would do if everything came good, and she would tell me stories about her work which made us laugh. When I wasn't with her, I worried about her terribly and I pined for her, and for Gabriel.

We are such a close family and we had always enjoyed having a family home, somewhere filled with drama and laughter, like Pal Gardens and Gabriel's house. Suddenly, there was no home for us all to come back to.

As ever, we were hardy and got on with our lives and still laughed a lot, but something had to give. We were the only ones who could get ourselves out of this mess, which only served to confirm to me, as if I needed confirmation, that everything I'd felt about having to look after myself when I was older was true.

Then, many months into my job with Christian Salvesen, in the spring of 1982, I stumbled upon the answer to our problems. My long-standing boyfriend was from Yorkshire, so I was spending a fair bit of time in Leeds and, quite simply, I fell head over heels in love with the city and the people. I just loved the way they bantered and joked and teased each other in a deadpan way.

So one rainy Saturday morning, I found myself standing outside an estate agent's window. My mind was elsewhere and I was simply looking disinterestedly when I spotted a smallish three-bedroomed semi with very pretty windows with criss-crossed leaded lights. It was such a lovely house: 2 Moor Park Villas in Headingley.

The price was £20,500, which seemed like a fortune to me, as I was earning less than £4,000 a year at the time. But I suddenly thought of Mum, living miserably in her lodgings. Suppose we combined our salaries and got a joint mortgage? That night, I went back to my digs and sat down and did what I always do when faced with a problem—I did some sums. It was clear to me that we could afford a mortgage of £17,000.

The problem was securing it. Back then, banks would only lend you about twice your annual salary and you had to put down a hefty cash deposit. With our salaries put together, Mum and I could afford to pay the mortgage each month, but neither of us had a penny of savings. Just then, when I needed financial help for the first time in my life, my big brother Anton stepped in. He had been working hard and saving and so, without hesitating, he offered to lend Mum and I the £4,500 deposit we needed to secure the house. Now all I had to do was to tell Mum about my grand plans.

This was a turning point in both our lives. What I have always loved about my mum is that she will try anything, so I hoped she would hear me out. Most women of 53 would have laughed, especially as the facts didn't exactly make it sound like the opportunity of a lifetime. Mum had never been to Yorkshire in her life. My job, by then, was in Lancashire; her job was in Windsor. We had no money. We had no furniture. The chances of success were just a little above zero. But Mum has never been daunted by any challenge. When I rang and told her that I had found a house for us to jointly buy, she considered the prospect for a minute and then, after a short hesitation, she said firmly, 'Well, as long as it is near a bus stop.'

That was her only condition of the move. She happily left the buying of the house and mortgage arrangements to me, so I beavered away to make sure everything worked out in the right way.

The first time she saw our beautiful, happy little house—or even set foot in Leeds—was the day we moved in. We drew up outside in a cloud of smoke, back in the rickety old Datsun once more. Trixie's friend Christine had sold us some curtains at a rock-bottom price, as well as a big four-seater sofa, which we squeezed into the front room. We had a home to call our own at last, but no money for anything else.

Sheets were pinned up over the bedroom windows for a while, and the single set of curtains that we bought from Trixie's friend were so ill-fitting that we had to close them with some clothes pegs every evening. Even after I had been on television for a long while, I would still come home from a day of recording and peg the hand-me-down curtains together before bed—my nightly ritual.

Mum and I managed to buy two second-hand beds, but we were hardly living in luxury. The house had remained untouched for decades by its former elderly inhabitants. Threadbare carpet lay in each room, in various nylon shades of ugh. In my bedroom, where the carpet was a faded blue, someone had once placed a hot iron face down, so as soon as you walked in, a scorched iron-shaped mark stood out like a beacon.

Wallpaper from the 70s hung peeling from the walls and the tiny bathroom had a sink which was somehow miraculously hanging on to the wall, despite the crack which ran down the middle. Our only heating came from some rusted radiators which clanked and complained and occasionally provided some warm air, while in my bare bedroom I relied on a one-bar electric heater which was positioned perilously above the head of my bed.

Mum got a job with a firm of accountants very quickly and our house slowly but surely started to become a home. We didn't have a washing machine, so every Sunday afternoon we would carry our washing to the local launderette—another ritual which continued for a good few years after I had started on *Countdown*.

To our neighbours, Mum and I must have looked like unlikely housemates. After all, most 20-year-olds do everything they can to move away from their parents and have an independent life. But here I was, not only choosing to live with Mum, but also sharing a mortgage with her. There was absolutely no doubt in my mind that our future was together. We got on so well and, after all we'd been through, I couldn't imagine any other way to live. I just wanted to be with her.

I had the home I had always wanted, my Mum was still with me and I had a good job with prospects. Then something happened which was to change our lives dramatically.

It all began because of Mum and her addiction to newspapers. We had only been in our house for a few weeks when she started getting the *Yorkshire Evening Post*. Each night, after work, she would scour every paragraph, cutting out any articles of interest to add to her endless pile of press cuttings.

One evening, as I sat watching television and she was poring over the front page of her *Yorkshire Evening Post*, she let out a sudden little 'Ooh, Carol' and sat up with a start.

'Oh, you must read this,' she urged. 'This is right up your street.'

To be honest, I wasn't really listening. *Coronation Street* had just begun and I thought her article was probably something about a new way to cook without having to prepare anything. She would exist on chocolate and the dried food they give to astronauts if it was up to her.

'What is it, Mum?' I asked, with one eye firmly fixed on the television.

'There's an article here saying that Yorkshire Television is looking for a girl, good at maths, to appear on a television quiz show they are launching.'

'And?'

'And you'd be perfect for the job.'

'I've got a job, Mum.'

'Well, just have a look at the article anyway. It's very interesting.'

She handed me the paper and pointed to a short article on the front page. I quickly cast my eye over it. Apparently, a producer at Yorkshire Television was desperately trying to find someone to come up with the answers in a 'numbers game' on a new quiz show called *Countdown*. The applicant, the article stated, must be good at mental arithmetic and be able to think on their feet. The previous contender, an attractive girl whose photograph was printed on the front page and was around the same age as me, had dropped out of the local test show to do a degree and now they were desperately looking for someone to fill her shoes.

'Why don't you apply for it?' Mum asked eagerly, as I handed the newspaper back to her.

'Oh, Mum!'

'Why not? I think you'd be very good at it.'

'Because, Mum, firstly, as I said, I have a job and a good job at that and secondly, they aren't going to give me a part on a TV show.'

'Why not? They are looking for "someone with brains and beauty" it says here, and you've certainly got those.

'Well, you would say that, wouldn't you? You're my mother,' I said laughing, and squirming.

'I still think you should give it a go. Who knows what will happen?'

'I'll tell you what will happen, Mum. Nothing.'

'Why not?'

'Because they don't put people like me on the telly, that's why. I've got a better chance of getting to the moon than landing a job on TV.'

And with that I stood up and walked over to the television to turn up the volume, hoping that Mum would change the subject. By the time *Corrie* finished, I was more concerned with what I was going to wear to impress the boyfriend that weekend. I had also forgotten that you should never underestimate the sheer determination and cunning of my Mum.

## A NUMBERS GAME

### My Mother's Greatest Work of Fiction

2 Moor Park Villas
Far Headingley
Leeds 6

13 August 1982

J Meade, Esq.
Yorkshire Television Limited
Television Centre
Leeds 3

Dear Mr Meade,
I read of your search for a Channel 4 hostess in the *Yorkshire Evening Post*. If it's brains and beauty you want, addition is no problem and I enclose a recent photo for you to judge the second qualification.

I am aged 21 and in June 1981 graduated from Cambridge University with a BA Honours degree in civil engineering. I have twelve O levels and A levels in maths, physics and economics. Since August last year, I have been employed by Christian Salvesen Ltd on a graduate management-training course, working for the technical director of the cold-storage division.

I am fairly keen on sport, but not a fanatic. I

rowed for my college's Ladies First VIII; and at present I jog, play squash and generally keep fit. In the summer of 1980 I worked for McAlpine's at the Dinorwig Pumped Storage Scheme in Snowdonia, as a junior site engineer in the underground section.

I know that you must be inundated with applications for this very sought-after job, but I feel I have nothing to lose by applying, and certainly everything to gain should I get it!

Anyway, here's hoping for an interview!

Yours truly,

Carol Jean Vorderman, BA (Cantab)

Nearly 30 years later, this letter still makes my toes curl with embarrassment. The whole thing was a forgery, typed up during a lunch break by the criminal mastermind otherwise known as my mother. Where she got the bit about how I loved playing squash from, goodness only knows. That night, she raced home with the letter, proudly showing me what she had written.

I nearly died. 'Mum! I can't believe you've done this,' I said in utter horror once I had read it. Mistaking my comment for praise, Mum looked really pleased with herself.

'Well, I knew you weren't going to do it yourself, so I thought I'd take the matter into my own hands. All you have to do is sign here. I left a space for your signature.'

There was no way I was going to sign the letter. The whole idea of it was ridiculous. But Mum just wouldn't have it. I told her again that people who appeared on television were big, big stars. I was an ordinary girl, in an ordinary house, with a clothes peg holding her curtains together, and was very happy with my lot. She didn't listen.

So the application letter, addressed to the producer, remained unsigned. Well, at least unsigned by me. Because the very next day, without me knowing, my mum forged my signature with a flourish, enclosed a copy of my graduation photograph (yes, the one with the bad perm and the cold sore) and posted it to Yorkshire Television—first class.

It took another few days for her to tell me what she had done. I just shook my head. There was no point getting angry with her because no-one was ever going to read the cringey thing. I was sure it would end up in a big box somewhere, in the corner of an office. I knew that I had no chance of ever hearing from Yorkshire Television.

In the early 80s, the television industry was totally different from the way it is today. Now, with people having access to hundreds of channels and reality shows airing on all of them, a lot of young hopefuls see the industry as an opportunity for instant fame. When my mum sent her letter, it couldn't have been more different. For a start, we only had three television stations, a fact that my children now find hard to believe. There was BBC1, BBC2 and ITV, and that was it.

Channel 4 wasn't launching until November 1982 and it was destined to be a big deal. Back then, television wasn't transmitted around the clock. At the start of that decade, we didn't have daytime television as we know it now. If you took a day off sick, there would be no nice, cosy magazine format to keep you company as you staved off the flu. There was no Anne and Nick, Richard and

Judy or Holly and Phil on hand to entertain. If you tuned in during the day, you had two options. Either you could watch some educational programme aimed at schoolchildren or those taking an Open University degree, or you would find yourself staring at the BBC test card with its now iconic image of a young girl in a red dress and matching headband playing noughts and crosses with a stuffed clown. There was certainly no such thing as 'surfing' television channels. Most of us had never seen a remote control. Remember how we actually used to have to get off the sofa to change the channel or turn the volume up or down?

In the dark ages of early 1982 we didn't even have breakfast television and when it was imported over to our shores from the States at the beginning of 1983 it was met with a mixture of consternation, derision and even suspicion. 'It won't last, you'll see,' a neighbour told me at the time, her lips pursed in disapproval. 'They can do what they want in America, but people over here won't want to watch the telly when they are having their breakfast. It's just not right.'

Less choice meant that the programmes we did watch united us. Our family, like millions of others across the country, would sit on the sofa after dinner and tune in to watch the classic television shows of the time: *The Morecambe & Wise Show*, *The Generation Game*, *Dallas*. Whatever you chose, you could guarantee that your friends and family would have watched the same thing. So the people who appeared on television at that time were living legends: Michael Parkinson, Terry Wogan, the two Ronnies, Noel Edmonds, David

Frost.

Unless they were actresses, the women who made it onto television clearly came from two totally different camps. There were the 'thinkers', many of whom were also very glamorous, who carried considerable clout, like Joan Bakewell, Angela Rippon, Esther Rantzen and Anna Ford. And then there were the dolly birds with beauty queen looks, tumbling hair and shimmering evening dresses.

Perhaps the biggest difference between then and now is that normal people—and certainly girls like me—didn't get on the television. There was no 'instant' fame. The few who did reach the heady heights of TV stardom had worked their way up in the tough working men's clubs circuit or on the cub-reporting trail with local newspapers for years. Celebrity was hard-earned at that time.

So in the weeks that followed I hardly thought about the letter and the job.

Then the phone rang . . .

'Carol, can you answer that?' Mum called from the kitchen.

It was early evening and I had just come home from work. Meanwhile, Mum had her hands full getting our tea ready. I was trying to take my coat off while I answered it, with one arm in and one arm out of the sleeves.

'Can I speak to Carol Vorderman?' said a voice with a broad Yorkshire accent.

'That's me. Carol speaking.' I said happily.

'Good. I'm calling from the *Countdown* office about your application to do the numbers.'

'Er, yes . . .'

'Well, we'll have to test your maths before we

take it any further. Are you around on Sunday afternoon?'

For a moment I was totally dumbstruck, still standing half in and half out of my coat. 'Er . . . yes . . . that would be great. What time?'

The man I was speaking to introduced himself as John Meade, the producer. By the time I put the phone down, Mum was hovering by my side, her apron on and our tea forgotten. My whole body was jangling with nerves, excitement and disbelief. I said, 'I've got a test on Sunday. A maths test,' and then laughed myself senseless at the madness of the situation.

Mum was so excited.

We laughed and laughed, leaping around and skipping and whooping like a couple of crazy kids.

Even then, I thought nothing would come of it. During the week, they sent me the rules of the numbers game, but they weren't the right ones and made the game seem much harder than it actually was. Put loosely, their rules said that every part of the answer had to flow as one long sum, which meant that you couldn't do two separate sums, like $6 \times 100 = 600$ and $4 \times 9 = 36$ and then add those answers together ($600 + 36 = 636$), which made most of the sums I'd been practising pretty difficult.

As I looked at the sums, the thought that they could lead me to appear on television seemed utterly ludicrous. In the studios of Yorkshire Television, where I was going to do my sums test, I knew that they recorded some of the biggest shows at the time. The great Les Dawson's programmes often came from there, as well as *Rising Damp* with Leonard Rossiter. *3-2-1* with Ted Rogers was a massive Saturday night show, even bigger than *The X Factor* is today. Then there was Jimmy Tarbuck and his huge comedy quiz shows, as well as the ratings winner, the Yorkshire-based soap opera *Emmerdale Farm*. In charge of the light entertainment department was the legendary Vernon Lawrence and reigning supreme alongside him were TV executives like Sir Paul Fox, John Fairley and John Willis, who'd made their names as great programme-makers.

Bizarrely, this planned new show, *Countdown*, came from the local news department, and it had been piloted over the summer for six weeks. The knocked-together set was made of plywood walls, a basic wooden desk and a large clock. For the pilot series Richard Whiteley, the presenter of the local news programme *Calendar*, had turned quizmaster and the cheap and cheerful show had been a surprise success.

When I turned up for the maths test, I knew absolutely nothing about television. I didn't have a clue what sort of thing I should wear, for a start, so I emptied out my wardrobe, trying to find something which looked smart among the overalls for work and the tight shorts and boob tubes for evening playtime. In the end, I settled for a pair of dark trousers and a plain top.

I arrived there that bright Sunday afternoon to find the building quiet and almost empty. Biting back my nerves, I walked up to reception and asked for John Meade.

John was a formidable man who looked so like a Mexican that he could have stepped straight from the set of a Clint Eastwood spaghetti western. He had olive skin, a large, drooping dark moustache,

86

longish black hair and wore a pair of Cuban-heeled boots. It was only when he opened his mouth that you knew he wasn't from Acapulco but was, in fact, a Yorkshireman. John sat me down and talked me through the programme. *Countdown*, he explained in a weary voice (he'd been through a lot of interviews by this time), was a to be a new quiz show based on a popular French game, which had been devised by a man called Armand Jammot and brought to England by a Belgian gentleman, Marcel Stellman. Marcel and his exquisite wife Jeannie were to become family to me over the years that followed, and I love them dearly.

'In France it's called *Des Chiffres et des Lettres*. That's "numbers and letters" to you and me, love,' John said by way of explanation. He went on to say that they'd had thousands of applications 'from models and actresses who can't add up' and also from teachers (they'd had to advertise in the *Guardian* supplement when they'd realised it wasn't going to be easy finding someone) and even a statistics academic who'd written 40 books on the subject, apparently. Nobody, it seemed, had been able to solve the numbers puzzle fast enough. John was running out of time. It was now the end of the summer, they were due in the studio to record very soon and *Countdown* was to go out on Channel 4 when it started transmitting in November.

John led me into an office and sat on one side of a big desk. He plonked me on the other side and shoved a tape into the new-fangled video machine which was linked to a TV.

'I'm going to show you a couple of the French shows and you'll see how they answer the numbers game, OK? And then I'll show you a few more, but

I'll stop the tape when they've picked the numbers and you work out the answer,' he growled.

'OK, boss,' I said.

When I saw the first of the French shows, it was obvious to me that the rules YTV had written up and sent me were wrong. I needed to know which rules we were going to play by, so I stopped John and said, 'Um, excuse me, can I just check something first please? Do the French play by different rules from the ones you're going to use on *Countdown*?'

'No, why?'

'Well, it's just that the rules you sent through are different, but if you want me to play by the French rules then that's fine. Let's start.'

'French rules?' he said, confused. 'What you just saw on the telly, that's what we're doing.'

That was the answer I wanted to hear, as it made the solutions ten times easier to find.

He played the numbers selection, stopped the tape and said, 'Right, you can start working it . . .'

But I interrupted him and said, 'Got that.'

'What do you mean you've got that?' he demanded.

'I've got the answer.'

'Have you?' he said in genuine astonishment. 'How did you do it then?'

So I showed him. I think he'd started with an easy one.

Second game. Same thing happened, within a second.

Third test. Took a bit longer, about five seconds, but I did it.

Now, by this time, I was getting into my stride and wanted to carry on, as I am a woman obsessed with mental arithmetic. But John Meade seemed anxious to get on with his day. He said, '*If* we ask you back for a screen test, would you be able to come in next week?'

'I'll have to get time off work, but yes,' I said, really interested now, as I liked the numbers game so much.

A few days later, John Beresford Courtney de Winter Meade (for that was what he claimed was his full name, although he was most often known simply as JB) invited me for a screen test.

I took the day off work and reported back to Yorkshire TV. By now, nerves were starting to set in, but the screen test was an anti-climax. I was taken into a small room, put in front of a camera and asked a whole series of normal questions— 'Where are you from?' 'What do you watch on the telly?'—while the camera recorded my answers. Then I went home again, still not knowing if I'd got the gig or not.

To be honest, I was trying not to expect too much so to me, this was a bit of an adventure that I could tell my mates about in the pub that weekend. I still believed it wouldn't come to anything.

The phone call came a few days later and I instantly recognised the Yorkshire accent on the other end of the line.

'Carol, It's John Meade from *Countdown* speaking.'

'Oh hello, John, how are you?' My heart suddenly stopped and I could feel the adrenalin pumping around my body. I wanted to know if I'd got the job, but at the same time I didn't want to know, because then the adventure would be over.

Luckily, John wasn't one to waste time with

small talk.

'You've got the job, love, can you come in and see me?'

Stunned, I stuttered, 'That's fantastic, John! I won't let you down, I promise. Bye.'

I was standing in the small, dark hallway at home. For a few seconds, my brain scrambled. Something extraordinary and gut-churningly different was turning my life upside down. And there was only one thing I could do.

'Muuuuuuuuuuuuuuuuuuuummmmmmmmmmmm-mmmmm!' I screamed.

*       *       *

Three weeks later, I found myself sitting meekly in the corner of a studio at Yorkshire TV on the first day of filming. I had always been a confident child and a pretty confident young woman, but this was a whole different ball game. The plan was to rehearse all day and then film our first ever show later that evening.

Very quickly though, things began to unravel. The pilot show had featured two 'hostesses', the stunning and very beautifully spoken Cathy Hytner managing the letters and Denise McFarland-Cruickshanks doing the numbers game.

Now there was to be a change. Meaders (as he later became known, after cricket-commentating legend Brian Johnston (Johnners) appeared on *Countdown*), for reasons known only to himself, had told Cathy that her services were no longer required. Her replacement, a gorgeous model called Beverley Isherwood who had been on *It's a Knockout*, turned up for the first day of recording.

But very early on in the day somebody—John Meade or the Channel 4 bosses, I don't know which—decided they wanted Cathy back on the programme.

I knew something was going on, but obviously I wasn't part of the hasty discussions. The executive producer, the great Frank Smith, and the commissioning editor, Cecil Korer, were debating what to do. In the end, John Meade scuttled off to ring Cathy and—as gruffly as he had fired her— begged her to return for filming the next morning. It was decided that for the first ever *Countdown*, Beverley would pick out the numbers to put on the board, with Richard reading them out. Cathy would manage the letters and I would answer the numbers game. Nothing was actually recorded that day as Cathy wasn't there.

My contract stated that I would be paid about £30 per show and I was contracted to record 40 shows. Sharing my job was the very brilliant Dr Linda Barrett, who had a PhD in theoretical mechanics and was also able to answer the numbers game very quickly. Linda was lovely. We were to alternate shows, so while I recorded one show, she would watch from the sidelines and would then jump in to take over on the next one.

The set had been slightly changed, but because no-one ever thought that *Countdown* would carry on for more than one or two series, it was a bit, well, crap. Whiteley and I loved that set and laughed about it for years after. The letters and numbers were cardboard cut-outs with magnetic strips on the back which stuck to the other bits of magnetic strip on the letters board—if you were lucky. We had a clock with the ability to time

60 seconds, with 60 lights to match, but when the production team realised they wouldn't be able to squeeze enough 60-second rounds into a half-hour show, they couldn't afford to make a new 30-second clock. So the original cheap 60-second clock had to remain—even though only half of it was ever used.

In the studio the next day, I got a good look at my new surroundings. The set design meant that Cathy couldn't see Richard Whiteley and he couldn't see her. I also had no earpiece and no link to the control room. So effectively, standing in my corner, I was totally isolated.

I felt very nervous. Everything was bright, fast and furious, with John Meade running around like a demented cowboy in the middle of all the confusion, adding to the chaos.

For my first day of recording, I had carefully chosen my favourite outfit: a pair of suede tan trousers and a mustard-coloured top. I was shown into a small dressing room, which Linda and I were to share with Beverley and Cathy. Not normally one to be backward in coming forward, I was still a bit too scared to strip off in front of the others, so I crept into the toilets to change in private. I didn't know the other girls well enough yet.

Then I was called into the make-up room. There, someone furiously worked on my hair, setting it in rollers and creating something that wasn't me. I looked in the mirror and, to my mind, a brunette Molly Sugden was staring back. But I didn't have time to fret, because I was suddenly whisked back into the studio.

With recording about to start, I was given absolutely no instructions whatsoever. I didn't even realise that when a red light went on above a camera, it meant that the picture from that camera was what was being transmitted.

I just tried to concentrate on doing the sums correctly and making sure that the audience would understand what on earth I was talking about. When I look back, it was a rabbit-caught-in-the-headlights style of presenting. But with no knowledge and no real idea of what I was supposed to do, I had to just make it up as I went along.

By then, I had changed my 'proper job' from being a management trainee at Christian Salvesen to selling the very first desktop computers at Tandy and I took a couple of days of holiday so that I could record the first programmes.

I recognised Richard Whiteley immediately. He was a big name in Yorkshire. He was a bit lofty and pompous when we first met, introducing himself by announcing, 'I am the quiz-master.' None of which helped my nerves.

Richard was still presenting the live, daily local news programme *Calendar*. He recorded *Countdown* with us in the afternoon, then ran over to the *Calendar* studio to spend an hour presenting the live show, while the rest of us had a tea break. After he'd finished the news, he would run back to the *Countdown* studio, ready for another show. This was the reason he became known as 'Twice Nightly Whiteley'—because he was on telly twice within a few hours—although years later he would love to hint that it was more to do with his antics in the bedroom and then claim that he'd regressed to 'Once Yearly, Nearly'. Kathy, his partner in later years, said, 'He was called Twice Nightly Whiteley as that man is a martyr to his bladder!'

Keeping track of two different programmes a day was hard, and Richard would often kick off *Countdown* by saying, 'Hello, and welcome to *Calendar* . . .' before realizing his mistake.

One day, he was extremely tired and started to introduce the numbers game as the letters game, and in part two he did it again. He shook his head and muttered, 'Now why do I keep doing that?' At which point, his earpiece was filled with John Meade's droll voice, speaking from the recording gallery: 'Because, Whiteley, you're a c***, that's why.' That story became *Countdown* legend, and we loved to hear it told.

That was what brought us together really, the fact that we could sling insults at each other in a funny and fond way—banter. There was no standing on ceremony and I loved it, as it took me back to the days with Gabriel.

Right from the start, everyone had a view about the *Countdown* theme tune, written especially for the programme by the seasoned television composer Alan Hawkshaw. But Alan had almost said no to one of the most lucrative commissions in TV history. The station's head of music, Keith Morgan, had asked him to write it. He was busy with Arthur C. Clarke's new series, but said he could just about manage to squeeze it in. With only a few weeks left until we were in the studio, after hearing nothing, Keith rang Alan to remind him about the theme tune.

Alan told him it was coming along nicely—without admitting that he hadn't actually started working on it properly. Now, with next to no time to write it, he had to come up with something fast. He went to the toilet and started writing the theme

94

tune there and then.

Years later, he told us that this was how he'd found the inspiration for the cheerful piddly-piddly-ping at the end. It actually came from the tiddly-tiddly-plip as he sat on his enamel throne!

This was a Hawkshaw technique employed many times. He wrote the tunes for *Grange Hill* and the *Dave Allen* comedy series on the same toilet seat and the music for Channel 4 news in his bath. Putting them all down on paper later on, as it were.

It was this theme tune—complete with Alan's toilet tinkling at the end—which played out at 4.45 p.m. on 2 November 1982.

In the weeks leading up to the first programme, the press had been full of what this new innovative and daring channel would be about and we all took part in photoshoots (that was a strange new experience for me, but not for Cathy and Beverley, whose job it was to be photographed constantly) and interviews for newspapers. The big day arrived and a few minutes before the appointed time of 4.45 p.m. the screen went completely black.

Mum, Anton and I gathered together on the sofa at home, to watch the first ever show, the first time anyone we'd ever known had been on the telly, and that someone was little Casa (my brother's nickname for me). To mark this big moment, we'd bought a VHS video recorder and a bottle of Champagne and three straws.

The room suddenly fell quiet as the new channel exploded into life with a rousing montage of film clips, and then, after the continuity announcer had welcomed everyone to the channel, the first show on Channel 4 began. They could have chosen something dramatic and powerful, or something musical and light—anything really, rather than a parlour game with some magnetic letters and numbers on a board and a big clock with a hand that didn't go all the way round—but they didn't and *Countdown* began. The theme music started playing, the letters twizzled across the screen in the title sequence and then suddenly, there on our screen, was Richard Whiteley: the first person to be seen on Channel 4.

'Hello, hello, good evening,' he began. 'And as the countdown to a brand-new channel ends, a brand-new *Countdown* begins. This *Countdown* is a quiz game that all of you can play at home, so if you think you're good with figures or figure you're good with letters, well, we think this could be the game for you, because it's all about sums and anagrams. So why not grab a pencil and paper right now and I'll give you the rules . . .'

And so Richard went on to explain the format and talked through the letters game, before turning to me. 'But *Countdown* isn't just about letters, it's about numbers as well and we figure we've got a pretty good figure ruling that part of the game too. Meet our vital statistician, Carol Vorderman. She's a Cambridge graduate and she works in computers!'

That was the big build-up and these were my first words. Wait for it. 'Um, good evening.' Oh yes, to earn my place in TV history, I really pulled out all the stops. It wasn't exactly an 'a star is born' moment. But I got my numbers right, so I was happy.

It felt truly surreal to watch myself on the television for the first time. To me, I looked barely recognisable in my mustard-coloured top and my Molly Sugden hair and I didn't sound like myself either. My voice seemed to have risen an octave and I came across as very shy, which I wasn't at all in real life. I realised that in trying to say the numbers slowly and clearly, I sounded painfully slow. Even *I* was shouting at myself from the sofa: 'Get on with it, woman!'

After the show, we emptied the Champagne bottle. 'Let's watch it again.' And so I got off the sofa, went to the video, pressed a button to rewind the tape and another to play it back. Nothing happened. The screen was completely blank. I tried again, and then again, but still nothing happened.

'Did someone forget to press record?' Mum asked. And with that we all burst out laughing.

## MY TV HOME

November 1982 felt like a time of great change: Thatcher was in power, the Miners' Strike was in full swing, the Falklands War had begun barely five months previously and Culture Club were riding high in the charts. Everyone tuned in to this new numbers and letters game because it was the very first show on a totally new channel. Big news in Britain in those days. We made television history as the first programme shown on Channel 4, and apparently we drew in over three and a half million viewers.

The next afternoon, we made history for a second time because our ratings dropped to

800,000 viewers, the biggest percentage loss of audience ever known. And the third show? Well, don't ask. The answer isn't pretty.

Many years later, it became one of our favourite stories. Whenever Richard and I told it, we'd laugh ourselves senseless. We were very proud of our tremendous record-breaking failure. But back then, in the first week of *Countdown*, no-one had any idea how the show had done. I was so naïve that I didn't even know what television ratings were.

The most important television critic at the time was Nina Myskow, who wrote for the *News of the World*. Everyone who worked on the show—from directors, producers and presenters to the props boys—waited with bated breath until Sunday, when we could finally read what she had made of our quirky little programme.

The feedback we'd had from various viewers' phone calls hadn't been particularly reassuring. Opinions had ranged from a straightforward 'It's awful' to complaints about the music—'What's that tune all about? It reminds me of a funeral I was at recently.' We weren't filled with confidence that this was a show with a bright future.

But there was an unspoken feeling that if Nina gave the show her approval, it was a sanction from on high and we stood a chance of carrying on. If she didn't like it—well, the thought was too dark to contemplate.

On Sunday, I hurried through my newspaper, trying to find her column. There it was: the word '*Countdown*'—hooray! But, quickly scanning the page, I could see it wasn't exactly what we needed. One of our contestants had offered the word 'wally' on the show and it had been disallowed, and Nina had latched on to the theme. There, in big, bold letters, she had voted Richard the 'Wally of the Week'.

And so the general drubbing continued, one critic saying: 'If *Countdown* is the best that Channel 4 has to offer, then take the show and the whole channel off air immediately.'

Luckily for us, at that time Channel 4 had much bigger problems than what to do with a quiz show that went out at 4.45 in the afternoon. We were well off their radar screens, so we kept our heads down and carried on with the business of filming, hoping that we might survive long enough for a second contract.

The Yorkshire Television studios where we filmed on Kirkstall Road, Leeds, was a large, purpose-built studio complex and, as time went on, we'd record each series in blocks of days every six weeks or so, which meant that we recorded five or six shows a day. The days were taxing, to say the least, and not just for us in front of the camera, but for the audience. They had to sit on uncomfortable chairs for up to four hours at a time and we'd often be found doing exercises together halfway through filming, to stop the pins and needles from setting in. I grew to love all that—having a laugh and a cup of tea and a Gypsy Cream with our gorgeous *Countdown* audience.

In those very early days at work, I was quite shy. I sat on the sidelines, watching and learning the business of television as everyone hustled and bustled around me. Cathy Hytner had been on a few shows and was quite experienced, and thankfully she took me under her wing.

There were endless studio behaviours to learn and rules to follow, as these were the days when the power of the broadcasting unions was at its peak. If I wanted to move my stool, for example, just a couple of feet away from where it was, I wasn't allowed to shuffle it over myself, even if I was off-camera. I had to get a union member to do it for me. It was a new world to me. For example, I didn't even realise, in my naïvety, that any talking at all during recording was forbidden. I remember chatting very quietly to the props boys, not realising that we were in Richard's view as he was presenting his bits to camera.

When filming was finished, he came over and said, very sternly, 'Would you mind not talking when I am trying to present the show? It is most distracting.' As totally in awe of him as I was, I was mortified.

I was still working at Tandy in Leeds, trying to sell computers, and on the days I was needed to record *Countdown*, I would use up my holiday allowance. None of us actually expected *Countdown* to be more than a short adventure, so there was no way I wanted to give up my day job. I really did need the money to pay the mortgage, and the rusty Datsun was breaking down so much that I carried a can of water in the boot to top up the radiator every day.

It did feel quite strange though, leading such a double life. One day I'd be in the television studio, having my make-up done, and the next I'd be on the bus to work with Mum, getting ready for another day of computer sales.

After a year, as *Countdown* became more popular and was re-commissioned, it became impossible to juggle both jobs. I had more studio dates than I had holiday allowance, so I took a big breath and thought, 'Well, I'm only 22 and if it all goes pear-shaped, I can always do something else.' Mum agreed, so that was it. I decided to give TV a go. I didn't truly expect a career to emerge, but I thought that I might have a year or two of fun and then I could train, perhaps, to be an accountant.

I continued earning about £30 an episode on *Countdown*, which would run for six months of the year on and off, and then the plan was to try to pick up TV and researcher work wherever I could to bump up my money. Obviously, I'd done my sums and between us, financially, Mum and I were just about OK. But giving up a full-time job with a guaranteed income was a tough decision. For a start, I had no idea how much longer the programme was going to last. 'Hang on to the day job!' Richard regularly liked to quip. 'We could all be back on the streets in a couple of weeks.'

By that time, I'd found a whole new group of friends in Leeds, outside of the television studios. My long-term boyfriend was a civil engineer who I'd met a few years before. He was a squidge off six foot six and the spitting image of Dolph Lundgren in *Rocky IV*. The problem for civil engineers was that to earn good money they had to work abroad and so he had long stints in the Middle East and Africa, which meant I was out and about quite a lot at parties with my girlfriends in the meantime.

One of our *Countdown* directors, David St-David Smith, was keen to help in my search for other TV, radio, writing or puzzle work. David was a tall, lean, wild Welshman, with long blond hair and a fondness for beer and mayhem. Everyone

101

loved David for his one-off sense of humour. I remember when he was called in front of the Bar Committee, yet again, this time for attempting to climb the bejewelled and sparkling Christmas tree. Under interrogation, David admitted he did it 'because it was there'.

Meanwhile that night, John Meade was playing a new word game—'The dictionary is the only place where . . . pride *doesn't* come before a fall'. We were all coming up with suggestions—'There are never tears *before* bedtime . . .' and then JB provided the winner: 'The dictionary is the only place where David doesn't come before the Bar Committee!' Drinks all round. David was filming over the Humber Bridge for another programme one day when the helicopter he was in crashed. He died in his late 30s, cameraman Graham Barker died with him, and it was a tragedy.

David had also directed *Calendar*, the local news programme which Richard presented, so he started to find me the odd assignment for the programme, like little films about how to decorate your house for Christmas. I also worked as a researcher for other televison shows. But it was tough working as a freelance. I wasn't a proper dolly bird, so the bosses didn't really think I had a future.

Rick Vanes was one of the original scriptwriters and he and John Meade would work hard on the puns and intros to the guests in Dictionary Corner. Rick was also the best—or should that be worst?—pub singer I've ever heard. His comedy party turn was to murder any song you gave him. It was priceless . . . or maybe worthless!

In the early days of *Countdown*, Gyles

Brandreth, who was guesting in Dictionary Corner, took me aside during a lunch break to give me some pearls of his unquestionable wisdom. 'A bright, wonderful Cambridge graduate like you could achieve much more with her life than working in television, Carol,' he said in his usual effusive way, which is why I like him so much. 'I'd find something else to do if I were you. This is an extremely fickle business. We'll be lucky if we have another few months. Mark my words.' It's a conversation I remind Gyles of from time to time, not least when I asked him to host my *Goodbye Countdown* show 26 years later.

Meanwhile, my mother, not content with getting me a job on television, was now working on getting me a slot on radio too. Not that she knew anyone in radio, but that wasn't going to stop her.

Our local radio station, Radio Aire, was holding a competition for listeners to write a song that would be played at the Lord Mayor's Parade. So my mother, who wouldn't know one end of an instrument from another, wrote a song called 'Oh Leeds We Love You'.

She roped everyone into singing it through a single microphone hooked up to her little tape recorder. Even my cousin Pamela, and her daughters, Emma and Kate, who'd since moved from North Wales to Harrogate, were ordered to the house to add their voices to the mix. Mum sent it in and Martin Kelner (now of Radio 5 Live) played it and duly awarded her the 'special prize for the most humorous entry'. As far as Mum was concerned, it was an experience that gave her an 'in' and so, eventually, I also ended up with a job on Radio Aire, working with James Whale, who is still a very dear friend, and my big buddy Peter Levy, who christened me 'Roots Vorderman' because of my peroxide highlights. Now that was progress—from Boots Vorderman at Cambridge to Roots Vorderman in Leeds.

I loved working at Radio Aire on weekends and having a show to myself, even though I was a novice. Shortly after I started there, I received a letter from a listener asking whether she might be able to bring her son into the studio one morning when I was on air, as he wanted to work in radio when he grew up. She said he wanted to act as my assistant for the day, bringing me cups of tea and so on. I was more than happy to oblige and, the following week, this cute, freckle-faced boy and his mum Vera came into the studio. My mother was doing the phone lines at the time, taking calls from listeners.

'So you want to work in radio when you are older?' I said to the angelic-looking ten-year-old boy when he arrived for work that day. He nodded shyly, half hiding behind his mother.

'And what's your name?' I asked.

'Chris. Chris Moyles,' he squeaked.

Who'd have thought it, little Moyles, the saviour of Radio 1! Such a sweet child.

Meanwhile, Richard Whiteley also decided to help me find some extra work. *Calendar* was looking for someone to present the weather and so he said he would put a word in for me, as he was having a lunch with Graham Ironside, a colourful Scotsman who was the head of local programming at YTV.

The following day, I asked Richard how the lunch had gone.

'Well, when the subject came up, I put your name into the ring and said, "What about my numbers girl then, Graham? She'd be perfect for the job. She's very good at standing at a board with a pen in her hand."'

'And what did he say?'

'He said . . .' Richard put on a very theatrical Scottish accent. ' "Ay, Richard, I know who ye mean. I've seen that wee lassie on the show and I'm telling ye now she has absolutely ne future in television whatsoever!" '

And with that, Richard collapsed with laughter. And so did I.

Richard himself was a legend at Yorkshire TV. He had trained at ITN and joined *Calendar* first as a reporter, before taking the helm of the show. In the course of his career, he interviewed every prime minister from Harold Macmillan to Tony Blair. Although, much to his annoyance, he was always best remembered during his time at *Calendar* not for his heavyweight political interviews, but for being bitten by a ferret. He was doing a live interview with the animal's handler when the ferret suddenly turned on Richard, sank his teeth into his hand and then hung there for an agonising 30 seconds until the pair were finally prised apart. It was a TV clip that would be repeated time and time again on various TV blunder shows. Years later, when he moved up to North Yorkshire with his love, Kathy, they named the house where guests would stay Ferret Hall.

At the beginning of 1984 all of us on *Countdown* were amazed to find that somehow we were still clinging onto a contract. Richard, John Meade and myself were invited to Monaco, to attend the series finale of *Des Chiffres et des Lettres*, the French quiz show on which *Countdown* was based. The event was to be hosted by Antenne 2, the French equivalent of the BBC. This was a wow moment for me and I couldn't wait. It was still all such an adventure.

The trip was memorable in several ways. We watched the show being recorded in a huge auditorium and afterwards went to a private dinner, where John Meade, the world's most outspoken Yorkshireman, somehow ended up sitting on a table next to the sister of Prince Rainier of Monaco.

The wine was flowing and, all of a sudden, out of nowhere, came this familiar booming Yorkshire voice, for everyone to hear. 'You might be good with wine, but you were a bit crap at Waterloo, weren't you?' The entire dining room froze in total shock. And then the voices started again. The great thing about John was that he had no idea what the big deal was.

Richard Whiteley, meanwhile, had other things on his mind. He had seen a hastily scribbled note on a pad in John's office back home. It said simply: 'New presenter'.

Richard thought, 'Oh, poor Carol. It is very harsh to sack her. She really isn't that bad, after all.' He went overboard to be extremely nice to me throughout our Monaco trip, not realising that the presenter whom John had been told to get rid of was Richard himself.

For the first year or so, ratings were OK, but they weren't great, and the TV bosses had decided that they liked the show but it needed a bigger name, like Bob Monkhouse, to present it. John had been told to go to the South of France and at the end of the weekend, break the news to Richard that he wasn't needed anymore.

On our last day in Monaco, John received a telex from Yorkshire. As Richard loved to describe it, we were in the hotel and the bellboy was calling out, 'Massage for Monsieur Mid! Massage for Monsieur Mid!' While Richard was thinking what a marvellous idea it was to order a massage, the rest of us realised the bellboy was actually saying, 'Message for Monsieur Meade.' Anyway, the envelope was handed to John and when he opened it, he saw it was from the managing director, Paul Fox, and it simply said: 'Congratulations to you and the team on getting two editions of *Countdown* into the Channel 4 top ten. Business as usual.'

In other words: 'Don't sack Whiteley, we're doing well.' For a teatime show to be doing that kind of business was astonishing. A year later, we had more editions in the top ten, and by the late 80s we *were* the top five shows on the channel, week after week, year after year, for well over a decade, beating all records before and since. *Countdown* was now secure for the foreseeable future, and I didn't have to become an accountant.

I was now 24 years old and I didn't feel anything like a celebrity. Each day, after filming, I still returned home to Mum with fish and chips from Brian's, the famous chippy in Headingley, the wooden clothes peg was still holding our curtains together in the front room and I still made a trip to the launderette most Sundays. The only difference was, I was sometimes recognised as I sat watching my smalls dry.

Meanwhile, Richard, settling comfortably into his

own role as quizmaster, had moved on from grey suits to more colourful jackets teamed with the most appallingly mismatched ties. The clash was apparent to everyone apart from Richard, who sincerely believed that he had a very good dress sense.

Our relationship remained a bit stiff on screen and I was still only answering the numbers games, so I didn't really have a chance to say much beyond '75 × 5 is 375'. It all changed one day when, during a show, Richard made a remark about an outfit I was wearing. I think he was mocking my shoulder pads, which was rich, coming from a man who was wearing red and yellow stripes at the time. I hit back quickly with: 'Oh, you can talk, dressed like a deckchair in that jacket.' With that, the entire studio audience burst out laughing, while members of the crew stifled their giggles. Nobody had ever dared to mention Richard's dress sense to him before.

After filming finished, Richard found me in the corridor and said sternly, 'I need a word with you.' I didn't have a clue what he was going to say, but I didn't have long to wait. 'I don't want you commenting on my jackets in future,' he said stiffly.

I opened my mouth to apologise, but Richard wasn't finished. He continued: 'These jackets are high quality and made from the very finest material. The cloth comes from Bradford and it is then dyed in Huddersfield and finally tailored in Leeds.'

I had to stand and look contrite throughout a long lecture on the clothing and materials industry across the Pennines. However, it was like a red rag to a bull for me, so the very next day, I made another little comment about his bad taste in jackets on air. Once again, the studio audience loved it and Richard frowned, but he didn't say anything. Eventually, once he realised that the jackets had become an ongoing joke, he started to enjoy it. Very slowly, the distance between us began to close and our proper friendship evolved. It was to become one of the most enduring relationships of my life and one that has probably provided me with more fun than any other. It still does, even writing this now, years after his death. I remember some of the stories and laugh . . . until I cry.

Richard's jackets just got worse and worse. Many viewers sincerely believed that the jackets were a novelty, a joke thought up by the producers and supplied by the costume department to give Richard his own unique comical identity. Nothing could be further from the truth. He would find the most hideous brightly spotted tie, hold it next to a clashing, stripy jacket and nod in deep satisfaction. He genuinely felt that his jackets, which had been specially made for him and were actually well-tailored, made him look distinguished. Many years later, he declared proudly, 'I'll have you know that my tailors have a photo of me in their front window.'

Struggling to keep a straight face, I jokingly replied, 'And when are they going into liquidation?'

While Richard's jackets shifted from grey to somewhere over the rainbow, *Countdown* gradually found its own identity too. After the first series, Dr Linda Barrett, who shared the numbers job with me, went back to working full-time as an academic. Next, Beverley went, leaving just Cathy and me and a variety of people in charge of the dictionary.

New faces arrived and some became great friends. On the first series in 1982, I met my Prince of Numbers, a bookie called Michael Wylie, who was a contestant who got through to our first ever *Countdown* final. Michael was from Edinburgh, brilliant with words and fast as you like with the numbers. In his first few shows he beat me on the numbers, which frankly I wasn't happy about at all. But as John Meade said, I didn't have to worry, as Michael wouldn't have fitted into my dresses. He was over 20 stones and I loved every ounce of him. John gave him a job as a researcher and he eventually became our producer and was with us for 25 years. We sparred over tens of thousands of numbers games throughout the years and, in my mind, he was the ultimate competitor. I judged a series on how many times I could beat him, not that it mattered at all to anyone but him and me. I was his 'Welsh witch' and he was my 'Scots git'. Michael died just a few days after my final *Countdown* was recorded in 2008, but that's another story.

In the office were Diane Barr and Lesley McKirdy, both good friends. Cindy Ritson was the PA in charge of all the timings and there was also a young man called Mark Nyman, who'd won a series as a contestant. His genius with words was heart-stopping. Just like Michael, Mark became a researcher and then a producer on the show, thanks initially to John Meade.

We were given Yorkshire television's first female

trainee camerawoman, Annie Peppiate. She became my camerawoman and together we would wait for Richard to start digging himself a huge verbal hole with one of his long, off-the-cuff ramblings. When he began talking, we would all start giggling at the same time and I would sometimes look up to see cameras shaking uncontrollably.

A young lad called Matt Rook was Richard's cameraman. His camera was positioned next to my numbers board, so when the clock started counting down, I would finish my sum and then talk to Matt. It never failed to drive Richard mad.

John Meade was an ever-present dynamic force in our lives. John was from Scarborough and he and Richard were Yorkshiremen through and through. They were hugely different on the surface, but in many ways very similar. They were very bright (although Whiters did manage to hide that for a lot of the time) and they were cheeky and irreverent. John was a great writer and, in different circumstances, he could easily have written wonderful dramas.

I loved Meaders. He wasn't the tallest man in television, but what he lacked in height, he more than made up for in heart. He wore his Yorkshireness on his sleeve and was one of the rudest, cheekiest, gruffest, kindest, funniest, most loyal blokes I've ever met. As I got to know him over the many, many years that he was in charge, he did some very naughty things and always got away with them. John also had a soft side and he married a perfectly lovely lady, Gill, who worked at the company. From that time, Gill was his angel.

Without John Meade in charge, I honestly

believe that *Countdown* wouldn't have stayed on air. He hated paperwork and he hated rules and he hated people interfering in his fiefdom. His idea of a day in the office was to turn up about 11 a.m., take the *Telegraph* crossword to the loo for an hour, ask the office if he had to sign anything, then go to the bar for a few hours, which is where he used to do his thinking and have his meetings. Later, he'd return to the office to see if there was anything else to sign and then back to the bar, or the pub, or a rugby match, and finally a taxi home—the taxi drivers of Leeds loved him and looked after him. Life was never dull when John Meade was around—and, in many ways, he reminded me of Gabriel. I missed Gabriel terribly and I knew he was very proud of me, but I couldn't go and visit him due to my loyalty to Mum. She hadn't spoken to him since the day we left Denbigh in 1981.

As *Countdown* continued to grow, a tremendous spirit developed which bound us together. Everyone—Richard, myself, John, every member of the crew, including our make-up girls and boys and the props boys (some were of retirement age, but they were always 'boys' to me)—started to take the mickey out of each other relentlessly. Every conversation was littered with insults which would leave us laughing till we cried.

Gradually, a crew which had been thrown together hastily grew to become a team—and then something more. A *Countdown* family. We laughed together, ate together and shared our secrets. Meanwhile, we couldn't believe our luck that our little show was getting bigger and bigger and people even started recognising Richard outside of

Yorkshire. But there was no danger of any of us becoming complacent or self-satisfied because John Meade was always there to pull us down a peg or ten, the self-appointed guardian of our egos.

Meaders was fiercely, fiercely competitive. It wasn't enough for *Countdown* to be growing in success. No, he wanted to make more shows per day than anyone else. When other programmes were recording up to three half-hour shows a day in the studio, Meaders made sure that we trumped them by recording five. This meant that three were recorded in the afternoon and two in the evening, following a morning of rehearsal.

After a while, even this wasn't enough for Meaders and he upped our schedule to six programmes a day (four in the afternoon and two in the evening). On the days when Meaders felt compelled to exert his power, he would make us record seven half-hour programmes a day (four in the afternoon and three in the evening) before we stumbled into the bar to recover.

Only once did he ever decide to make us record eight shows in a day. It was a feat which reduced us all to silent shells of our former selves. Even Meaders was totally shattered. He never tried it again, mercifully, but it took us and our audience ages to recover from our longest ever day.

Various celebrity guests would appear on the show and we would meet up for lunch before the recording. Kenneth Williams was a regular in those early days and really helped us to make our mark. Keith Barron was, and always will be, one of my favourites. Then there was Sylvia Sims, Stephen Fry, Rick Wakeman, the legendary rock god, Sir

113

Terry Wogan, who loved the show, Richard Digance, a great comic, actor Martin Jarvis . . . The list ran into hundreds as the years rolled on.

Meaders would always tell the guest of the day that he never drank on studio days. But when we got to the dining room, they would see a bottle of wine perched in front of him. The few who dared to question this were waved aside by an impatient flick of Meaders' hand. He would dismiss the question by explaining that 'wine isn't booze'. Somehow, in the crazy world of our much-loved producer, only spirits and beer counted as alcohol. And so it was that inside our *Countdown* world, the wine continued to flow. Richard and I, however, never drank until the shows were over. Can you imagine how many three-letter words we'd be getting otherwise?

Over time, I started to try to spread my wings. Always have a Plan B. One job I applied for was for a continuity announcer at Border Television. With my copy of the *Stage* newspaper beside me, I sat down and wrote an application letter. I told the Dear Sir or Madam that it had always been my dream to announce programmes for Border Television—my long-term ambition in life. I was using my mother's technique of 'flattery will get you everywhere', but it didn't work in this case and, unsurprisingly, I didn't even get called for an interview. It was one of dozens of jobs that I applied for—unsuccessfully—as I tried to find myself more work.

But eventually, I'd been working hard on all the other non-*Countdown* shows, learning my trade, and now had enough day jobs at Yorkshire Television to warrant a full-time contract.

*Countdown* went to almost 150 shows a year and I was in demand as a researcher and presenter on education and children's shows. So, with a new agent, I managed to get a contract for a whopping £20,000 per year. It was unbelievable.

I found myself working as a researcher on a programme idea of my own. The programme was called *So We Bought a Computer* and the idea had come from my work at Tandy. These were the days before PCs were widespread, when the concept of owning a home computer and knowing what to do with it was state-of-the-art stuff.

Channel 4 had commissioned the programme as part of their education brief, so I worked for weeks as a researcher, pulling the stories for the show together. It was the perfect scenario for me: the *Countdown* office was upstairs in the same building, so I'd go up for a chat in my tea break to see what was happening. I learned how to be a proper TV researcher, writing detailed notes and directions for film crews, and it gave me the grounding for a career as a producer and then eventually as the owner of a small TV production company.

Because of my research, our little house in Leeds was crammed with computers of all shapes and sizes and one day I came home from work early to find some visitors. The house had a pretty front door with big diamond-shaped panes of glass and just one Yale lock, which we left on the latch on a hot day.

As I walked the few yards from our gate to the front door, I saw that one of the panes of glass had been smashed. Then, just as it dawned on me what had happened, a strange face appeared at the door. I screamed, realising that there were burglars in my house. I was so mad that someone was in our house, I scrambled for my key, screaming foul language at them all the time. When I got in, I chased one of the men out of the back door and then the other one ran down the stairs and out of the front. They were off so quickly I couldn't catch them, but they left behind my suitcases, which they'd packed full of computers. Had they managed to take them, Mum and I would have been in serious trouble, as they were on loan from the manufacturers and weren't insured.

*Countdown* remained my TV home and, very slowly, in the mid 80s, there began to be changes to the team. After about three years, when Cathy Hytner left, John Meade started looking around for a new hostess. The first to take the job was a beautiful blonde model from Manchester called Karen Levy. She was with us for about a year and then left, later becoming Mrs Graeme Souness. The next hostess was an actress who did one series and then decided that she wanted to return to acting, I believe.

John Meade had been in his element when he first had to conduct interviews for the job. He'd liked all these models turning up. The second time, he had been bored, and now he was faced with yet another round and he was trying to palm the job off onto someone else.

So it was—at our annual Christmas lunch at a restaurant in Leeds—that John Meade sat with his head in his hands and slurred his concerns to a very bleary-eyed Richard Whiteley. This lunch, just like all the others, had begun at midday and was still going on eight hours later.

116

Our table was lined with the remains of countless bottles of booze and only the hardcore few remained: myself, Richard, Rick Vanes, our brilliant scriptwriter, and Meaders. John Meade groaned, 'Hostesses. Bloody hell, Whiteley, I can't interview any more of them.'

Richard, my great champion even when very, very drunk, slurred back, 'What about Carol? I think she could do the letters.'

John Meade belched loudly and contentedly. 'She thinks she's too bloody good to do the letters.' He paused and added darkly, 'Cambridge and all that.'

I slurred back, 'Shnot so. I don't think I'm too good. I can do the letters.'

John hiccupped. 'What makes you think you can do letters?'

I replied, with as much indignation as my very drunken state would allow, 'I know my alphabet,' and then I started to recite it. Very slowly—and wrongly.

John Meade held up his hand with a groan. 'Ohhhh, that will do. You can do the bloody letters.'

We were so incredibly drunk that I didn't think anyone would remember the conversation. So when we came back in January to record the next series, I was genuinely stunned to find out that I would be doing the letters as well as the numbers.

John Meade came over to me and cackled an evil laugh. 'You're doing the letters, Vorders, and we're not paying you a single penny more. I've saved myself a helluva lot of money.'

And so, with that, my new vowels-and-consonants role began.

117

'It's just you and me now, Vorders,' Richard said as we walked towards the studio that morning. 'Just you and me, little one!' And we held hands because we knew it was going to be alright.

## STUCK IN A MOMENT

By the summer of 1985, life was sweet indeed. And then I went and spoilt it all by making a big mistake. I got married on the rebound, to a man I hardly knew. We were two young people who got carried away in the moment, but it should never have ended in a wedding.

The daft thing was that I was so happy at the time. I was enjoying *Countdown*, working hard on lots of other things, living happily with Mum in our little house, and going out every weekend with friends.

I had friends at Yorkshire Television. I had friends from Radio Aire, like Liz Kershaw, Peter Levy, James Whale and Christa Ackroyd, who went on to present *Calendar* with Richard for over a decade and is now one of my dearest friends.

I also had a non-work group of friends who were all Leeds Uni graduate types in their mid to late 20s. Our social life revolved around the Regent pub in a suburb of Leeds, where we'd meet on a Friday night and often end up singing loudly until we were finally thrown out. With the pub closed, we would go hunting for a party, often dossing on somebody's floor and finally staggering home happy two days later, on a Sunday evening.

Life was easier. My Datsun had given up the

ghost and I had to literally roll it down a hill into a garage, where I bought a brand-new Ford Orion with a loan. I'd been on *Countdown* for about four years and was starting to make a name for myself in TV circles, although not every venture had been successful.

I'd been to see a TV boss in London. I was very nervous, but was determined to start putting my show reel around and thought that maybe, with my growing experience on education and local news programes and children's TV, there might be a job for me there. He was very important and in charge of some huge entertainment shows. He was over an hour late for our appointment (not a good sign) and then, when his secretary asked me to go into his office, he put his feet up on the table, looked me up and down and said, 'Sorry, love, your tits aren't big enough for TV.' So if anyone ever tries to tell you that television isn't sexist, just laugh!

But my mistake wasn't the partying. It was doing the one thing that was to bring these good times crashing to an end and would mean moving from my beloved Leeds.

I met and became engaged to a stranger within six crazy weeks. And it all happened because, for the first time in my life, I was on the rebound.

I had, since my teenage days, always had long-lasting relationships. However, my long-term, on-off boyfriend of five or six years had moved to work in New Zealand and called me out of the blue one day to tell me that he had found a new girlfriend. I didn't know what to say, although admittedly we were in an 'off' bit of the 'on-off' at the time. It was an odd experience. I suppose, with this relationship, I had always thought that one day the 'on' bit would take over. I was 24 and suddenly properly single. I had a great job on telly (which, incidentally, the on-off had never been that impressed with, particularly as we'd known each other since I was about 19). I was quite broken-hearted, not that I admitted that to the on-off.

So when my Leeds friends introduced me just a couple of weeks later to a lively young naval officer called Chris Mather, I was only too ready to have a good time. Within six weeks, Chris had proposed and I had accepted.

I thought I should let my ex know—I didn't want him finding out through mutual friends—so I rang him on the other side of the world, saying pompously, 'I thought you should know that I'm engaged now.' Maybe I half hoped that he would say, 'Don't do it, I'll come back and rescue you,' but no grand declarations were made. Instead, he said, 'I hope you'll be very happy.'

I remember feeling an anxious emptiness inside, which should have told me something, but instead my wedding to a young man I really didn't know well enough was just a matter of weeks away and my life felt like a rollercoaster.

Looking back, it seems ridiculous that the situation got so far, so quickly. We met in the late summer, were engaged in early October and the wedding was set for the Sunday before Christmas. His family welcomed me fully into the fold. I had always been cautious about anything important before, but now I was suddenly hurtling into a marriage with no real thought about the consequences.

Other people were concerned at how quickly it was all moving. John Meade and Richard Whiteley both took me to one side and asked me, quietly, 'Are you sure that you are doing the right thing?' I assured them that I was, with a certainty that, deep down, I didn't really feel. Yet another dumb and stubborn instance when I should have listened to others who knew better. Mind you, Richard was married briefly to a girl called Candy and, as he often used to tell us, when Candy left him he wore a black tie on *Calendar*, as a form of mourning the end of his marriage. He got very annoyed when no-one noticed after a year of this, so he gave up and went back to ties of full colour.

Mum must have secretly had her doubts—after all, Chris and I barely knew each other—but she would only say what she has always said throughout my life: 'Do whatever makes you happy.' Not exactly good advice. Here was a huge fork in the road of life coming up, and I took the wrong path.

The week before the wedding, Chris went on his stag weekend and I went on my hen weekend. It was a great three-day party for everyone else, but even though I danced and played the fool, it was a miserable affair for me. Sensing that something was wrong, my friends all kept asking, 'Are you *sure* you want to get married?' No, I wasn't sure. But what was I going to do? I didn't have a clue.

This wasn't fair to Chris or to me, but I didn't have the courage to stop it all. To this day, I know that if I'd still had Gabriel in my life, as the father figure I so badly needed, he would have taken control of the situation. He would have seen the madness, sensed my unhappiness, dragged Chris to one side and said, 'Listen, young man, this is crazy. I'm putting a stop to it now.'

But Gabriel was no longer there with his bear hugs and his brashness and his unashamed emotion. And to make matters even worse, just when I needed a father the most, the man who actually was my father turned his back on me one more time.

When I first became engaged to Chris, I thought of Tony Vorderman. It was the first time I had ever sat down, as an adult, and really considered him. Trixie had made contact with our father in more recent years and through her I met one of our half-sisters, Karen, when I was in my early 20s. I liked her. The family resemblance was immediately obvious. She had the same eyes.

As we talked, I realised that Karen had enjoyed a happy childhood with a loving and devoted father. While Tony had totally failed us, he had managed to be the perfect dad to her and her sister. Now, at the age of 24, I decided to hold out an olive branch to my father and invite him to the wedding. It was a sweeping gesture which I thought would make everyone happy. A wedding was supposed to bring families together after all. Yet another dumb move, as it turned out.

He had never been in touch when I was growing up, but surely now, after all these years, just as I was about to walk down the aisle, Tony Vorderman would want to join in the family celebration.

Once the engagement had been announced, it was Mum who invited him, his second wife and the two girls on my behalf. She rang and left a message with his wife to say that I was getting married and wanted to invite them to the ceremony. Mum didn't hear back and so she rang again two days later, and this time Tony answered the phone.

The conversation was short and curt, almost as short as the one so many years ago when he had cut us out of his life for the first time. Mum said, 'Carol is getting married and she would like you and your family to come along.'

He didn't even pause for thought. All he said was, 'I don't think so.'

Mum was so disgusted that she put the phone down immediately. Having taught me as a child to cope with his rejection, she now had to tell me that he didn't want to know me as an adult either. It did hurt, but I was angry more than anything else. I swore that I would blank him from my mind from then on—and for many years, I did.

The upset didn't help the turmoil that I was experiencing in the weeks before my wedding. When I came back from my hen weekend, I was miserable and stressed. When I finally blurted out the truth to Mum, she supported me totally. She even typed up and printed notices to send out to the wedding guests which read: 'Jean Vorderman regrets that the marriage of her daughter Carol to Chris Mather will no longer be taking place.' But the cards were never sent.

In truth, I was all over the place. Every nerve in my body was screaming that getting married at this time was the wrong thing for me to do. I steeled myself to cancel it, but in the end, I bottled out. Mainly because I didn't want to let anyone down and, most particularly, I didn't want to hurt Chris. Also—and this seems like madness now—I had booked a big wedding reception and the thought of ringing the hotel manager just a few days before the wedding and saying, 'This isn't going ahead' made me sick with anxiety. I was very young and

I'd never had to organise anything like this before.

I told Chris about my doubts and he came up to Leeds immediately. We talked about everything and eventually he managed to persuade me to go ahead.

But I don't think I slept in the days leading up to my wedding. Each night, I would lie awake and try to somehow think straight. I felt so guilty, and even though I'd now said I was going ahead, I still felt it wasn't going to be right for either of us. It was something that should never have gone so far.

It was like being a small ship, tossed around in the middle of a storm. I didn't buy a wedding dress. Instead, I simply borrowed a beautiful, long, white dress from a friend of Trixie's. I also borrowed another outfit from the *3-2-1* TV show's costume department for the evening bash. It was all mesh and had sequins covering the important bits.

I walked down the aisle and said my vows.

That afternoon, I drank plenty at the reception. It was followed by a disco in the evening, and my girlfriends produced deely-boppers for us to wear on our heads. They were all the rage back then—small, glittery, antenna-like balls which bounced stupidly on wires sticking up from a plastic hairband. I think I still had mine on when I clambered onto the stage to sing along to one of my favourite comedic songs—'It's Raining Men' by the Weather Girls—not the best song for a bride to be singing at her wedding.

Eventually, I was hauled off the stage. But a borrowed dress, ridiculous bouncing deely-boppers and the song which had been my signature dancing tune when I was single summed up the whole business. There was no honeymoon.

We went to Wigan to stay with Chris's family over Christmas, and by this time the marriage was already in difficulty. Afterwards, we went back to the house in Leeds which I shared with Mum. After a couple of months, Mum moved into a flat across the road, but our marriage unravelled quickly. We were just wrong for each other—completely. To this day, I have the greatest admiration for anyone who walks out before a wedding because they know that things aren't right. It isn't necessarily an act of cowardice, as it is so often perceived.

Now we were living with our mistake. I have a clear memory of sitting on the big sofa at home, aged 25, thinking that my life as I had known it was over. My closest friends—Richard Whiteley included—knew that things weren't right with me. But I did want to try to make the marriage work, in spite of everything.

It didn't. A year later, I walked away and went to stay with my sister Trixie, who was back in Prestatyn. I decided a completely clean break was best and never spoke to Chris again.

The marriage itself, and the consequent break-up, affected me badly for a long time. I felt a complete failure. I had wanted to be married just once in my life and live the happy-ever-after dream. I'd been so sure of everything until that point, but this was where all the parts of myself I had relied on in the past—the work ethic, the thinking things through, the passion, the laughter, the confidence and determination—just escaped me. It is hard when you are a confident person, so in control, the person others come to with their problems, and then suddenly, through no-one else's fault but your own, you do something so obviously wrong. It takes time to forgive yourself. I am sure that Chris has found someone far more suited to him than I was and is very happily married now and I am sorry for the unhappiness that happened.

We had to sell the house in Leeds which Mum and I had bought together years earlier, and that upset me greatly, on top of everything else. I was never to live in Leeds full-time again. I was getting work in London, and felt that I had to move on. Again. Moving on has never concerned me, and I've done it all of my life, but I know that I would have been happy staying in Leeds. Going back every few weeks to record *Countdown* for the next 20 years gave me my 'Leeds fix', but leaving there remains a regret.

So, after staying with my sister for a couple of months, commuting to work from Prestatyn, I eventually went to stay with Mum in the one-bedroom flat Anton had bought for her, across the road from our old house.

For the first few weeks, she and I shared her room, sleeping side by side in two single beds. As if that wasn't cramped enough, when Anton came to join us after another operation on his cleft palate and lip, he had the bedroom and Mum and I camped in the lounge.

'Here we go again, back to square one!' I laughed as we got into our makeshift beds that night. 'Do you think we will always be living like this, Mum? With you and I sharing a room when things don't go right for us?'

On the face of things, life went on. Work was going from strength to strength and provided a healthy distraction from everything else. Meanwhile, thanks to the support of my family and friends, bit by bit, I came out from under my shell and regained some of the confidence I had lost over that year.

Starting to work down in London as a temporary means of not having to return to Leeds meant I was heading in a new direction. And thanks to that, I found two men who have played significant roles in my life. The first was my manager and best friend John Miles, a complete gentleman, who has looked after me now for nearly 25 years. And the second was my husband Paddy, the father of our two children, Katie and Cameron, who are the centre of my world.

## HAPPY, DREAMY DAYS

*Countdown* continued to grow in popularity. It was particularly watched and loved by students, retired people and those who were off ill from work for a day to two. 'Ooh, Carol love, I was snuggled up in bed with you the other afternoon when I had the flu, did you notice?' is one of my favourites. I must have heard it a thousand times and it still makes me smile.

The laughter kept coming, and so did the *Countdown* contracts. My first move into prime-time television came when, in 1987, I was asked to co-present a programme for BBC2 called *Take Nobody's Word for It*, named after the motto of the Royal Society, the oldest and most venerable scientific institution in the world. I hosted it alongside the uniquely twinkling Professor Ian Fells from Newcastle University and the programme featured us performing lots of scientific experiments, most of which could be replicated at home. It was something new. We had two producers, the very funny Patrick Titley, who also directed the programmes, and George Auckland, who was the most enthusiastic science producer ever. When we went to George's house, every spare inch was filled with would-be rockets or the bits and pieces of his many home-grown experiments. The programme was, I think we'd all admit, George's brainchild.

We recorded the show at BBC Bristol, where we would have a day's rehearsal, followed by one full day in the studio with five television cameras trained on us while we carried out the demonstrations. One time, the cameras were filming and I was busily demonstrating yet another experiment, with our usual black backdrop and flame-throwers and dry ice to give added dramatic effect. The security guard was sitting in his normal seat in the corner of the studio.

Except this time, the flame-throwers set fire to the curtains behind me. The security guard was facing the other way and was understandably oblivious to the flames which were curling behind me. I was so engrossed in my experiment that I didn't smell the black smoke.

Incredibly, not one person in the studio noticed the minor problem that we were, in fact, on fire. It was only Patrick Titley, sitting up in the gallery, who saw the growing flames on the screens.

I had no earpiece, but Patrick was linked through the headphones to one of the cameramen, who suddenly rushed forward and grabbed a fire extinguisher, much to the astonishment of the rest of us. It was the only time in my career that we have almost burned a studio down.

*Take Nobody's Word for It* won a number of British and international awards for science and educational programming. *Countdown*, however, never won a thing in all its years, which Richard and I eventually thought was funny, but more of that later.

At this time, I was still dealing with the split from Chris Mather and was travelling to London a lot more for work. Pretty soon, I managed to wangle myself another presenting job, this time on the massively popular Saturday morning children's show *The Wide Awake Club*, which was broadcast live from the studios of TV-am in London.

It meant travelling to London on Fridays to rehearse with the main presenters, Tommy Boyd, Timmy Mallett and Michaela Strachan. Every Saturday, I would do an experiment live from 'Carol's Lab', my own science corner within the studio.

We knew there would be millions of parents sleeping in while their children sat and watched television, so sometimes, out of sheer devilment, Tommy used to say on air, 'Go and wake Mummy and Daddy up and tell them that the story about the dolphins is coming soon . . .' We'd all sit and smile at the cameras, knowing that in homes across the country, tiny feet would be thudding upstairs and little voices would be screaming, 'Wake up! The dolphins are coming!'

Timmy was at the height of his fame and was going out with Lynda, an Australian girl who'd come over to stay with him for a couple of weeks on her travelling break and, like a lot of Australians, had never left. I liked them both immediately. It was Timmy who introduced me to his agent John Miles, who was to become, and still is, one of my greatest friends and a big influence in my life.

My agent in London was very good, but there were changes at the agency and I thought that I needed someone who 'got me': an engine-loving, geeky, workaholic, alright-looking northern girl— surely there was a future for her somewhere?

John Miles is a Bristol man, born and bred. He decided to stay in Bristol in the 60s instead of moving to London, where most agents are based, recognising that he could do most of his work on the phone without having to waste time at endless showbiz lunches. My kind of agent.

I asked the man in charge of contracts at Yorkshire Television, Filip Cieslik, if he knew John. He said that John was, in his view, the best presenters' agent in the country and would do me proud. Mind you, realising that he might have to be negotiating with John in the future about my *Countdown* contract, he also said, 'I'm probably shooting myself in the foot telling you that, aren't I?'

John only ever represented about a dozen people at a time and he had a small number of big TV stars on his hands, like Keith Floyd. I went down to Bristol to see him, hoping that he'd like me enough to take me on. And to this day, I'm so grateful that he did.

John is a gentleman in the truest sense of the word. He's kind and thoughtful and a very clever

130

businessman who likes to push boundaries. I knew in an instant that I wanted him to be my agent, but I had no idea just how far we would travel together in the years to come. Unlike most other agents, who would immediately have wanted a huge percentage of everything I was already earning, John said that he wouldn't take anything from that income, only from any new contracts he negotiated. He didn't ask me to sign a contract— we still haven't got one nearly 25 years later. In fact, he has now been an agent for 50 years in total and has never had a contract with any of his clients. He is, above all things, a man you can trust. With John beside me and his wonderful assistant, Mandy Berry supporting him in the office, everything moved up two gears and then eventually off the scale completely.

Whatever story I tell you in this book from now on, rest assured that even if his name isn't mentioned, John played some part in it. We speak at least twice a day, even when we're on holiday, and his family are part of my family, and I hope that my family are also part of his.

Back in the early days of *The Wide Awake Club*, I was constantly schlepping from Mum's flat in Leeds down to London and needed somewhere to lay my weary head for a couple of nights a week. That's how I ended up firmly ensconced in Peter Stringfellow's satin sheets . . .

It happened because one of my best friends, Kate Andrews, a nurse I'd met in Leeds who later became godmother to my daughter Katie, had moved down to London. There, in the hospital where she worked, she had looked after the mother of Coral Stringfellow, the wife of flamboyant nightclub owner Peter.

Although Coral's mother, Carrie, sadly passed away, Coral struck up a friendship with Kate, who then moved into Coral's flat in Marylebone Road, pretty soon after Peter had moved out. I found myself staying there as a regular guest, because Coral is generous to a fault and wouldn't hear of me staying anywhere else.

The flat was absolutely enormous. It boasted six or seven bedrooms and whenever I stayed over for filming, Coral kindly gave me the bedroom at the very end of the hall. The vast bed was always dressed in shiny satin sheets, and as I get bored easily and I love to muck around, I made up a new sport. Before I got into bed for the night, I would take a run from the hallway, building up as much speed as possible before hurling myself onto the satin sheets.

At speed, satin turns a giant bed into the equivalent of a bobsleigh run. I would slide straight over the giant bed and fly off the other side, coming to an abrupt halt when I crashed straight into the bedroom wall. No sport is complete without fellow competitors, and occasionally a guest or two would take on the satin challenge.

Coral is an extraordinary woman. She had helped Peter build up his first empire of nightclubs in Sheffield, before moving down to London. She is petite, like a delicate doll, age-defiant and fiery, but perhaps her greatest gift of all—apart from throwing parties—is gathering people: famous people, eccentric people, titled people, young people and old people.

Each morning I would wake and stumble into the kitchen to find someone like the actress Diane

Keen sitting serenely at the table, listening to a Russian classical musician strumming his guitar, while a West End star would be brewing a cup of tea. Even the moon-walking astronaut Buzz Aldrin and his wife were visitors. Different faces, famous or not, filled the flat day and night. There was so much noise and so much entertainment that there seemed little point in actually sleeping. So when I got back to the flat from TV-am after rehearsals on a Friday, I would often stay up all night and then go to a live broadcast of *The Wide Awake Club* still merry from the night before. They were happy, carefree days and I still had to pinch myself that my mum's secret letter to *Countdown* had led to such a great set of jobs and wonderful new friends and experiences.

I was now divorced and settling back into singledom. It was around this time that a friend from Cambridge, Kumu Ratnatunga (she of the venereologist father), was getting married to her beau, Count Rupert Ruvigny, who had been at Oxford University. They'd met training to be accountants at Price Waterhouse. Kumu is Buddhist and Rupert a Catholic, so there were to be a number of ceremonies and parties. I was honoured when she asked me to be a bridesmaid.

Now, because there were a number of bridesmaids, including some very young ones, the dresses had to suit all of us. I ended up in a pretty silk number, but it did have huge blue and white stripes and looked a bit like the Argentinian football strip. In fact, the stripes were so bold, I would have outshone one of Richard Whiteley's classic deckchair jackets.

But during the reception, a wedding guest made

his way to my side. He smiled, looked me up and down slowly and declared, somewhat laconically, 'You look like a walking sofa.'

It really wasn't what I was expecting, but I liked him immediately. He introduced himself as Paddy King, a friend of Kumu's, and he had a sharp brain and an even sharper sense of humour. Shortly after the wedding, we started to date.

I was travelling backwards and forwards from London to Leeds, driving myself up and down the motorway endlessly. Meanwhile, John Miles had started to work his magic and the job offers were piling up.

Paddy and I had been together about a year when my dream assignment came up. I was asked to fly to Australia for three months to record *Postcards from Down Under*. It really was the opportunity of a lifetime and, in making the programme, I tried everything from rounding up cattle in a helicopter, to scuba diving with moray eels, white-water rafting and ballooning over the famous Alice Springs. I also had to eat witchetty grubs, which looked like giant caterpillars and had been baked in a hole in the very hot, dusty ground. They were put into the ground and changed instantly from wriggly things to being stiff as a board. 'Now you eat them,' I was told by our Aboriginal guide. Well, let me tell you, they tasted just like sticks of scrambled eggs. Good food, if a little scary.

The film was originally commissioned by the Queensland Tourist Board, but the BBC then bought it for the token sum of one pound and it was broadcast as a travel show. I was offered the job of anchoring the ITV show *Wish You Were Here* some years later and was sorely tempted to take it, simply because of the great time I'd had in Australia. I said no in the end, but I still wonder if I should have said yes.

Paddy joined me in Australia and when we came back, he proposed. We were married in 1990, in Ringwood near Bournemouth, where his parents Godfrey and Margaret lived. We had a wonderful weekend, with guests coming in from all over the country. The weather was perfect, and this time the ceremony was for real. I even had enough cash by then to order my wedding dress from a place in Chelsea. It was certainly a very different scenario from my first wedding. Richard Whiteley came (there's no show without Punch after all) and for years after on *Countdown* he used to say, 'I've been to *all* of Carol's weddings.' Cheeky monkey. Paddy and I went to Salcombe for our honeymoon, and went back many times over the years.

Mum was still living in Leeds, where I went to work on *Countdown* most weeks, so I saw her all the time. In 1987 my workload had increased so much that I needed a secretary, and who better—and keener—than my Mum? She became my first full-blown employee and she's been nothing but trouble ever since!

Paddy and I settled down happily in our new lives as man and wife in trendy Barnes, south-west London, in what was boldly described by the estate agents as a 'mews cottage'. This description absolutely fascinated me, because where I came from the same house would have been described as a small two-up, two-down. The agent's notes said it had 'a butterfly garden', which meant that no-one had cut the grass for ten years and so butterflies lived there. The house cost about £150,000, compared to the £20,000 it would have cost in Leeds. And even for that hugely inflated sum, you still couldn't park your car anywhere near the front door. I was beginning to understand the very real differences between the north and south.

The wealth in London in those Yuppie days of the 80s and early 90s staggered me. I stepped out onto a zebra crossing one day and a young man in a Porsche screeched to a halt, stuck his head out of the window and yelled, 'I'm rich—get out of my way!' Idiot.

Somehow, I didn't feel I could buy into that life and we began to think about moving out of London, so that we could get slightly more house for our money and hopefully find somewhere to raise a family. We found our answer in the little village of Holyport, near Maidenhead.

In 1991, we fell in love with Bryony Cottage. It was a detached cottage which had been added to over the years. There was a beautiful wisteria arch outside the front door, which took my breath away. A pretty magnolia tree framed the front garden and everyone used the side door into the kitchen as the main entrance.

When I was a little girl, I had dreamed of owning a solid house. I remember walking from our road, Palmeira Gardens, to the next road along, which boasted big, detached 1930s houses with decent gardens, and I imagined myself one day living in a large house just like these. Something that couldn't be taken away from me, where I would never have to flee my bedroom in the early hours of the morning. This need for the firm knowledge that I owned something that

136

couldn't be taken away was always there.

Here now, with Bryony Cottage, my dream was about to come true. It had five bedrooms, though two of them were tiny box rooms. Downstairs, it was a peculiar shape. There was a very long, narrow lounge and a kitchen which boasted a lovely circular bay window, where we put a round pine table.

On the day we moved in, there was a slight delay with the legal papers. The removal men had already arrived with all our furniture, which they unloaded onto our front lawn. I sat outside in the sunshine, amid all the disarray, feeling deliriously happy. I could hardly believe that something this wonderful was going to be ours.

But Paddy and I weren't alone on the lawn. No, we'd asked Mum to leave her flat in Leeds and come down to live with us. Neither Mum nor I really wanted to be apart, and it seemed the perfect solution. And it wasn't just the three of us. Trixie had moved back to North Wales and had split up with her husband Francis, so he came to Byrony Cottage too for a while. With friends wandering in and out, it was a lively and happy house.

In December 1991, a test confirmed that another part of the dream was on its way. I was pregnant with our first baby. I had no idea, because you don't until it happens, of the change that a child would make to everything. The world shifts from its axis, never to return. But our daughter's opening chapter was not an easy one.

# UNCONDITIONAL LOVE

I was definitely pregnant. There was no doubting that. Any romantic thoughts I might have had about pregnancy—images of myself wafting around in spotless white linen, with a neat little bump, shining hair and the sort of wistful, contented countenance which you see in a White Company catalogue—were just notions in my head. I spent virtually the whole time with my head in a bucket or down a loo, trying to carry on working in between the almost non-stop waves of nausea.

Other mothers-to-be bloomed. I, on the other hand, ballooned. Every inch of my body swelled up: my ankles, my legs, my neck and my face. I was pregnant from my toes right up to my nose, or so it seemed. For the usual reasons of not wanting to tempt fate, Paddy and I didn't tell anyone I was pregnant for 14 weeks, apart from close family. But everyone must have guessed because I was beginning to look like Shrek: green-faced and bloated.

When I told John Meade and the gang on *Countdown*, they decided to record as many programmes as they could before I had the baby, so that they could carry on screening the shows well into my maternity leave.

The baby was due in mid July 1992, and we finished recording in April. Because we had pre-recorded so many programmes, I was actually pregnant on screen until mid-October, making mine the longest pregnancy in television history, much to the delight of Terry Wogan, who regularly referred to it during his Radio 2 show, telling his listeners it was an elephantine pregnancy. 'For how long is this woman going to be pregnant?!' he would giggle.

I, meanwhile, was thinking the same thing. The pregnancy had not started smoothly and because we were trying to finish as many programmes as possible, managing my workload was difficult. I would be on my feet, for 12 hours every day, smiling and trying to pretend that I didn't want to be on the sofa with a cup of tea. I did find it particularly hard in the later months of pregnancy.

Back at the hotel, I would flop on the bed, so exhausted that I couldn't move. Meanwhile, on the non-*Countdown* days, I was working hard on a whole host of other programmes and projects, including a BBC1 quiz show with Kenny Everett called *Gibberish*, on which Keith Barron and I were regulars. As Keith never quite grasped the rules, it descended into chaos most days. I had also become a governor of the new Dixons City Technology College, a secondary school in Bradford, West Yorkshire, and was indulging my lifelong love of education. The school's results were incredible.

Added to that, I was making some education programmes for the BBC and hosting countless awards ceremonies and corporate events. To cap it all, I'd set up a business a few years earlier, something which was always in my Plan B, in case the presenting jobs started to wind down. The business made revision videos for National Curriculum and GCSE Maths and English. The house was covered in Post-it notes with maths questions scribbled all over them as I worked on the videos. Once they had been recorded and edited, they went on sale in WHSmith, Woolworths and the Avon catalogue, among other places. I learned a lot in those days about the business of, well, business.

Work on all these extra activities started once I was home from the day job, giving me many more hours work in the evenings. When the *Countdown* recordings ended in April, I hoped that I could start to unwind slightly and enjoy the remaining eight weeks of my pregnancy, but life sometimes has a habit of turning around and biting you just when you are least expecting it.

By the first week of May, our house was uncharacteristically empty. Mum and Francis, Trixie's former husband, who was still living with us at the time, had gone for a short holiday to Holland to visit my brother Anton. Then Paddy set off for a two-day conference in Bournemouth. The baby wasn't due for another two months, so we all thought the timing was perfect. I, meanwhile, was hugely distracted with some issues at the video production company. We had had to resort to lawyers and the stress was immense.

On 11 May 1992 I drove myself to London early in the morning. I was seven months pregnant and I had a host of meetings, including one with the lawyers. I found myself sitting in a stifling hot meeting room, listening to legal advice and trying to focus on the problem.

After many physically and emotionally draining hours, I stumbled outside into the fresh air. It was around six o'clock in the evening, and I set off to drive home.

I was still feeling totally stressed when I left the

Chiswick flyover on the M4 going west out of London and joined the main part of the motorway. 'Nearly home,' I thought. I remember driving behind a heavy lorry which had a large load on the back. The lorry was in the middle lane and I was in the fast lane. Then suddenly, as I was driving along at around 70 miles an hour, a huge plank of wood fell off the back of the lorry and bounced right into my path.

I had a split second to react, but time stood still and I was able to see the full potential horror of the situation. While I was braking, I quite rationally thought, 'If I hit the wood, the car will blow a tyre and I will crash into the central reservation.'

I knew I had to swerve to avoid it, but as I pulled hard on the steering wheel, I was thinking, 'If I hit somebody now, I might end up dead. Please don't let there be a car in the middle lane. Please don't let there be a car.' Mercifully, my prayers were answered. I braked hard and as my car skidded left; there was nothing alongside to crash into.

The near miss left me feeling physically limp. My head started pounding, my heart was thumping, my whole body felt cold and I was drenched with sweat. My hands were shaking so badly that I gripped the steering wheel as tightly as I could. I actually wanted to stop the car by the roadside and get out, to try to gulp down some air, but I knew that, badly shaken as I was, I had to somehow get home.

When I finally drew up at the house, it was nearly eight o'clock. I stopped the engine and felt so exhausted and ill that I could hardly step from the car. The cottage was silent and in darkness. I knew that Mum and Francis were flying back that night, but it would be hours before they were due home.

I rang my friend Lynda Mallett, Timmy's wife, who was also pregnant at the time. As we talked, I mentioned in passing that I was having stomach gripes. Lynda offered to come over, because I was on my own, but I insisted that I was fine.

When I put down the phone, I switched on the television, just in time for the *News at Ten*. Then, just as Trevor Macdonald came on the screen, I felt a savage pain flashing across my stomach. I wasn't unduly worried, but I decided to call the hospital where I was booked in to give birth in July. I spoke to a kindly midwife and she said, 'How long is it between pains?' I told her that I wasn't having pains which came and went; I just had a really bad ache in my stomach. She reassured me, saying, 'I'm sure it is nothing. It could be Braxton Hicks contractions. Call us back if you think there is a problem.'

I put the phone down, stood up to switch the television off and staggered slowly up the stairs. As I stood in our bedroom, my waters broke in an unmistakeable gush of warm fluid. I didn't have time to react, because I was suddenly hit by a pain in my stomach so intense that it doubled me up. I collapsed onto the bed and, through my tears of agony, all I could think of was ringing Paddy. He didn't have a mobile and when I called the hotel in Bournemouth where he was staying, he wasn't in his room.

I waited while the receptionist went to find him, the pain in my stomach was making me catch my breath. Finally, they tracked him down in the

142

restaurant and he came to the phone. I told him what had happened and tried to say, 'Don't worry, I'm sure it will be fine,' in between the waves of agony. But Paddy just said, 'I'm coming right now—I'll have to borrow a car.'

Now I had to sit and wait on my own, in the dark. Paddy was going to be hours and I had no way of getting hold of Mum and Francis. I was totally on my own. How ironic that our house was always crammed full of people and laughter and noise, but now, when I needed others around me more than I had ever done before, I was utterly, totally alone.

I concentrated on trying to keep calm and anticipate the waves of pain, while fighting back the panic which was threatening to engulf me. I had no idea what else to do and I didn't want to ring 999. I didn't want to bother the emergency services; I felt that others were probably in more need than I was.

Mum and Francis got back at about 11 o'clock. They walked in smiling and laughing, but dropped everything when they saw me. It was obvious now that I needed to get to hospital, and as fast as possible. They led me outside to the car—I was bent over and in so much pain that I could only just manage to climb into the back seat.

We arrived at the hospital to find the consultant waiting. He quickly checked me and announced that I was ten centimetres dilated. Then the real nightmare started. The consultant turned to me and said, '*You* will be fine if you have the baby here, but the baby may not survive. We have no special baby care unit. We need to get you to Ascot where they have the right equipment.'

Someone asked if they should call an ambulance to transfer me, but the consultant shook his head. He said, 'We haven't got time. The baby is on its way. Get in a car and go as fast as you can and I will drive there too and meet you at the other end.'

As I was wheeled down to reception, Paddy turned up in a stranger's car. He'd run into the bar at his hotel, accosted some fellow delegate from the conference who he hardly knew and persuaded the poor man to hand over his car keys. Paddy had then broken all land speed records by hammering up the motorway back home.

I was led back to the car by Paddy and a midwife and once more climbed into the back seat, with the midwife by my side. By now, I was screaming in pain and real fear for the safety of our baby. Paddy and I didn't have a clue how to find the hospital in Ascot, but Francis jumped in his car with Mum and, because he knew the area well, said he would lead us there.

There then followed the car chase from hell. Francis led us through the back roads of Windsor's royal estate, through the Great Park and down unfamiliar dark lanes. We couldn't afford to lose sight of his car ahead, because we would be totally stuck in darkness. At the same time, each contraction was ripping through my body and I was trying to breathe through the pain. All I could think of was the two-months premature baby arriving in the back of the car. 'Please don't come now. Please don't die,' I was urging it silently.

We reached the emergency doors of the hospital just as another massive contraction tore through me. I was now fighting the urge to push. I can remember being loaded onto a trolley in the darkness and wheeled quickly down a corridor straight into a delivery room.

I was beside myself with pain. I was given gas and air, but before it had taken effect, the baby, our daughter, was suddenly born. It was 12.15 a.m. and we had been in the hospital for just under ten minutes. My pains had only really started two hours earlier and here she was.

There was a tiny cry and then they placed her in my arms very briefly. No bonding, no moment of defining love. Just terrible fear. I had never seen a baby as tiny as this—she was 4 lb 5 oz—and all I could think was: 'Will she survive?'

I had hardly any time to take in her features before they whisked her out of the room and straight to the neonatal intensive care unit, to stabilise her. I was left in a state of total shock. The baby should still be safely protected inside my womb. Eight weeks premature, she was now fighting for her life.

All throughout my pregnancy, I had imagined the moment of giving birth, of seeing my baby's face, of holding my newborn child for the first time. Our first cuddle. Our first meeting. Instead, there had been pain, shock and a tiny red baby who had been taken from me before we'd even had the chance to say hello. Never in my wildest dreams had I imagined that this—what should have been the happiest moment in my life so far—would turn into a fearful nightmare.

The next hour was perhaps the longest hour of my life, while I waited with Paddy, Mum and Francis for news of our baby girl. Then a doctor came to tell us that she was on a ventilator and we were taken to the neonatal intensive care unit to meet our daughter properly for the first time.

The unit was hushed. Nurses slid silently between the rows of incubators and the only sounds were the blips of the machines keeping tiny babies alive. I was led to an incubator and there I saw her properly for the very first time.

At that moment, my heart just stopped. Inside the incubator was our baby, her minute arms covered in needles, a tiny woollen hat on her head to keep her warm and her face obscured by tubes and tape. I saw a little hand—the size of a doll's hand, so tiny that her palm was smaller than my thumbnail.

Her chest was heaving up and down in an effort to breathe. In that moment, I was utterly lost. I had never seen such a helpless, desperate and brave little thing as this. My heart was stolen.

I was hit by a wave of unconditional love. My life now belonged to her. I would give mine to save hers in an instant. All my instincts were to pick her up, cuddle her and protect her from the world. Instead, it was the incubator that was protecting her and keeping her alive.

There was nothing to do except sink down into a chair beside the incubator and watch as this tiny creature battled for her life. Over the next few days, the only useful thing I could do was to express milk which was then fed to her through a tube in her nose. The baby unit had a special fridge, used for storing breast milk from new mothers. Inside sat row upon row of neatly labelled jars. Name of mother. Name of baby. Date milk expressed. Each sterile jar telling its own story of shock and sadness. Each jar came from mothers who could not hold their own babies in their arms, or bond with them as they breastfed.

Around me, over the next few days and weeks, I became aware of other white-faced parents sitting beside incubators, urging tiny babies to fight on, some of them much smaller than our daughter. And all around us, day after day, was the knowledge that death was sometimes the outcome. Babies who were too small to survive died after the bravest of fights. The sound of parents crying is one which I'll never forget. You'd come to know these parents and then their baby died and you'd be filled with the most awful sadness. And guilt, because your baby was still alive and that's all you were praying for.

We named her Katherine Margaret Gina—to be known as Katie. To this day, I don't know who sent flowers or cards after she was born, because my whole life centred around her incubator. I had always been strong, but now I was in pieces. I was allowed to put my hand through the window of the incubator and Katie would grip it fiercely with her own tiny fingers. That brief physical contact would leave me reeling.

Having to leave Katie behind at the hospital a few days after her birth was horrible, but there were no beds available. I had never felt so empty before. My arms ached to hold her. Paddy and I drove home in silence, taking some of the balloons and cards sent by well-wishers. We both felt wretched and all I wanted to do was to change my clothes and head straight back to the hospital to be with my daughter.

The house felt eerily quiet and still. I went upstairs to have a shower and paused outside Katie's nursery. It had been decorated in a pristine white with daisy patterns and there was a beautiful swinging cradle sitting untouched in the middle of the room. We'd had no idea whether our baby was to be a boy or a girl, so white had seemed the safest bet. I didn't want to go inside. I didn't want to tempt fate.

So my new routine began. Each day I would wake at six o'clock, dress quickly and head straight for the hospital to sit beside Katie's incubator in an agonising vigil. Every evening I would bid her farewell and leave, in tears, for the silent drive back home. Every night and every morning I rang the hospital to find out how she had fared while I hadn't been by her side. Sleep became a thing of the past, a luxury I could no longer enjoy. Every night was spent lying awake, desperate to be back with her.

It was to be a tough fight. Katie developed jaundice and then her weight dropped further, leaving her even more bird-like and vulnerable as she lay in her incubator.

I was eventually allowed my first, all-too-brief cuddle with my daughter. I had imagined that this would be a wonderful moment, the chance to see her little face clearly for the first time and to drink in her wonderful baby smell.

But, in reality, I was utterly, utterly petrified. She was so tiny that she would have fitted snugly into Paddy's outstretched palm. Katie was connected to dozens of tubes and wires and I hardly dared to breathe, so scared was I of harming her.

Over the next few weeks, the nurses in the baby unit began to show me, very slowly, how to mother such a tiny baby: how to change her nappies, how to clean her with a sterile cotton wool ball and how to cradle her against my chest.

After a month, the doctors began to talk about 'when' Katie would be coming home. Not 'if', but 'when'. It was my first indication that all was going to be well. Until now, everything we did—and everything she did—was regulated by trained doctors and nurses, who helped in every way they could and supported all of the parents so wonderfully, but never gave anyone false hope. They'd seen too much on that unit. I had surrendered control the second she was born.

So now I made the first decision about Katie. Realising that she didn't have any baby clothes at home which were small enough to fit her, I decided to go to the local Mothercare and buy her a couple of babygrows.

It was a bustling store in Maidenhead and there, in the premature baby section, I found a single tiny babygrow. I held it up in its special packet and then glanced around me. For the first time, I saw other new mums with their babies. I saw babies gurgling in slings, babies kicking their chubby little legs in prams, new parents tenderly hugging each other as they peered into the prams to admire their sons and daughters.

It hit me like a stone and I suddenly started crying. I couldn't stop. If anyone thought it was strange for a woman to be hugging a babygrow to her chest and sobbing in the middle of the store, they didn't say.

I didn't envy their happiness, their joy and their togetherness. I simply longed to be pushing my own daughter in a pram, or holding her in my arms. I wanted her so much.

Back in the baby unit, tears were understood. All of us mothers spent day after day willing our babies to thrive and to grow. Every small step was a huge achievement. The removal of just one wire. Then the decrease in the level of oxygen needed to help them to breathe. The first cuddle. The first bath. The first attempts to breastfeed a tiny, fragile creature so weak that it could hardly suck. These achievements became our daily rituals, and we shared our happiness, our joy and—in some cases—our sorrow.

After about six exhausting weeks, Katie was finally declared ready and fit to come home. Paddy and I set off in the car that morning to pick her up, for the first time smiling and talking as we approached the hospital.

We took a baby seat for a newborn with us, but Katie, who we gingerly placed in it, was still so small that the straps, even fastened at their tightest setting, were loose. We drove home so slowly and carefully that other drivers behind us were probably cursing us.

We didn't care. Our daughter was coming home. At last. Back at the house, Mum and Francis had put up balloons. It was such a happy day and for two weeks we basked in the wonder of our baby girl. I doted on her and couldn't believe just how lucky we were. She was an angel and I didn't want to be away from her, not even in another room. The summer was hotting up and we'd take her for walks down the very quiet country lane where we lived.

Two weeks after she got back from hospital was a particularly warm day, so I put Katie in her new Silver Cross pram in the garden. We had a pretty back garden, with a patio to one side, next to an old eight-foot-high stone wall. We sat on the patio beside our daughter in her pram, gazing at her in total love and awe. I moved the pram into the shade of the wall which separated our garden from the one next door. The wall was nearly two feet thick and had been built many years before with a mixture of rubble, bricks and mortar.

Katie slept contentedly and when Mum called us in for tea, I hesitated, torn. It seemed a shame to move the baby when she was so happy, sleeping in the fresh air, safely in shade. But in the end, I pushed the pram to the back door, picked her up and stepped inside.

As we sat eating, there was suddenly a tremendous roar and a crash—so loud that I thought for one crazy moment that a bomb had gone off. The ground beneath our feet shook and we stared at each other in horror.

We went back outside and stood stock-still. There, where the huge wall had stood, was a giant pile of rubble. Minutes earlier, our baby daughter had lain in her pram in the shadow of the wall. Without a doubt, if I had not moved Katie at that moment, she would not have survived.

I dissolved into tears and hugged her close, shaking at the enormity of what had almost happened. Katie slept on—her dark hair, her wise little face, her flawless skin unharmed.

To this day, the memory still shakes me up and has me reaching out for the beautiful young woman who is my daughter. The baby who fought to survive and beat the odds. Not once, but twice.

# WOMAN OF THE WORLD

I went back to work when Katie was three months old. Walking back onto the set of *Countdown* again was like going back to school after the summer holiday; the team never usually spent that long apart. I toyed with the idea of bringing Katie up to Leeds with me, but Mum convinced me, and I think she was right, that routine was important for Katie, and also for me.

Looking back, I don't know if I would have been able to leave Katie, if Mum hadn't been at home to look after her. This was an old-fashioned, three-generation, 'family looking after family' home that we'd made together. I probably wouldn't have gone back to work while she was so young if I'd had to leave her with a nanny.

*Countdown* was now a huge success. It was the biggest show on Channel 4, in spite of being broadcast in the afternoon, when audiences are traditionally smaller than in the evening. Our viewing figures had hit at least four million viewers every day, sometimes as many as five million, and yet it wasn't 'showbiz'. That was its charm, I suspect. Richard and I bumbled through our days, loving every minute of it.

And the contracts got bigger as the ratings went up. But many presenters on shows with far fewer viewers were earning much, much more than us, as their shows came from the light entertainment and not the factual department. An absurd fact in TV which still exists today.

By 1992 I was better off financially than I had

ever imagined, but I still wanted to work for more security. The memory of my childhood burned deep. And in television absolutely nothing is guaranteed. How many TV shows go on for decades? You have to take the work while it's there, especially if you're a woman. So, for all those reasons, it was back to television for me. And, luckily, I loved my work.

Richard was passionate about politics and was pleased when I told him I'd met Prime Minister John Major, who had just won the 1992 General Election. I was surprised by how handsome John Major was, far better-looking and a lot taller in the flesh than on the telly. I think I'd grown used to his Spitting Image puppet.

Before Katie was born, I'd started co-hosting the children's show *How 2*, the updated version of the classic *How!* with Jack Hargreaves (he of the pipe and beard), which I'd watched as a child and loved, and was working alongside Fred Dinenage and Gareth 'Gaz Top' Jones. I'd been asked to do it by one of the most successful and brilliant children's TV producers—Tim Edmunds.

We generally split the items three ways. I would present most of the items based on science or technology, Gareth would do any of the 'young bloke' stuff and Fred would tackle anything else that came up, the 'leftovers', he called them.

And he literally did one day, when I was given an item to present: 'How would you survive in a jungle?' In other words, what would you eat? Now, this was back in the early 90s, a good decade before *I'm a Celebrity . . . Get Me Out of Here!* burst onto our screens along with various kangaroo-testicle-munching competitors.

In rehearsal we only pretended the 'food' was there. But during the recording, when all the cameras were rolling and I lifted the lid of the silver salver to reveal my 'dinner' underneath, reality hit home. There, sitting under my nose, was a plate of fried locusts. I almost threw up.

There was absolutely no way on earth I was going to eat them. Not even washed down with a side order of ants in a chilli sauce, following the appetizer of crunchy beetles.

I just couldn't swallow any of the insects in front of me. Fred came to my rescue. Like the true gentleman he was, he offered to munch his way through it, while I did the talking. He was only going to do it once, so it was 'first take or bust'.

The second that the director shouted, 'Cut!' Fred made a very strange noise, rushed to the side of the studio and spat out the lot. What a star!

Away from the television studios, I was also presenting corporate and training videos, which were anything but dry and boring. For Vauxhall, I learned the art of driving at the same time as talking into three cameras fixed to the car (respect to Jeremy Clarkson—it isn't as easy as it looks) and for Land Rover, I found myself taking off-roaders up mountainsides, tackling climbs so steep that my insides felt like they were trailing 20 feet behind me.

I went on a new Royal Navy frigate, which had been designed with wonky walls to reduce its radar signature, and we fired missiles. I stood just feet from Harrier Hawk jets as they took off time and time again. I was nearly blasted out of my boots. Here, in the wind and the rain, among some of the most interesting machines that technology had ever produced, I felt truly at home. Life on Planet Celebrity—what to wear, who to be seen with, where to go—I had little interest in it. This was my natural state.

So 1992 might have been the Queen's 'annus horribilis', with Princess Diana shortly to announce that she wanted a divorce, but for me, not so far away from Windsor Castle in Maidenhead, my life was blossoming.

GMTV took over from TV-am on 1 January 1993, with Fiona Armstrong providing what was called at the time 'the F factor'. I had been asked to be the education correspondent and so would work there when necessary, about one day a week. Education has always been one of my passions. It is, beyond question, the best way to change a nation and the chances of those who live there, and it had changed my life years earlier.

Eamonn Holmes and Lorraine Kelly were brought in. I'd met a young and handsome Eamonn many times about six years earlier at BBC Manchester, when he was hosting a morning show called *Open Air* for BBC1, and we'd always got on well.

Meanwhile, I was also busy juggling running a business with about 20 employees and, most importantly, being a mum to our baby girl.

September 1993 saw the most surreal job of my career to date: presenting the controversial World Chess Championship between Russian World Champion Garry Kasparov and British Grandmaster Nigel Short on Channel 4. The prize money was over £1 million. Nigel was the first Brit to have a chance of taking the title, so this was big news at home.

Kasparov had been the world champion since 1985. Now aged 30, he was a handsome, brooding genius whose battles with Anatoly Karpov were legendary. The official governing body for chess at the time was FIDE, but the chess world was buzzing. Kasparov, never one to hold back his thoughts, had been stripped of his title in March because he and Nigel had set up their own organisation, the Professional Chess Association, in competition with FIDE. It was fantastically exciting. To a professional chess player, the board is a battlefield and a loss is akin to death.

The series of 24 games was to be held at the Savoy Theatre in London and was sponsored by *The Times*. The event was held largely thanks to the work of Grandmaster Raymond Keene. Chess had never been broadcast live before—and we were about to find out why.

A set was made behind the players on stage, which is where the commentators and I would sit. Up in the gods of the theatre, a temporary editing gallery was erected, where the producers and editors could line up their shots and direct the cameras.

The executive producer chosen for the championship was an extraordinary man called Rocky Oldham, who had worked with megastar rock groups for years. Exactly why Rocky said yes to being in charge of a live chess event was a mystery, but his energy and passion made us all believe that we really could make ground-breaking television. He was amazing.

There are strict time control rules in competition chess and these were to play a dramatic part in the very first game of the championship. Not that we were aware of it at the time. Each player is allocated 40 moves in two hours, followed by a further 20 moves in one hour. At that stage, if the game has not been completed, there was to be an adjournment followed by a session of quick-fire moves up to a final time limit at which point the game would be declared a draw. The players each have a chess clock which counts down the minutes and is stopped after each move is made. The whole scene took me back to my days in Prestatyn when I was a young child and my brother Anton and I would wile away many hours a week just on one game. Anton's chess clock was one of his prize possessions and was polished and put away every night.

When we went out live for the first time, the game—or rather, my challenge of commentating on the game—slowly descended into chaos. Play was progressing and in the studio, in between analysis and comments on the tactics employed by Kasparov and Short, we were chatting away, not realising how quickly we were approaching a dramatic climax. 'What were we having for tea that night?' 'How were the kids?' Then our grandmasters—Raymond Keene, Jonathan Speelman and Daniel King—said, 'Quick, quick! You should be explaining this!'

Aaaargh! Time in the first period of play was running out for both players, and with 15 minutes left on his clock, Kasparov offered a draw after his 38th move. Short refused but he had even less time available for his moves. The game continued. The studio came to life and I leapt in with my commentary.

Just as Nigel Short went to pick up his chess

piece to make his 39th move, he paused, a delay which cost him a vital second. By the time he hit the button to stop his clock, it was too late—Nigel was out of time and Kasparov had won.

In the commentary box, with over a million viewers watching, the final few minutes of confusion and indecision seemed to last for hours. I was saying, 'And he's moving,' while my mind was screaming, 'What am I going to say next?' Never in my experience of live television has a silence lasted so long. I remember saying, 'And the clock is tick, tick, ticking as we wait for Nigel Short to play his move.' What a stupid thing to say.

The story led news channels around the world. Slow-motion action replays of a chess move? Yes, indeed. And whose stupid commentary was going on in the background? Mine. I've had better moments.

The whole experience of watching these two brilliant men battle with their wits was akin to watching Muhammad Ali and George Foreman in the ring. Not quite the Rumble in the Jungle, but a meaty contest nevertheless. And the charming, deeply romantic Kasparov was the equivalent of Ali. Adored by his fans and the undisputed king of his game, he oozed power and went on to win the championship by some margin.

Such was Kasparov's influence that he persuaded Boris Yeltsin to allow us to fly to Russia a year later to film the first Kremlin Stars World Speed Chess Championship from inside the walls of that amazing citadel. This was big stuff.

It was now 1994 and Moscow was only just opening up to visitors from the West. By day, I went to the Kremlin to film the chess challenge and each night we were whisked into restaurants which were hidden behind seemingly derelict doorways set in crumbling walls. Inside, women sat swathed in furs and laden with huge diamonds, while full orchestras played, waiters served five-course dinners and bodyguards with machine guns stood outside. It was like walking onto the set of a Bond movie. I'd never thought chess would give me such enthralling moments.

This was all great fun and exciting but if you are trying endlessly to cram 28 hours of work into every 24-hour day, something has to give, and in the end it did. One day, when I was 33 years old, I was sitting at my desk at home working on some spreadsheets when I had a funny feeling on the right-hand side of my face, like it was going numb. I ignored it. Then my neck, on the right side only, started to feel numb. I ignored that as well. Then it happened to my right arm and very quickly the numbness started to spread down the right side of my body. Mum was at home and I told her. She rang the doctor's surgery in our village and they said to come in straightaway. I'll never forget the doctor saying, 'I think you're having a stroke. I'll ring for an ambulance.'

So now I was worried and I fainted. Minutes later, the ambulance arrived. I had no idea what was going on. When I got to the hospital I was scanned and monitored, but nothing could be found. I was there for about four days, until the numbness started to recede. 'A virus' was eventually blamed, but the consultant said that he was seeing more and more of it in people in their 30s with careers; they were simply too stressed for too long. I should have taken it as a warning, but

159

when you're busy juggling work with being a wife and mother and trying to do everything to the best of your ability, you just get back on the bike and start pedalling again.

*    *    *

And so the next TV adventure began. Unknown to me, a BBC focus group was underway, looking at the station's flagship science programme, *Tomorrow's World*. It was presented by Judith Hann at that time, but from somewhere on high, the decision was made to revamp the long-running and popular show. This happens all the time in telly; sometimes it works for you and sometimes against you.

When the focus-group findings came back, three-quarters of those questioned had stated that they wanted me to present *Tomorrow's World*, or so I was told. The new editor of the show, Edward Briffa, rang my agent John Miles to ask if I would consider presenting the programme.

*Tomorrow's World* wanted me to commit to three days each week, which was a lot at the time, as I was already more than full-time on everything else. But I have always believed it's worth investigating every option open to you; you never know where you will end up.

The idea was that I would be the anchorwoman in the studio, while also filming my own reports out on location.

A little while after I said that I was interested, one executive turned around and announced, 'We are going to build you into one of the biggest faces on the BBC.' He paused and then added, 'So we need you to give up *Countdown*, as you are perceived as a daytime hostess and not taken seriously enough.' You can imagine how well that went down! I was annoyed that negotiations had taken place and absolutely no mention had ever been made of me sacrificing my beloved *Countdown*.

No promises of prime-time fame and all the trappings of success were worth turning my back on the show I loved more than any other. So I said no, without hesitation, and expected that this would bring a sudden end to all our talks. Instead, the BBC came back, upped their offer and said that I would be allowed to continue with *Countdown* and *How 2*.

So, as negotiations for the final contract continued, in September 1994, I began my new job as the host of *Tomorrow's World*. I was working so many hours at this time that I never had a chance to do anything other than work or be a mum. I certainly never had time to go to the hairdresser, so I used to cut my own hair at home with a pair of office scissors. I got rumbled, though, when I had a photoshoot for my first front cover of the *Radio Times*. I'd cut my hair in the bathroom specially for the occasion. Millions of copies were printed and when I saw one I realised that my fringe was about an inch shorter on one side than on the other and looked hysterical. I tried to make out that I was ahead of the trend with the asymmetric fringe, but really it was because I was rubbish with scissors.

On *Tomorrow's World*, I found myself immersed in some of the most fascinating filming I had ever been a part of.

I met a most wonderful mathematician at

Cambridge, Professor John Daugman, the inventor of the iris-recognition system, which we are now beginning to see in passport control. Far more accurate than fingerprinting and a phenomenal piece of mathematics. John was a chess fan and totally engaging. We talked about the 1993 Kasparov/Short match and the Kremlin Stars, and I could have stayed there filming for a week, but a day was all we had and the crew dragged me off back home.

I also went to a university in America where scientists were pioneering new bullet-proof vests made out of spiders' webs. We shot at vest-clad mannequins and the vests resisted the impact. We filmed in vast forests in Michigan and in laboratories at the cutting edge of science. This was my perfect show and I loved it even when peculiar things happened

Back in London, at the BBC TV Centre, I would spend a day filming the links between the various reports. I naïvely thought that this would be a very simple process. Well, it isn't rocket science, standing in front of a camera with an autocue which has the script on it in big, typed letters and scrolls up in front of you.

But one day I quickly became aware that something wasn't quite right. In fact, I realised this as I uttered my very first sentence. I smiled into the camera and said, 'Hello and welcome to *Tomorrow's World.*'

Someone stepped forward. 'Can we do that again, please?'

I obliged. 'Hello and welcome to *Tomorrow's World.*'

There was a pause in the studio. A sense of

unease. I couldn't understand it. Another voice said, 'Can we do this again, please?'

I was genuinely puzzled. Pulling my smile on again, I beamed at the camera. 'Hello and welcome to *Tomorrow's World*.'

This time, there wasn't even a pause. It was becoming clear that something I was doing—or saying—simply wasn't right.

A tense floor manager stepped forward. 'Please wait, Carol. One of the producers is coming down to speak to you.'

By the time the producer in question arrived from the production gallery, I was genuinely confused. One glance at his face told me that all was not well. He looked at me seriously and shook his head slightly. I really thought I had done something terribly wrong. He said gravely, 'Carol, I need to talk to you because "hello" and "welcome" are two entirely different forms of greeting and the nuance between these separate forms of greeting must be correct. You must emphasise the differences much more, and pause, but not for too long. "

What? I burst out laughing. This *had* to be a joke. I actually looked around the studio, half expecting Noel Edmonds to come leaping out of the wings to announce a Gotcha. But he didn't. I couldn't help but chuckle.

It was a hilarious introduction to how, in some people's eyes, the devil really is in the detail.

I loved the freedom and the fun of going away on assignment as a team, with a cameraman, sound engineer and producer. It was early in 1995, while I was in Australia, that a contractual storm broke.

In September 1994, a couple of weeks *after* I had

started filming for *Tomorrow's World* and the BBC had issued a press release with the headline 'CAROL IS BBC 1's NEW WOMAN OF THE WORLD', the BBC had sent through a draft contract which included a clause to say that I couldn't present any commercials.

This had never been discussed in negotiations prior to me starting.

Had it been, I would have had to refuse the job, as I already had contracts for commercials and I had never made any secret of this—to the BBC or to anyone else. Indeed, I had been promoting products for some time.

John Miles was aware of my existing commitments of course, and was often in ongoing discussions with advertising companies with regard to TV commercials and endorsements.

So John Miles wrote back to the BBC to explain it would not be possible to sign the contract with the clause relating to commercial endorsements.

He left messages and sent letters but nothing came back from the BBC at all, so I just carried on hosting the show without a signed BBC contract.

I was being paid my fee and, as far as I was concerned, the BBC was aware of my situation and all was going well until early 1995. I made a TV commercial for Ariel and it had started to be broadcast.

I went to Australia to make some films for *Tomorrow's World*. When I got back to the hotel after a day's filming outside of Sydney, my telephone rang. It was the BBC. They wanted me to fly home for an urgent meeting in London to discuss the embarrassment they felt was being caused by the airing of the Ariel advert. Although I tried to point out that no-one had mentioned this to me before and that no contract had been signed saying that I could not appear in adverts, it became clear to me that I needed to fly straight home and that sorting the whole thing out, as far as the BBC was concerned, was now an immediate priority.

I was upset, particularly as I had to tell the camera crew that I was returning home early. Negotiations had already begun with John by the time my plane landed in London. The BBC offered to effectively let the matter drop if the Ariel advertisements were immediately pulled. Ariel—not surprisingly—didn't want this, and neither did I. This was, as far as I was concerned, non-negotiable: I had signed a contract with Saatchi to make up to three Ariel adverts and I was not prepared to renege on that deal.

Rumour has it that someone connected with the BBC saw the Ariel advert I had already made and thought it 'inappropriate'. The BBC said, unequivocally, that I should not be filming advertisements if I was presenting *Tomorrow's World*. In response, I pointed out that Noel Edmonds, while hosting his *Noel's House Party* programme every Saturday on BBC1, was advertising Maxwell House coffee and Terry Wogan was happily fronting an ad for a utility company—both high-profile BBC personalities, both advertising commercial products without any problem from on high. The BBC responded by saying that it didn't count as they (Noel and Terry), were working for the light entertainment department. They stated it was different for me as I was presenting a factual programme.

So I pointed out that Gary Rhodes, who was

working for the factual department presenting cookery shows, was at that very moment advertising Tate & Lyle sugar. The BBC responded, 'But Gary is a cook, which is different from what you do.' As far as I was concerned, it was the same thing. He cooked and advertised sugar; I presented a science programme and advertised washing powder—no difference at all, as far as I could see. It felt like there was one rule for me and a different rule for everyone else.

The BBC finally agreed that they would accept the current situation with this Ariel advert running and they would even accept the advert being repeated at a later date, but if Ariel wanted to take up the option on another advert then the BBC and I would have to part company. So, in February 1995, five months after I had begun work on *Tomorrow's World*, I finally signed a contract with the BBC. This seemed fair to me, as it allowed me to keep my promise to Ariel in the event that they wanted to make another advert (although it seemed odd that the BBC did not object to the continuing broadcast of the advert which I had already made or indeed any repeats of it).

Just over a month before the end of the series in the summer, we had the phone call from Saatchi, to say that Ariel had considered the campaign to be such a success that they wanted to take up the option for another TV advert, which they were entitled to do under my contract with them. This, of course, meant that the BBC would be entitled to terminate my contract. I had hoped that the BBC might wait until our contract expired naturally within weeks or, at the very least, that the BBC and I would be able to issue a joint statement that because of a prior contractual obligation, we had mutually agreed to part company. But it was not be. The press got hold of the story quickly and, before I had any time to issue a statement, it was being widely reported that I had been 'sacked'. Although not true—the BBC had legitimately terminated our contract, not sacked me—in all the furore, it did indeed feel as if I had been sacked. And it was horrible. I felt like I was standing completely alone.

Unsurprisingly, after all the fuss, the BBC weren't falling over themselves to work with me on other projects which had been in the pipeline and I suddenly found that my previously full diary was looking quite empty. I just didn't know what to do. I sat at my desk, sobbing and frustrated. So I decided to fight my corner. I wrote an article in the *Sun* asking why I was singled out and I quoted all the other BBC personalities who were presenting adverts at that time and for whom no similar rule applied.

The article created a storm. *TW* continued with another handful of shows until the end of the series, but ratings dropped significantly. Within weeks, my column in the *Radio Times* about science stories had been cancelled. I had also signed up for a new education series for the autumn of 1995. I was removed from this series and paid off, even though that contract had no mention of adverts. It felt like such a waste.

Meanwhile, I carried on with *Countdown* and my other programmes. Then, in August, just before the new series of *Tomorrow's World* was due to return, the telephone in my dressing room at *Countdown* rang while I was having my make-up done. It was Phil Dolling, the highly likeable deputy editor of *Tomorrow's World*. I was delighted to hear from him. He wondered if I would consider discussing a return to the show. I virtually had to pick myself up off the floor, I was laughing so much. I told him I would be more than happy to discuss the possibility of returning, as I loved the programme so much.

Phil arranged a meeting between me and the BBC. I thought long and hard about the prospect of returning before I went. Yes, I decided, it was best to let bygones be bygones. I could rejoin the programme and we could put the whole incident behind us and concentrate on making the show once more.

I was feeling fairly positive as I went into the room, and I felt even more so when I was told that the BBC had been consulting a lot of research groups since my departure and, as a result, were offering me my job back. However, I was then warned that if the story of my possible return got into the press, the whole deal was off. As I'd had nothing to do with the initial press coverage following the termination of my contract by the BBC, I was upset at the suggestion and it made me think twice. After a few weeks and more debate about adverts, I decided not to return to *TW*. But I remember it vividly as the first time I had been let go from a programme. I was only the second presenter, I think, that this had ever happened to at the BBC. And the rules about adverts have changed significantly since then.

At the same time, we were moving house from Bryony Cottage to a bigger property, one completely beyond anything I'd even dreamed about before. The new house had just had a huge, bare extension built on and we needed builders there for quite a few months more.

Because it took a while to get new TV contracts going, I had some weeks to write a maths book for Dorling Kindersley called *How Maths Works*. The book was about the beauty of maths and included maths experiments that children and their parents could do at home. It went on to sell around the world for over a decade. I was very proud of that book.

Time was racing on ever faster. Katie was a beautiful, happy, kind little girl and we would bake cakes every day that I was home. I used to weigh everything out for her and put the ingredients into little bowls, like they do on cookery shows. From the age of 18 months, she knew exactly what to do and the order in which to do it. She is now a brilliant baker, and I used to do sums with her too. Knowing that it was likely people would ask her about maths during her growing-up years if they knew she was my daughter, I reckoned that she needed to be as good as she could be, so that she could answer all their questions. She's turned out to be a natural at that too. My mum looked after her magnificently for the periods when I was away, and that was my own comfort blanket.

Once I'd had the chance to pick myself up after the *Tomorrow's World* debacle, I had to start again. They say that what doesn't kill you makes you stronger and I guess it's true, to a certain extent.

About a year later, the BBC and I 'made up' and, at a time when *The X-Files* had taken a grip on the nation, I was asked to host a series about supposedly unexplained phenomena. *Out of This*

169

*World* took me back to prime-time on BBC1 and from there the offers rolled in once more. Within a couple of years, the list of shows grew, and all the time *Countdown* carried on, as Channel 4's number one programme.

Excitement. Adventure. Exhaustion beyond belief. And hotel rooms which morphed into one. My 30s were dominated by work. But Paddy, my husband, was exactly the same and so were many of my friends, who had spilled out from universities and straight into careers which brought them money and success.

We adored Katie and when we weren't working punishingly long hours, our lives revolved around her.

Together we cherished her first few words, her first steps and the sudden change from babyhood to round-faced toddler. Whenever I got home early enough from a busy day of filming, I would take Katie in my arms and try to convince myself that I could have it all. What a joke.

In reality, I was driven not so much by ambition but by fear. A fear that one day I could lose everything. Being dropped by the BBC had brought it all back to me. There had been many times when everything had been taken away: by my father and then when Mum left Gabriel many times. In my head, I'd go back to the room opposite the jail in Leicester, the one with the broken window, and the student lodgings Mum lived in when she was 53 and my divorce from Chris, and on it went. My absolute priority in life by then was to look after my extended family and I was damned well going to do it. It drove me on.

And then, amidst more and more work and

contracts, I became pregnant for a second time and we were delighted.

Our beautiful baby boy, Cameron King, was born in February 1997. This time there were no problems with prematurity, as there had been with Katie, and Cameron and I could bond immediately. In fact, Cameron and I have smiled endlessly at each other since that day. But work carried on. Three weeks later, I was back at work on the very first midweek National Lottery programme with Carol Smillie, who became a good friend. There was also *Hot Gadgets*, *Points of View* and then the big one, *Mysteries with Carol Vorderman*. Clare Pizey was the producer of *Mysteries*. Hugely talented and a laugh a second, she and I fell into an instant friendship, although trying to stop giggling at production meetings with Clare was a problem. We travelled around the world filming folk with strange stories. Some had wanted to freeze their bodies after death (or just before death, in one case). I went to Rome with a cheeky boy, Ash Atalla, who became the producer of *The Office* in later years. He was always trouble, even then! We attempted to check out haunted homes and investigate the influence dolphins could have on the chronically ill. The stories were certainly varied. In 1997 the shows were pulling in huge audiences, up to ten million viewers a night.

It was incredible how things had accelerated. It was almost as if being let go from *Tomorrow's World* was something that had been meant to happen. But the pace of work, although welcome and exciting, was taking its toll.

# DETOX AND DRESSES

So how does it get to the stage where you are on national television every day, but you don't recognise the person staring back at you in the mirror? Who is this bloated, tired old bird with a wonky haircut and hamster cheeks?

In the 90s, after I'd had Katie, I had started to hide behind certain clothes: a pair of safe black trousers and long jackets which covered my bum. My workload rocketed, but I was more and more tired, picking up food and eating it without thinking, without even knowing I'd eaten it most of the time. It was a robotic action. When I'm tired, and particularly when I'm stressed, I need food.

Professionally, I was, to the outside world, a soaring success. The highest-paid woman on television, by all accounts. Privately, my self-esteem was dropping fast and I was stuck in a vicious cycle. The more work I took on, the more tired I became, the more I reached out for comfort food. The more weight I put on, the worse I felt. And so the cycle continued. For about seven or eight years.

In my student days and my 20s, I had remained naturally slim. At five foot six, I was a size 8–10, which fitted my frame perfectly. I go in at the waist and very much out behind, with what we call in our family the Vorderman bottom. Even Anton has a Vorderman bottom. When instructors shouted, 'Clench!' in aerobics lessons, I used to say, 'I *am* clenching,' and they'd laugh.

Then came Katie. I was 31, not a geriatric

mother (as medics like to call you over the age of 35). I ballooned to a size 16 when I was expecting her, but that had seemed acceptable. I was eating for two, as everybody nicely tells you, and I was very puffy. I blithely assumed that the weight would drop off once the baby was born, but soon found out that rule is for a different species of female.

I am a very lively person, bouncing around and generally making a bit of mischief in one form or another, but that all stopped when I was pregnant. I physically couldn't be like that anymore.

Other mums had told me that if you breastfed, your body would twang back to pre-baby shape within weeks. Calories would be devoured and my old energy levels would come surging forward. In fact, the very opposite happened. I found it incredibly hard to lose the baby weight. Furthermore, I was hit by a wave of permanent tiredness which was to stay with me throughout my 30s.

Months after Katie's birth, I was still a size 14–16 and was wearing many of the clothes I had worn during my pregnancy. I started all sorts of diets, but a mounting workload and the very business of being torn between life as a mum and life at work consigned me to failure.

I tried SlimFast, Rosemary Conley, the cabbage soup diet (one of Richard Whiteley's favourites, so we know how successful that diet was!), anything the tabloids printed. But I couldn't stick to any of them for more than a day and a half, as yet another week of being away from home, having Katie to worry about and a business to run, took priority.

My body felt alien to me. I really didn't like the

way I looked, and I hated the way that it made me feel even more. So I reached out for a disguise—choosing clothes which would hide my weight gain.

It was like a uniform I wore every day. It consisted of a pair of very well-cut, designer black trousers, which had been given to me by a stylist when I'd worked on an Ariel commercial, and a wardrobe full of long jackets, which I hoped served as camouflage for both my bottom and stomach. I couldn't remember the last time I had worn a dress or a skirt and blouse nipped in at the waist with a belt.

Being overweight when you're on the box is quite a lonely business. I couldn't join WeightWatchers, because I was either working or looking after my daughter. Anyway, it would have been in the papers within a nanosecond. In the days before the internet, there were no online slimming groups or information to help people who wanted to lose weight.

Finally, years after Katie was born, when I was removed from *Tomorrow's World*, I had a slug of time freed up, so I hired a personal trainer. I started to watch what I ate and 'treated' myself to running around the park three times a week, being encouraged (i.e. shouted at) by my lovely female trainer.

Slowly but surely, the pounds began to drop off. And then, in 1996, four years after Katie was born, I found out that I was pregnant again. Of course, I was utterly delighted. We had wanted a brother or sister for Katie for a long time, but it had taken a few years to happen.

The personal trainer went off into the sunset, while I settled down to enjoy my second pregnancy. It was much easier than the first. I didn't feel nearly as sick and although I piled on weight, I wasn't quite the human balloon that I had been when I was pregnant with Katie.

Cameron was born on 11 February 1997. Not premature. No issues. No panic. He was healthy and beautiful. I'd worried terribly about him being premature and, as I was now what is regarded medically as an 'old mother' at 36, I'd had scans galore to check that everything was alright. I'd had a sneaky peek at one very detailed ultrasound scan which proved undeniably that he was going to be a boy. I didn't tell anyone, not even Paddy, but I was thrilled. How lucky were we, not only to be having a second child, but also one who looked healthy and a boy to match our gorgeous girl, who was by then a constant source of joy?

But now the two stones I'd put on during the pregnancy wouldn't shift. Again. And with a young child and a new baby, the process of losing weight seemed tougher than ever before. When I was at home with the children, I would automatically finish off any food from their plates. Well, it's easy to do, isn't it, just a few mouthfuls before you chuck the rest in the bin? Then, when Paddy returned hours later, I would serve him up a huge helping of pasta with a rich, creamy sauce, loading my own plate with a large portion to match. It meant that I would eat two lots of food in the evening and do nothing to burn off the calories.

By the end of the week, when Paddy and I would both be physically shattered, we would simply opt for a Chinese or Indian takeaway. It became a habit to eat too much of the wrong type of food. Probably three takeaways a week became the norm.

By now, we were living in a big house in Maidenhead and Mum was still living with us, thank goodness. We had loads of rooms, big gardens and a meadow, and a business annexe with room for two secretaries, Mum and Robin (who was now Francis's partner—yes, I know our family is complicated). I had a team of people: a nanny, a housekeeper, a cleaner, two secretaries, a man who 'did', gardeners, and you name it. Whenever I came home, the house was packed. I was utterly exhausted, but I was at the top of my game in terms of work.

When I was working, my eating habits were becoming worse. I would have to leave the house at 5 a.m., and instead of eating a sensible breakfast to keep me going, I would bolt down the first of many coffees with sugar and maybe a croissant. I needed the sugar to stay awake.

By the time I had driven to the studio or location, I would be utterly famished and would find my way straight to the canteen or the catering bus. Then I would gorge on a big, fat bacon and fried egg buttie, washed down with the first of 12 cups of tea.

By mid-morning, I would be famished once more and so exhausted that I needed a sugar hit, so I would grab a bar of chocolate or a biscuit to keep me going. When you're in the studio or on location, all this stuff is very readily available; it's the normal fare. Lunch would be on the run—a sandwich and a bag of crisps eaten hastily between shoots—followed by more chocolate later in the afternoon to get me through the rest of the day.

On the drive home, to keep my concentration

levels up, I'd snack on sugary foods from service stations, and by the time I made it through the door and had dealt with the kids, I would have something from the microwave and then that comforting little bowl of Crunchy Nut Cornflakes just before bed. I was eating in a bid to fight the exhaustion and to boost my blood sugar. I was eating out of habit and to forget the growing frustration about my weight and shape.

They say that the camera never lies. Well, let me assure you that it does. Constantly. Appearing on camera adds at least one dress size to how you look. I always laughed when people in the *Countdown* audience said, 'Ooh, Carol, you're not half as fat as you look on the telly, love,' when I walked into the studio. They were always surprised by how much smaller I seemed in the flesh. But I felt middle-aged and exhausted, and I was heading towards my 40s.

Something had to break the cycle. And, in the end, it took an old friend to turn this whole thing around. I had invited a friend from Leeds, Liz, to come and stay. We had seen in the New Year, welcoming in 1999, together five months earlier, and Liz had been looking tired at that time— exactly the way I felt. So when she bounced through the door the following summer, I almost had to do a double-take.

It wasn't just that she looked slimmer—which she certainly did. She looked absolutely glowing: her hair, her skin, her shining eyes. She had found something that I had long lost—and I was desperate to know more.

Liz, it turned out, had tried a new eating system which was being promoted by my gentle friend Ko

177

Chohan. I knew that Ko swore by Dr Robert Gray's Cleansing Programme, but I remained a cynic. I couldn't see how adding powder to a drink could change the way you looked. But then again, Liz was right in front of me, looking fresh, bright and alive. She insisted there was no magic potion, just a powder which contained a seaweed protein and fibre and which helped to clear out the colon of old packed waste materials, which most people carry round with them. She claimed that the powder drinks, used with a meal plan, had transformed her.

I still didn't know quite what to think, but I simply had nothing to lose. I got hold of the powder and started my new regime. For a month, I had to stick to a strict diet of brown rice, fruit and vegetables. Alcohol was banned, and so was wheat, meat and dairy. So determined was I not to fall off the wagon that I cleared out the larder one morning, pulling out every tempting little snack and replacing them with sultanas and fresh fruit. The first week was absolute agony. My stomach was swollen and bloated and so solid that it felt like a drum. Meanwhile, I had swapped my continuous cups of tea and coffee for a strict no-caffeine diet. Deprived so suddenly of my daily caffeine fix, I was literally going through cold turkey.

Then, after that first week of misery and discomfort, an extraordinary thing happened. Weight started to drop off me, but bigger changes happened which were far more important than the weight. After ten days, my eyes started to look brighter, my skin was clearer and my energy levels began to climb. Best of all, instead of lying awake for hours with my head buzzing, I started to sleep peacefully through the nights. I knew nutritionists might dismiss what was happening to my body, but I couldn't. The change was so wonderful and I had needed it so badly.

When I started the diet, I must have weighed about 11 stone. Five weeks later, I was somewhere nearer 9. I was thrilled. I wasn't afraid to look at my own reflection anymore and felt that the old Carol, the one with the energy, was back. More importantly, the self esteem which had been at rock bottom was climbing. I loved the feeling. For the first time in ages, I was back in control of my body.

To be honest, I had no intention of telling anyone in the press that I had been on a diet. I happened to be doing an interview for the *TV Times*, to launch a new series on ITV. It was lunchtime and I was sitting in the canteen eating my lunch—a plate of steamed vegetables with lots of soy sauce and mustard.

The journalist asked me if I was on a diet and I began to tell her about what I'd been doing. It was just chatting really, but it turned out to be the main theme of her finished article.

I had posed for a photograph, which made the front cover of the *TV Times*. My hair was cut short and curled on top and I was in a long dress and wearing roller skates. It was where I met someone who became a great friend, the make-up artist Karen Alder. Karen had lived in Sheffield and this was her first professional job and she was very nervous, particularly as she only had about half an hour to do the whole look. Often, it can easily take two or three hours. The shoot had been exciting and fun, and the energy I felt was clear in the picture.

It caused a bit of a stir and made lots of front pages. And it took me utterly by surprise. After years of feeling so unhappy about being big and bloated, the last thing I ever expected was to be congratulated on the way I looked.

Within two days, letters started coming through the door, some addressed simply to Carol Vorderman, England. I sat down to read them and ended up with tears falling down my face. Here, in countless letters and cards, were the most secret thoughts, fears and sometimes self-loathing of thousands of women.

In every story I read, I could see my own experience. Marriage. Work. Children. Exhaustion. Snacking. Weight again. Insecurity. Dismay. Everyone who'd written to me had lost themselves in the same way that I had lost myself. And they all wanted to do something about it. Like me, they longed for a change. And like me, they would try more or less anything in order to change their lives and their looks. The letters came from women in all walks of life. Nurses. Teachers. Factory workers. Working mums. Stay-at-home mums. I wrote back to as many as I could, but it was hard to know what to say. At that point, I didn't feel able to give advice, other than to tell them what I had done.

Two years later, I worked with Ko Chohan on a book which contained a diet plan: *Carol Vorderman's 28 Day Detox Plan*. It included a shopping list of what to buy and when it came out sales of blueberries and corn-based pasta went through the roof. It was one of the year's bestselling books.

I hope the writers of all those heartfelt letters found the same happiness that I did. I started to wear my old clothes again. I felt young. My maternity outfits found their way to charity shops. Eventually, as confidence in my new-look body grew, I decided to invest in a whole new wardrobe. It had been years since I had been able to wear dresses and skirts, and now I wanted more. I chose some new trouser suits, but these ones were figure-hugging and flattering. And when it came to going out, I had dresses which were very daring, with plunging necklines and bold colours.

In May 2000 I was invited to attend the annual BAFTA TV awards. Des Lynam was to host the event and I would be presenting one of the awards.

I hadn't planned what I was going to wear. A few weeks before the ceremony I went to Browns, a trendy clothes shop in London. I was flicking around the rails on the top floor when I saw this lovely, bright-blue, shirt top. I asked the assistant whether I could quickly try it on. 'It's not a top,' she informed me. 'It's a dress.' And so I tried on the Emanuel Ungaro dress and thought it would be good for an eventual summer holiday.

I didn't give the blue dress a second thought until the day of the BAFTAs. It was a very hot day and I'd been sunbathing in the garden and playing with the kids. When I came in to get ready for the ceremony, I realised that I was going to conk out with heat in the dress I'd decided to wear. These gigs start really early, as it takes hours to get everybody inside, so we were all asked to arrive at around four in the afternoon. I suddenly remembered the little blue Ungaro number in my wardrobe. By now, I was running late, so I had about half an hour to get dressed, check myself in the mirror and then dash for the taxi for the hour's drive into London.

I knew that the red carpet was going to be busy and I didn't think anyone would be particularly interested in me, other than the obligatory taking of a photo for the archives. After all, I wasn't used to anyone taking any notice of what I wore—that's normally reserved for the actresses and glamour pusses.

I stepped onto the red carpet and the paparazzi started clicking away, calling out my name so I would stop and pose for photographs, which they do to everyone until they get bored of you and the next, more interesting person comes along.

The next morning, I was honestly stunned to see myself—and my tiny blue dress—on the front page of every single tabloid. The reactions to my outfit could best be described as mixed. Newspaper editors and columnists seemed amazed and affronted in equal measure that a woman my age would dare to wear such a number. It wasn't the dress itself which ignited such passion, it was the fact that someone of 39 years of age was showing a bit of leg.

The *Daily Mail* invited two of its leading columnists to debate the fact in one of those 'should she, shouldn't she' articles. I was working at Granada two days later and Matthew Kelly and I were sitting in the make-up room watching BBC1, only to see Kilroy declare that he was devoting a whole show to the subject! We corpsed. How hysterically funny! In fact, they not only devoted the entire episode to it, they even had a copy of the dress flown in from Paris to show viewers exactly what I had dared to wear.

Looking back, I can see where they were coming from. The dress was quite revealing, not least because it was strapless and so I had to spend most of the evening hoisting it up. And to be fair, it was a little shorter than anything you'd have seen me wearing on *Countdown*. But that said, it was only a dress.

I assumed that after a couple of days all the interest in my choice of clothes would eventually die down. But no. Pictures of the dress appeared every day in one national paper or another for over a year. *That* dress is still somewhere in my wardrobe and I swear I'll wear it again. One day.

But it was the response I had from women all over the country that really meant something to me. Day after day, letters would arrive at *Countdown*, asking for advice. They had seen me on television every day for the past 18 years and they had watched me gain weight and then lose it. My body shape had changed in front of a whole nation of judges. And they knew—and I knew—just how hard the fight had been.

I'd love to say that everything became easier from then on, that I maintained my size 8 effortlessly. But that would not be entirely true. When we moved to London, I thought it was best to hire a personal trainer again. It's much easier to do some exercise if you know you have no choice but to go to the gym. I met Sarah Williams—or Cruella, as I call her—and she would whip me into shape within weeks when I got out of hand.

Although my weight does fluctuate, I don't own a pair of scales. I judge my weight on a pair of trousers which are utterly unforgiving. These trousers never lie. They are green, satin and made by Versace. I wore them once for a show and they looked amazing. I couldn't sit down with them on, but as I only had to stand in front of the camera anyway, that didn't bother me.

I've used these trousers to judge my weight for the last ten years. They fit nicely if I am a size 8–10, so if I can't pull up the zip, fasten the top button or—emergency measures required—even get them over my bum, I know I need to diet. I am now a comfortable size 10 and have been for the last decade, but sometimes it's a loose size 10 and sometimes a very tight one.

Through being overweight—lacking self esteem and hiding behind my clothes—and then learning that I could change it, I have come to understand very well what so many other women go through. And how what we eat can affect our health for the better.

## PRIME TIME

There are some moments in your life when you realise the thing you are doing right now, this very second, really isn't a very good idea. Most of those times, thankfully, you can make your apologies and sidle away. But for me, unfortunately, the realisation came when I was wearing fishnet tights, thigh-high boots and a curly black wig. On national television.

It was Nigel Hall, the producer, who had bamboozled me with charm and persuaded me to take part in *Celebrity Stars in Their Eyes* in 1998. I can't ever say no to Nigel. It heralded the start of the whole celebrity programme genre and Frank Skinner, myself and others were the guinea pigs. Matthew Kelly, the presenter, was a friend of mine, so that gave me some comfort. Whatever my reason for saying yes, I can safely say that nothing would ever convince me to do it again.

I can't remember who persuaded me that it was a great idea to appear as Cher—in truth, I have a really horrible feeling that it was me who came up with that idea—but it was tantamount to a catastrophe and the memory of that day makes me cringe, even now. When I look at pictures of myself dressed as Cher, with my wild hair and slightly crazed look, I realise I look less like the singer and more like an extra from *The Rocky Horror Picture Show*.

I had always enjoyed singing in the past. In fact, probably right up until the moment I recorded the show. At one point, back in the 80s, I had moonlighted as a singer with a band in Leeds called Dawn Chorus and the Blue Tits, which was fronted by the DJ Liz Kershaw. We had been offered a deal with Polydor Records as, thanks mainly to Liz, we had managed to convince them that we could hold a tune. Well, Liz could anyway.

With this in mind, I thought I'd be able to pull off just one song for *Celebrity Stars in Their Eyes*, and in rehearsals my rendition of Cher's hit 'The Shoop Shoop Song' seemed to work quite nicely. But, of course, that was in rehearsals. On the night itself, it was another matter completely. No sooner had I announced that famous line from the show— 'Tonight, Matthew, I'm going to be . . .' pause for a drum roll '. . . Cher!'—everything that could

185

possibly go wrong did go wrong.

When Matthew announced me and the doors to the stage drew back and it was time for me to walk out, there was so much dry ice filling the air that I couldn't see. I could barely make my way to the centre of the steps I had to walk down and my choice of towering footwear didn't exactly help matters. So I tottered, rather than strode, into position. On top of this, the audience was cheering so much at seeing me I couldn't hear the backing track. I missed the cue to the start of the song, which was disastrous because I then had to struggle to catch up. And because I couldn't actually hear myself when I started singing, I was completely out of key as well. It was truly horrendous in every single way, and I had to be stopped halfway through the song to go back and start again. I went around the back of the set and did the whole thing again and, once more, I couldn't hear the backing track and started in the wrong place and was out of time with the music. So we stopped again. By now, my body had actually gone into a state of shock. I couldn't speak and tears were involuntarily running down my cheeks. I somehow managed to tell the floor manger that I couldn't hear the track, so he said, 'Don't worry, we have the shot of you walking out, so just start at the top of the steps and in silence.' But now I couldn't remember the first note and the music director had to come down to remind me. Eventually, I staggered my way through it. Matthew was lost for words. He was not the only one. The audience sat in a kind of stunned silence, as if they could hardly believe the horror which had unfurled in front of their eyes in the name of light entertainment. It had been—for both them and me—more like light torture.

When the show was broadcast weeks later, my family gathered to watch in our own front room. I couldn't watch my bit, so I left the room while it was on. When I was called back in for the next contestant, who'd appeared for years in *Les Miserables*, triumphantly sing the Spandau Ballet song 'Gold', nobody said anything. Eventually, I said, 'What was I like then?'

'Well,' they replied, 'stick to the day job, Carol. But never mind, it's a good job not many people will be watching.'

'They're right,' I thought, until we saw the ratings the next day—more than 15 million people had tuned in! I was teased relentlessly and cringed for years.

I'd been on telly for almost 20 years by this point and had met many other presenters, some of whom had become friends. One was Jill Dando. I had hosted the first series of a show called *The Antiques Inspectors* and the second series had gone to Jill. Jill had met Alan Farthing, a surgeon and a gentleman, and was deliriously happy. Jill and Alan had come to our New Year's Eve party in Maidenhead to welcome in 1999. Theirs was to be a life full of laughter and joy; they were meant to be together.

The first programme of the new series of *The Antiques Inspectors* was transmitted on 25 April 1999 and when I was being driven up to Leeds the next day, I tried Jill's phone to have a chat about it, but I couldn't get through. I eventually got to the *Countdown* studio, unpacked my suitcases and went into our little green room for lunch. One of the producers came in and said, 'Jill Dando has been shot.' I couldn't take it in, not for months afterwards. Not Jill! Why? All these years later, I still find it difficult to comprehend, that Jill died that day. Alan asked all those who were to have been invited to their wedding to come to Jill's funeral in Weston-super-Mare. It was one of the saddest days I've ever experienced. Jill was completely decent and lovely and cheeky and perfect, and I think the television industry has been much poorer without her influence and presence.

\*     \*     \*

The BBC had been good to me once the dust had settled after *Tomorrow's World* and were now booking me for many shows, including *Points of View, Mysteries* and the midweek National Lottery programme, which were all going well. Then the boss of ITV, the incredible David Liddiment, decided that I might be more suited to his channel. It was a brave move for both of us. For me to take on a show on prime-time ITV was tantamount to a slap in the face for the BBC, I suppose, but they weren't prepared to guarantee me a future and ITV was. John Miles managed to negotiate what I think to this day is a unique double and I ended up with two exclusive contracts with different channels.

Channel 4 was worried that I might present another daytime show in opposition to *Countdown*, something I would actually never have contemplated. They offered me a huge five-year contract for 1,275 shows, where I would be exclusive to them between lunchtime and 6 p.m. ITV wanted me for prime-time only, so they were happy with an exclusive contract for me to broadcast on ITV outside these hours.

The work piled in, and I absolutely loved the shows I was making. Funnily enough, my first ITV programme was a science-based show called *What Will They Think of Next?* and it was run by a mid-ranking producer called Helen Warner, who was heavily involved in me leaving *Countdown* ten years later, when she became the head of daytime at Channel 4.

*Countdown* was still Channel 4's biggest show and even though I was at that time all over the magazines and prime-time telly promoting other programmes, I knew that *Countdown* would always be my home. Richard used to say, 'I'm very proud of you, little one, very proud indeed.'

Mind you, when I was the subject of *This is Your Life* with Michael Aspel in the late 90s, he also said, 'How they managed to stretch the programme to half an hour with your story is amazing. Now there's good TV production!' And I hit him and he laughed and we carried on.

Carol Smillie was hosting the massive hit *Changing Rooms* on BBC1, so when I hosted *Carol Vorderman's Better Homes* on ITV, she and I would ring each other up and tease each other mercilessly. These programmes were the real birth of home-makeover and quick-fix shows. Nothing like *Better Homes* had ever been shown before, in terms of the scale of the makeovers, and it involved a filming schedule which was run with military-style precision.

We had to film two makeovers for each show,

which meant choosing families who lived relatively close to each other. The idea was that we would perform actual building work rather than just decorate. The chosen couples would be given a list of possible home improvements and would pick what they thought would be best for their houses. Then they would move out for five days while our team of builders moved in to complete the transformation—be it a conservatory, kitchen extension or a new bathroom. Finally, at the end of a very hectic week—and often just minutes after the builders had cleared away—the couple would return for the final big 'reveal'.

We'd film their stunned, happy reaction and then interview an estate agent, who would review the work and estimate by how much the house had actually gone up in value as a result of our transformation.

Presenting the show was definitely not for the faint-hearted. I filmed in snow, in ice, wet concrete and falling plaster. But it whisked me back to the happy days of my own childhood, when my beloved Gabriel would sit in the back yard, covered in brick dust, happily teaching me how to build brick walls.

On *Better Homes*, unlike on light entertainment programmes, there were no Winnebagos, no make-up artist or clothes stylist, so the only way I could put on my make-up would be to find a spare bedroom—often piled high with furniture from the rooms we'd already cleared—and squat down with a tiny child's Barbie mirror to quickly apply my foundation and mascara.

As with any busy production, we made full use of our 'runners', often young school leavers or university students who want to break into TV.

Once, when we were filming in Yorkshire, I stumbled out of bed at 4 a.m. at home in Maidenhead, caught the 6 a.m. flight from Heathrow to Manchester and stood outside the airport, waiting for the trusty *Better Homes* van, driven by our latest runner, to pick me up and take me to the first location.

There was no sign of it. After half an hour or so, I rang the producer and creator of the programme, Nigel Mercer. Nigel sounded confused. 'He left here hours ago, Carol. He's got to be there soon.'

So I stood and waited. And waited.

Eventually, very conscious of the hours slipping away, it became obvious that the poor runner was hopelessly lost (these were the days before sat nav), so I rang him, asked what road he was on and told him to wait. Then I jumped into a cab and headed off to find the van—with *Better Homes* painted brightly down its side—which was parked in a layby. I opened the door, told the runner to move over and jumped behind the wheel.

An hour later, we screamed into our *Better Homes* street and when I jumped down from the driver's seat, I could see the astonished faces of the family who we were due to film that day. They obviously thought that I doubled as television presenter and white van driver, a budget cut which, thankfully, no-one suggested to the television bosses at the time.

That first ever series of *Better Homes* caused a television sensation. In some cases, the transformations were extraordinary. We had a truly great team, including designers like George Bond, who had an unbelievably good eye for superb design, teams of builders and our special boys Neil and Adrian Rayment, who went on to become the evil twins in the Hollywood blockbuster *The Matrix Reloaded*. They spent most of their time with us in dungarees, so the difference must have been astounding for them.

I will never forget one programme where a designer added a stunning new conservatory and garden to a particular house and listening to the family happily admire the work when it was revealed to them. The job added tens of thousands of pounds to the value of the property and as we packed our things away and drove into the sunset, we assumed that the owners would be grateful.

Not so. Shortly afterwards, the production office received a disgruntled phone call from the homeowner, who said he wished to log a serious complaint. There was a horrified silence in the office, as the team waited to hear what had happened. Had the beautiful conservatory come crashing down? Had cracks appeared in the fresh plasterwork? He paused before delivering his crushing verdict. 'I'm ringing to complain because I suspect that one of your crew has stolen our mop and bucket.'

While the production person struggled to find words to reply, the man continued, 'I'll have you know that we have been out to price a replacement and want the full amount repaid.' Needless to say, they didn't get a new mop and bucket from us.

But most of our families were genuinely deserving and thrilled with the results. My favourite job was when we went to the house of a remarkable woman called Jean Forrest, who had fostered 600 children over the years in Littlehampton. She had recently lost her beloved husband and if anyone deserved our help, it was this modest and unassuming lady, who had previously won a Pride of Britain award.

We transformed her kitchen, back room and garden, and the entire team put their absolute all into this job. Right at the end, once we'd revealed her new downstairs, she came to film a final interview in the garden.

Jean was utterly, utterly overwhelmed. We sat on a bench and she told us how much her husband used to love sitting in the garden. With that, she began to quietly sob. It was impossible not to be moved. I started to cry, and then the cameraman, the soundman and the producer. We all stood there, wiping our tears away, while behind us a group of foster children whooped with joy. It was a day of absolute emotional extremes. How I wish all television programmes could work their magic in such a way!

At ITV, David Liddiment and Grant Mansfield, head of factual programmes, were on a roll and their peak-time audience share was rising in an unprecedented way. With that came more shows. *Better Homes* had a spin-off series, *Better Gardens*. There was also a great, live, Friday-night programme called *Find a Fortune*, produced by my old friend Clare Pizey, a brand-new show called *Stars and Their Lives*, where celebrities told their personal stories, and many other shows besides.

There was a bit of a moan going round at the time, with critics saying that you couldn't switch on the TV without seeing Vorderman, which I suppose was true, especially as *Countdown* was, of course, still running five days a week, but all the shows were doing well. *Stars and Their Lives* and

*Better Homes* were often hitting ten million viewers. As far as I was concerned, I was doing my job and was very lucky to have the chance to do it too.

But nothing has ever moved me, exhausted me or inspired me more than the *Daily Mirror*'s Pride of Britain Awards. Funnily enough, for one of the most watched ceremonies in the year, this didn't start off as a television project.

It was the brainchild of a brilliant executive on the *Mirror*, Peter Willis, who suggested that the paper should host awards to acknowledge and celebrate the absolute best in Britain.

In 1999 I was writing a weekly column for the newspaper about the internet and one day the deputy editor, Tina Weaver, rang me to say they'd had the idea to host a ceremony called Pride of Britain, which would take place at London's Dorchester Hotel a few weeks later. There would be awards for sportsperson of the year, actress of the year, businessman of the year, and so on, and the event would be attended by celebrity guests.

Over the next couple of weeks, Peter Willis and his team hit the telephones and rang every single celebrity they had ever met to invite them to the awards. I was asked to host the star-studded event and the whole thing would be reported in the newspaper the following day.

It was casual to the point of chaos. I was given a script a few hours in advance and I had a very short rehearsal beforehand. There was no autocue, no cameras and just a lectern to rest my notes on; the whole thing felt small, comfortable and very friendly. It was only when proceedings started and I stood by my microphone that I had a chance to look at the people sitting at their tables. What I saw was astonishing.

Paul McCartney sat right in front of me, near to Cherie Blair and the Spice Girls. On another table, Cilla Black smiled gracefully around her, while Bobby Charlton, Lennox Lewis and Mick Hucknall waited for the awards to start.

I had been to many show business awards in the past, but they had always been restricted to one area: sport, music, film or television. Never had I been at a ceremony which combined every single aspect of fame and achievement. Never had I seen so many superstars gathered together under one roof.

The event kicked off and the mood was good. Everyone clapped as Queen Noor of Jordan accepted a special peacekeeping award presented by Prime Minister Tony Blair, on behalf of her late husband, His Majesty King Hussein of Jordan. Everyone applauded when an award went to boxer Lennox Lewis. Richard Branson was businessman of the year, Michael Owen young sportsman of the year and the team of scientists behind Viagra won the award for inventor of the year.

But it was when a series of special awards was announced for a group of people leading ordinary lives who had overcome extreme odds that something strange happened in the room. Nobody said a word. Celebrities and non-celebrities alike now suddenly fell silent.

The first of these awards was given to a group of survivors from the Omagh bombing, which had ripped apart a high street and a community in Northern Ireland. As the remarkable stories of bravery and triumph over evil emerged, the whole room froze. One young girl, Donna-Marie McGillion, received an award for outstanding bravery. She had been shopping with her fiancé when the bomb had gone off and had suffered 65 per cent third-degree burns and was in a coma for six weeks. Her fiancé, meanwhile, spent eight weeks in hospital after suffering 35 per cent third-degree burns. Donna said, 'I won't let the bombers destroy me, otherwise they have won.'

More unsung heroes collected awards. A young man, Daniel Gallimore, had gone to the aid of someone who was being beaten up. Daniel was then severely attacked by the gang and left for dead on the pavement. When he eventually came out of a six-week coma, he found that he had lost his sight in both eyes and was suffering from debilitating memory loss. He was in hospital for a year, but now he was rebuilding his life and raising money for charities. When his brother came on stage to speak about Daniel, whom he loved with all his heart, many of us were overwhelmed with emotion.

A young student doctor, Helen Smith, who had lost both legs and part of an arm after being struck down by meningococcal septicaemia, stepped forward to receive an award presented by Heather Mills, the model who had found fame after losing her leg in a road accident.

By now, I had tears running down my cheeks. I really couldn't help it. As she came onto the stage, Heather threw me a napkin and as I wiped my eyes, I saw hankies out at every single table. Famous pop stars, politicians and sportsmen and women were all unashamedly crying. Sir Paul McCartney was staring at Heather intently. She

196

did, in fact, look stunning in tight trousers and a pretty top. It was the first time they saw each other.

Many stars accepted awards that night, but the occasion, unexpectedly, had been taken over by the unsung heroes. After every award these extraordinary men and women received, there were huge standing ovations which lasted five minutes each time. I had never experienced such a strong well of emotion. It was like a tidal wave which swept the room, leaving us all sobbing and fighting for breath.

By the time the awards had finished, two things were clear: that it had been a unique ceremony and that the real champions that day had not been the celebrities, the sporting legends or the business-empire builders, but the men, women and children who had won their awards through acts of courage and love.

I was absolutely convinced that this event should be televised. Somehow, we had to share the unique atmosphere that had filled the room with a wider audience. So the next day, I rang Grant Mansfield and told him about it.

I arranged a meeting between Grant, Peter Willis and the editor of the *Mirror* and from this first meeting, the awards were eventually commissioned. It is still the highest-rated awards show on TV years later. This was when I first began working closely with Peter, a man who seemingly devotes his life to the Pride of Britain Awards and without whom the whole operation would come to a juddering halt.

The ceremony was televised for the first time the following year, at the Hilton Hotel in Park Lane. Once more, the room was filled wall-to-wall with A-list celebrities, but now we had lights, cameras, a script and run-throughs.

This time, we focused entirely on the real-life unsung heroes and, once again, their achievements sent a wave of emotion through the room. One beautiful young girl, Michelle Lewis, 17, had raised almost a million pounds for Alder Hey Hospital, where my brother Anton had undergone several of his operations to correct his severe cleft lip and palate.

The show was wonderful when things ran smoothly—and even better when they didn't. Robbie Williams presented an award to a little girl who adored him. He bent down, gave her a kiss and the whole audience melted. Then I asked her, 'Would you like Robbie to give you another kiss?' At which point she shook her head firmly and said, 'No!' which set the whole audience off in hysterics.

We gave an award to a remarkable lady called Alex Bell, who had adopted seven children with Down's Syndrome. She had told us that she didn't want the children to come to the event, because the excitement might be too much for them. But, with a huge amount of organising, we arranged for all seven of them to be there, hiding backstage. When Alex received her award, the entire family ran forward shouting, 'Muuuuuum!' and screaming with excitement. It took a whole fifteen minutes for the joyful chaos on the stage to end. Alex was trying to calm her brood and the audience and I were just cheering them on and loving every second of it. Makes me cry now just remembering how much they loved their mum.

Filming the Pride of Britain involves days of intense work with the bosses Tim Miller and Tom

Gould. On the big day, I snatch just four hours of sleep and arrive at rehearsals at 7 a.m., using the first of a series of scripts which will be constantly changed throughout the day. There is too much to think about to eat anything, so by the time it's all recorded, at around 11.30 p.m., food isn't always easy to come by.

A couple of years ago, when the hunger surge hit me, I wandered into the green rooms to see if anyone had left any biscuits or fruit. We were filming at the LWT studios in London's South Bank and the lovely man in charge of the green rooms, Terry, ran off to see if he could find some bread and cheese. While he was gone, I stood alone and waited, winding down from the awards. Who should walk past but Paul O'Grady, with his arm around the legendary Dame Shirley Bassey.

He spotted me and both of them came in to say hello. I said that I was waiting to have something to eat and Dame Shirley waved her arm and said, 'Let's have a drink.' Within minutes, someone had found an entire case of Champagne for us. My hunger forgotten, I found myself sitting on the high stools in the small green room with Shirley, Paul and Terry.

Over the next four hours, as we became more and more tipsy, she sang all the songs from her shows—an incredible personal cabaret, just for us. And when Shirley sat down for a rest, Paul would spring up and perform a one-man comedy cabaret act which had us in stitches. By the time we fell out of there, it was four in the morning and I was aching with laughter.

The next day, I was appearing on Paul O'Grady's show on Channel 4, to talk about the

Pride of Britain Awards. 'Wasn't it great with Shirley last night?' I said when I saw him. 'I've got the evidence,' I added, and we ended up showing some of the photos I'd taken on my phone to his audience.

*Stars and Their Lives* was special. It was made by Hanrahan Media, an independent production company based in the Midlands, the boss was Will Hanrahan himself, the cheekiest Scouser around and a great journalist and broadcaster. Without fail, when I was standing backstage and the announcer was saying, 'Please welcome your host . . .' Will would say down my earpiece, 'They are ready for you in make-up, fat bum.'

We told the life stories of people like Bob Monkhouse, Chris Tarrant and the legendary Barry White, whose family was flown over from the USA to surprise him (that was incredible). But one show grabbed headlines around the world. By that time, it was known that Paul McCartney was dating Heather Mills, whom he'd first clapped eyes on at the Pride of Britain Awards about a year earlier. The show was about Heather and, unknown to her, Paul had agreed to come on and talk about her work with victims of landmines. So cut to the corridor by my little dressing room. There walks past the Beatle who my sister had been in love with since 1965. I could see what she saw in him immediately.

Any personal questions about their feelings for each other weren't planned. Heather had started talking about how romantic he was, and he said that when he saw her on the Pride of Britain he thought 'very beautiful, a true fine momma . . .'

'When I heard her speak I was very impressed

with her speaking, so I found her phone number. We had three or four meetings . . . All prim and proper . . . And I played it cool to start with . . .'

And then Heather said 'At one of the last meetings, I saw him eyeing up my bum . . . He is a gorgeous man.'

And then when I asked her 'What do you think of him?'

She said ' . . . I love him.'

He joked 'On national telly?'

And then said 'I love her too.'

They laughed so much and they did look so soft together and finally they kissed.

The clip led news programmes around the world and whole chat shows were devoted to it. Paul and Heather, as we know, went on to marry and then divorce and my sister still hasn't really forgiven me.

In the year 2000 I made my mother very proud. I was awarded an MBE for 'services to broadcasting' by Her Majesty the Queen in her Birthday Honours List. 'Two consonants and a vowel, from Her Majesty, no less,' I joked when I told Richard Whiteley the news.

On 12 December 2000, less than a fortnight before my 40th birthday, Mum, my sister Trixie, my daughter Katie and I made our way to Buckingham Palace for the investiture. I wish I could say I'd planned my outfit, but life was so hectic I'd forgotten a handbag, so I had to make do with my old rucksack, which went everywhere with me and was so big I could stuff anything into it— not exactly the height of glamour.

It was the most beautifully orchestrated ceremony. We were all held in another room and each group was received in turn, starting with the

Knights of the Realm, followed by CBEs, OBEs and then MBEs. I had a great two hours with lots of other very excited MBEs-to-be. We'd all been carefully instructed, in the nicest way possible, that when Her Majesty holds out her gloved hand to you, that means it's the end of the conversation—in other words, it would be time to step back and let the next person receive their honour.

My heart slightly missed a beat when it was my turn to stand in front of the Queen. We exchanged a few words—she mentioned my television work and I mentioned *Countdown* (well, if I hadn't, Richard would have killed me).

'Have you ever watched it, Ma'am?' I ventured.

'I don't really have much time to watch television,' she said. 'Tell me, though . . . is it on after the racing?' Her eyes twinkled. The gloved hand came out. And I was gone.

After the ceremony, we all headed to Langan's for a slap-up lunch and I'd literally only just sat down at my place when my mobile rang. It was Richard.

'Well?' He could barely breathe, he was so excited.

'Well what?'

'Did you ask her?'

'Ask her what?'

'Stop teasing me, Vorders! Did you ask the Queen whether she watched *Countdown*? I need to know!'

'Yes, I did, Whiters, and she said she'd never heard of it.' I always liked to tease him.

'I don't believe you,' he laughed.

# HAVING IT ALL?

At the beginning of 2000, I opened my diary for the year ahead and counted the days that I had free to spend with the family. There were just 12 plus some Sundays. The rest was an exhausting, non-stop, groundhog day of work, meetings, filming and guilt—guilt which nagged away at me constantly.

When I was at work, I felt guilty that I wasn't at home with my children. When I was at home with my children, I felt guilty that I wasn't working. It was a never-ending, ever-turning hamster wheel and I know every working mother has to swallow back the guilt as she kisses her children and sets off once more with her heart in her boots.

But it was a choice I had made and I was committed to it. The work, once I was there, was fun and exciting, but I was, I now admit, hammering at the door bearing the sign 'You Can't Have It All'. I was hosting five different series on prime-time ITV, on top of *Countdown*, and the schedule was unrelenting. There was even a day, apparently, when I appeared on BBC1, BBC2, ITV and Channel 4, hosting different shows (including some repeats) within a few hours of each other.

I would be up each morning at 5 a.m. and get myself dressed and ready before spending some snatched moments with Katie and Cam, if they had woken early.

The days would have an almost comical pace to them and while I thrived on adrenaline and was aware of how lucky I was to have all this work, it also took its toll. My diary was now so tight we would film two *Better Homes* programmes at the same time, which meant four makeovers per week (two per show). By 6 a.m. Paul Grant, the lovely driver I spent loads of time with between 1999 and 2005, would have arrived and he would take me to the first town where *Better Homes* was being filmed, say Cheltenham. On the way, I would make phone calls, check my emails and diary and do some newspaper or magazine interviews. When we arrived at the set, I would meet the family and then disappear into the house to put on my make-up and do my hair. Then I would run through the building plans for the two houses we would be redesigning in Cheltenham.

Quickly, I would run upstairs and get changed into outfit number two of the day. I'd go downstairs, film the interviews with the families and the designers and then I would change into another outfit to talk to the builders, who would already have started to knock down bits of walls and pull up floors.

As soon as this take was over and the director satisfied, I would jump into the *Better Homes* van and travel for an hour to a nearby town, say Gloucester, where the second programme was being simultaneously recorded. Here, I'd find a room to quickly change into yet another outfit, film the interview with the excited families, change once more into a fresh outfit and record chats with the designers working on this episode.

Next, I would jump into the van, travel back to film in Cheltenham and change once more to interview the designers about their progress. As soon as this was in the can, I would hop into the van again and race back to location number two. I would change outfits—yet again!—and interview the second team working on this separate project.

Finally, Paul would arrive to take me home and I would work in the back of the car. I would walk through the door at any time from 8 to 11 p.m. and run to kiss the children if they were still awake. Then I'd take all the outfits I had worn upstairs, to hang them up and label them for continuity, and choose more outfits for the next day of filming. I'd still have to do an hour or so in my office to catch up with paperwork before falling into bed myself.

The next morning at 5 a. m. would find me on my way to catch a plane at Heathrow to Manchester to record a different show, say *Stars and Their Lives*. After a day of rehearsals and production meetings, we would record the show in the evening and finally I would get into the car and Paul would drive me home while I worked on my computer in the back seat. Whatever I could get through in the car was one less thing to do when I got home. I'd stagger back in through the door at midnight, with just five hours to go before the next day of work. This was my world at least six days a week, often running for weeks without a day off.

Believe me, I'm not complaining. It was my life and I chose to live it that way. I was well paid, I enjoyed what I did and I knew I had to take the work while it was there. This was, after all, the era of having it all. Of trying to be a perfect cook and domestic goddess. The perfect wife or partner. And the consummate professional at work.

After a generation of bright women like my mother, most of whom had never had the chance to climb the career ladder, we were the first to truly show how we could succeed. And succeed we did. But at what cost? My head would pound from tiredness and my heart would sometimes feel as if it had been wrenched from my body whenever I thought of my son and daughter back home.

I honestly did all I could to ensure that the children were happy. Firstly, they were being cared for by my mother, and no-one other than Paddy and I could have loved them more than Nana. No matter where I was working, I always tried to get back to our family home outside Maidenhead to see Katie and Cameron before they went to bed.

One day there had been an accident on the motorway and I was stuck in traffic for three and a half hours. All I wanted to do was be with the children. Instead, by the time I got home, they were in bed. My brain felt so hot it was as if it was frying.

I walked in through the front door and went straight upstairs. There, Cameron lay on the bed, asleep. His little cheeks were rosy, his lashes curled over his closed eyes and his soft breaths were barely audible. He was three years old and he was heart-wrenchingly beautiful. As I gazed at his face, I felt an overwhelming rush of love—and despair. I'd hardly seen my beautiful little child all week. It hit me like a physical blow. Mum came in to find me standing at the doorway, in some kind of state of shock.

I turned to her, so upset that I could hardly speak. 'I can't do this anymore. I can't work like this. I can't be away from the children. I'm going to give it up. This is just too much for me to cope with. I hate being away. That's it. I'm out of this.'

If I was expecting sympathy and comforting

arms around me, I was mistaken. My little mother said, 'Do you think that after all we've gone through, me raising you and putting you through university and looking after your children and seeing you work so hard, I am going to let you give it up when you are at your peak? Nobody could love these children more than me. They are fine. I know you, madam, you'd be climbing the walls with boredom if you stayed at home all day.'

I was utterly speechless. It was the only time in her life that Mum has ever told me what to do. She always used to say, 'Whatever makes you happy.' What happened there then?

So I did what I was told and back to work I went—little realising that the tightrope between work and home was about to snap.

*       *       *

In 2000, my husband Paddy and I agreed to separate. It wasn't an easy decision and there were many horrible days—divorce isn't pleasant. Eventually, by the summer, the press found out and the story appeared on the front pages. Paddy and I were still both living in our house in Maidenhead at the time, but not 'together' and we co-ordinated as much as possible so that we saw the children, but little of each other during this difficult period. Eventually Paddy moved to his own house in 2001. Two years later in 2003 he married Susan and they live happily together with Susan's two daughters Camilla and Clementine. Paddy continues to be a good father to our children and they remain a very important part of his life.

We did agree, though, that we would continue to keep our children out of the press until they were adults. And, all things considered, the children have enjoyed anonymity. You won't (except between these pages, as I couldn't do an autobiography and not include them) see photos of either Katie or Cameron as small children, when my TV profile was at its height. They are not spoiled. They are both growing up into kind and normal young people with big hearts, we really are a very happy family.

The protection of children was something which dominated my life for over a year. It all began because I wrote a column about the internet every week in the *Mirror*. Little Sarah Payne had been murdered in July 2000 and this created a torrent of letters to the column from parents who were worried about the sort of people their children were meeting in internet chat rooms.

It was obviously a growing problem, but as yet a problem which no-one had really raised in the media. The explosion of the internet meant that chat rooms had opened up a world in which children could meet and converse. But it had also opened a door for paedophiles to enter the very same chat rooms and to begin to identify and 'groom' potential victims.

Politicians were also becoming aware of this threat and when I was invited to join a debate held at the Houses of Parliament, I jumped at the chance. Most of the internet service providers were there and I wanted the opportunity to urge them to enforce rigorous checks.

In the event, the debate was heated and emotional. I said my bit and sat down, then representatives of the internet service providers spoke. I felt they were pretty dismissive of the concerns. Finally, a minister stood up and the conclusion seemed to be that, basically, nothing much could be done.

This caused many of the members of the audience, including me, to erupt. That was when I became aware of a small group of campaigners who had been working on this issue for some time. We met up afterwards and had tea in the House of Commons together. Led by an inspirational man called John Carr, they were as horrified as I at the evil that was emerging from internet chat rooms.

I promised to do everything that I possibly could to highlight the campaign in order to help them. Their aim was to introduce a new law to make grooming children on the internet illegal. I spoke to mothers whose children had been tricked into secret meetings with paedophiles. The sickening truth was that, even if the paedophile had met up with the child (and some had been found with all sorts of implements and devices on them which showed their physical intent), until the child was actually harmed or abused, no crime had technically been committed. The police were helpless.

I proposed a special report for *Tonight with Trevor Macdonald* and they agreed to air it as a two-part special. I threw myself into the project. The subject consumes you when you see the pain of the innocent.

Manchester Police led the way by developing a special unit to deal with online child abuse. However, their funding was so tight that the computers available for the officers to use were the ones they had actually impounded from known paedophiles.

The programmes caused the sensation we'd hoped for and, eventually, after much work and pressure from the dedicated campaigners, they managed to change the law. The Home Office put groups of campaigners and internet industry people together. I was privileged to sit on one of the task force committees and, finally, the government agreed to make grooming a child online an illegal act, the first law of this kind in the world. Now the police didn't have to sit back and wait until these monsters abused children. They could be caught and brought to justice before more young lives were destroyed. I was proud to be able to help this group of committed campaigners and am grateful to them for the results they achieved to protect all of our children.

In May 2000, David Liddiment, the boss of ITV, asked if I'd take part in the very first *Celebrity Who Wants to Be a Millionaire?* Gulp. It couldn't be that hard, could it?

*Millionaire* had been on air for a couple of years and was getting great viewing figures. It was the first and only *Celebrity Millionaire* where you had to do it by yourself. I always tease my mates who go on it now in twosomes, as they have the other person to blame if it all goes wrong—which they do, often. So there I was, after a lot of encouragement from the producer, Colman Hutchinson, up against Kirsty Young, then of *Five News*, and I managed to get to the £250,000 question, having used all of my lifelines, including one where Richard Whiteley was my phone-a-friend and he ran out of time after 30 seconds (you'd think, after all those years on *Countdown*, he'd have known what 30 seconds felt like).

The £250,000 question was about a Shakespearean character called Sir Toby Belch—which play was he in? Well, I guessed that with a crude name like Toby Belch, it wouldn't have been a Shakespearean tragedy and there were only two plays up on the board which were comedies. One of them was *The Merchant of Venice* (which we'd read at school) and the other was *Twelfth Night* (which I'd no idea about at all). I was playing for a tiny charity I was patron of called Express Link Up and £125,000 was more money than they could possibly have dreamed of at the time. Express Link Up gave children who were in hospital for long-term care, computers for their education. I decided not to risk getting the answer wrong and took the £125,000 instead, but said what I thought the answer was—*Twelfth Night*. Chris Tarrant declared the answer was indeed *Twelfth Night* and that I could have won £250,000 had I played on. At which point, I said, as a laugh, 'Well, Shakespeare's boring anyway.'

Oh my. You'd have thought I'd committed an act of untold evil, the way the literati press reacted. Front page of the *Daily Telegraph*, amongst others, the next day for daring to criticise the Bard. I rang the editor, Charles Moore, and told him how thrilled I was to receive such prominent coverage and also to appear as the lead item in the editorial inside. Marvellous. Double-page features were written in national newspapers by professors of literature about my ignorance. *Newsnight* devoted virtually half of one programme to this outrage and, generally, it was referred to for years after.

Makes me laugh really. In comparison, it is perceived as normal for us to say how dull maths is in our media and not an eyebrow is raised. Ever.

By the way, I won more than Kirsty from *Five News*. Not that I'm competitive or anything, you understand!

*    *    *

By 2001, Des Kelly, who was the deputy editor of the *Mirror*, and I had become an item. Des is lively and very handsome with twinkling blue eyes.

I also decided that I no longer wanted any more wasted hours of travel to keep me from being a mum, so we moved to London. It meant saying goodbye to a nice home with a big garden, but what we missed in greenery, we more than gained in the extra hours we spent together.

Des, Katie, Cameron and I moved into a large apartment in London together in 2002, and obviously Mum came too. I could not exist without Mum by my side and she moved into a flat in the same block. Typically, she never questioned the move and never looked back to life in Berkshire. She packed her bags with great excitement and together we headed for a whole new adventure.

The difference was immediate. Cameron's school was nearby and whenever I could, I would jump on a bike and ride there with him.

For the first time in a decade, I started to relax about television work. I sought no new projects and eased up my workload, so that I could spend more time with the children. Gradually, the balance which had eluded me for all those years, the work–life see-saw which had left me permanently giddy before, began to even out. I didn't spend hours in cars, as most of my work was based in London. I couldn't have it all, and I knew that now.

A year after we moved, Mum wasn't looking too well. On Christmas Day, with all my family and Des's family around, she had to go back to her flat to rest, which just wasn't like her at all. We were all worried.

She went to her GP and was waiting to go for an ultrasound scan. A month later she went to the Well Woman Clinic at Guy's Hospital in south London. There they discovered a large tumour which needed immediate removal. Mum had suspected ovarian cancer, and the signs weren't good. My brother, sister and I had had no suspicions of her problems being linked to cancer. There was no history of ovarian cancer in the family, so it came completely out of the blue.

Ovarian cancer is known as the whispering cancer, as its symptoms are identical to those of many other common illnesses, such as irritable bowel syndrome. In this way, it disguises itself until often the cancers are very well developed. Mum's was bad and her condition meant that she was rushed into St Thomas's Hospital for an urgent operation the very next day.

We were completely rocked, in a state of turmoil. Mum had always been healthy and had always been there for us. It all happened so fast, we didn't get a chance to think about it. One day she was, in our minds, 'not well' and the next day she was seriously ill with suspected cancer. We fretted and worried and found out as much as we could and tried to comfort her. But I think, in her way, she was actually trying to comfort us. She was very poorly, but extremely brave and not teary at all, just as strong as she had always been when we were growing up.

The two surgeons who operated on her, and to whom we are eternally grateful, were Miss Shanti Raju and Mr Philip Townsend. Mum had undergone a partial hysterectomy 20 years previously but now needed her ovaries and the tumour removed. We were all with her, fussing around, while she was made ready for her operation, worrying but trying hard not to show it, making jokes when we could and pretending that everything was relatively normal, when really our world seemed to be collapsing. Occasionally we'd catch each other's eye and then it was hard, as we couldn't disguise what we were feeling inside. The operation seemed to be successful and the tumour was taken out. It was huge, weighing three pounds, and was described to us as being the size of a melon.

She had the operation during the day and was then kept in the recovery room next to the theatre for endless hours, as there were complications. It's soul-destroying sitting in waiting rooms, unable to do anything, helpless. So Trixie, Anton and I started to plan who would do what while she was receiving what we thought would be the inevitable sequence of chemotherapy and/or radiotherapy treatment in the months to come. Trixie lives in North Wales and Anton lives in Holland and so the arrangements were complicated, but all of us were prepared to give everything up to look after Mum. Making these plans kept us busy and it was in those moments that the three of us realised just how much we depended on each other.

Then, in the dead of night, when hospital corridors take on a quiet glow and sounds echo louder, we were told that the complications had worsened and she would need a second emergency operation. Again, we waited for what seemed an eternity. We had talked ourselves out. What to say now? We feared the worst. She seemed so small now, so petite and birdlike and very poorly. Mum had the second operation and stayed in the recovery room for 3 days until her body seemed able to start to cope with the shock of the operation and the removal of the massive cancer. That first night we sat still, praying, exhausted by it all, wanting to do something. But there was nothing we were equipped to do other than look after each other. Eventually, she was allowed back up to a room in the High Dependencey Unit. The porter who wheeled her upstairs with us all in tow, turned to me and said, 'Hello, Carol. I know I'm not supposed to ask because of hospital rules, but can I have your autograph, please?' I looked at Mum, who smiled weakly and nodded, so I asked him why it was against the rules. He said, 'Well, I was wheeling Paul O'Grady back upstairs after his heart bypass and I asked him for his autograph and I got into trouble.' I howled with laughter. The thought of Paul, hours after his huge op, having to lift his arm to sign was too much to bear. When I next saw him, Paul told me it was absolutely true. Just as well he'd been poorly, otherwise you could imagine the language.

Mum was in hospital for days recovering from her two operations, while we waited for the results of her histology report, which was the detailed analysis of the tumour itself. Only after that had been done could a plan of treatment be put together.

Then came the incredible news that her cancer was what is known as a granulosa cell tumour. The cancer can have malignant potential, but if it does spread, it may take up to 30 years to reappear. Seeing as Mum was already in her 70s by this point, the doctors said that the chances of secondary cancers were so low that there would be no need for chemotherapy or radiotherapy at all. This was amazing news and Trixie, Anton and I were overcome with joy. To us, it meant that she was safe again. Our Mum would be around for a long time to come and we had more years to tell her just how much we love her.

\*         \*         \*

On *Top Gear* in 2003, I had a chance to be a Star in a Reasonably Priced Car. I love *Top Gear* and if I was a bloke I would have plagued every single BBC executive to get on the show, but girls don't seem to get jobs like that. The morning was a washout, with floods everywhere causing road diversions on the way to the airfield where the filming takes place.

We reached *Top Gear* Nirvana. Eventually. But the track was wet and I was so disappointed. I love driving; I have adored engines and super cars since the days of watching my step-brother stock car racing in North Wales in the 70s. Over the years, I've acted as a rally marshall and have generally driven round tracks too fast making technology shows.

216

*Top Gear* brought out my most competitive streak. I really wanted to be the fastest Star in a Reasonably Priced Car, but with water on the track I didn't stand a chance. Dry track equals fast track; wet track equals timed oblivion. But not to be outdone, I sat and waited in the passenger seat for my teacher, the great and wondrous one clad in white: the Stig. I was trying desperately to catch a glimpse of what he looked like through a gap in his helmet, but he was too fast for me and even though I begged him to tell me his name or give me a sneaky peek at his face, he wouldn't. But he did do one thing which was superb—he taught me how to do a handbrake turn. Round and round we went. 'Can we do it again, Mr Stig, please? And again? And again?'

Eventually, after he'd shown me around the course a few times, he had to disappear to the Stig cabin. Now I was on my own. As the crew has to reposition the single camera to get shots of you at various points on the track to edit together for the final film, you have about half a dozen attempts at getting your best time. So I threw the car around the track and pushed it as best as I could. When I reached my final approach into Gambon corner, I got a bit cocky and ended up in the grass, which of course the crew loved, but I knew I'd done quite well in the early rounds on my wet track.

When it was time for the chat with Jeremy, I managed to dig out some facts from my engineering degree days (the Wankel engine was always one that made us laugh) and tried to foil him on the merits of superchargers, not Clarkson's favourite subject. But let's cut to the bit that we all love best: the lap time in a Reasonably Priced Car.

217

It was agreed that the moist nature of the track meant that my time would be many seconds slower than if I'd gone round in the dry. And then it was revealed. I couldn't wait to hear it, perched on the edge of the old car seats in the studio. I was confirmed, with a time of 1 minute 51.2 seconds, as 'the fastest driver in the wet by a massive four seconds'. To this day, I'm desperate to go back on a dry day and take it by storm. All hail *Top Gear*!

There were a lot of celeb style events for Des and I to go to in those days. It was quite strange for me to find myself in a position where designers wanted to lend me dresses. I usually said, 'Yes, please,' especially for big events which I was presenting. One time I was hosting the Pride of Britain Awards and was being pampered by one of my best friends, Karen Alder, who had years earlier re-designed my 'look'. Another pal, Claire Harries, who is a clothes stylist, had borrowed so much stuff for me to wear. As soon as I got back to my dressing room, I held out my arms and every single item was carefully stripped from me. First of all, the long diamond earrings and matching necklace and bracelets, worth tens of thousands of pounds, were removed by the PR lady from Theo Fennell, the jeweller. Next, the sound department stole away with my earpiece and microphones (two, just in case one of them breaks down during the recording). Then Clare unzipped the borrowed dress, made me step out of it and packed it away in its suit carrier. The shoes, which I thought they could have left on, were the next to go, and then the hairpieces. It was like being stripped by piranhas and I was left in just my false eyelashes and underwear, the only items that actually

218

belonged to me. Talk about Cinderella!

And while we're on the subject of sequins and hairpieces, in 2004 I was asked to join the second series of *Strictly Come Dancing*. My partner was World Latin Champion Paul Killick and what he couldn't do with his bendy bits wasn't worth knowing. He was magnificent, and I wasn't. So much so that when we performed the rumba in the second week, I fractured my rib in the final throw. The pictures look magnificent—there was I, in an 'is she wearing anything at all?' type of body-hugging dress, draped all over him, bending back with my head touching the floor—but the reality was totally different.

I didn't realise I had been hurt until the adrenaline started to leave my body a couple of hours later, in my dressing room. I simply couldn't get up from the sofa. I had to slip down onto my knees on the floor and grab onto something to haul myself upright. The next day, I was in agony and thought I'd pulled a muscle, so I traipsed off to the doctor for painkillers. A week or so later, it was no better and I had to go to the hospital for a scan. And there it was: a fractured rib. Pathetic. Mind you, it amused Richard Whiteley no end and I used to get members of the *Countdown* studio audience to feel the huge, egg-shaped lump on my back which grew while the rib was reforming, to remind myself just what an interesting experience it had been.

*           *           *

In 2005, Des's family and my family went to the Caribbean, which is near to being heaven on earth.

219

I was doing a little bit of work at the time and we had a ball. My sister had bought a number puzzles book for Katie on the internet and she gave it to her to keep her occupied by the pool one afternoon.

It was a thin book full of what looked like number crosswords. After a few hours, I asked Katie what she thought and there was no reply; so I asked again, still no answer, and I thought it was a bit odd. I was intrigued, so I went to lie next to her on her sunbed. 'Hello, lovely girl, let me see one of your puzzles.' And at that moment I took my first look at a Sudoku grid and was instantly hooked, transfixed by a bunch of numbers in a $9 \times 9$ square. No colour, no fancy pictures, just pure logic. Beautiful.

Katie wouldn't part with the book, so I had to draw out my own grid and copy the numbers down on a piece of paper before I could have a go. I didn't understand the very simple rules at first, so my first Sudoku took me about four hours to complete, but I was also scribbling notes as to how I could do it faster next time. This was the start of an obsession. I would enter my own little Sudoku world and everything else disappeared: all thoughts, worries, concerns, plans, everything melted away. The total concentration was something I'd rarely experienced before, except in a game of chess.

Then my brother Anton, who was also on holiday with us, got involved and every morning we would sit down before breakfast and draw out Sudoku grids on blank pieces of paper and then spend all day sorting them out and solving them, not competing with each other, but against ourselves. Within two days, I'd progressed on to harder ones. I knew that this was something completely different to any other type of number puzzle I'd tried before (and there had been many). This was so simple to explain and yet could be so difficult to complete—in many ways it was like *Countdown*.

John Miles, his family and some friends were staying on another island nearby and came to see us for the day. We had a wonderful time driving around in the old golf carts and when I told John about my new obsession and that I wanted to write a book about how to do it, so I could teach people the tricks I'd been analysing, he looked at me, somewhat bemused. I was raving about how Sudoku was going to be a phenomenon and we needed to get this book on the shelves as quickly as possible, as I just had a gut feeling that, although only *The Times* was running the puzzle, it had the potential to explode.

John was eventually convinced and when he got back to the UK he rang Dame Gail Rebuck, the exceptional chief executive of the publishers Random House, and said, 'Gail, we'll do a deal if you can get it out in six weeks.'

Gail said, 'We'll do it in five weeks,' and so that was that. I knew I could write the book within a fortnight. This was a battle against the clock—we had to be on the shelves as soon as possible, before the Sudoku explosion happened. So, for two weeks, our apartment was transformed into Sudoku Central, with pages of puzzles everywhere, and I worked through the nights to get it done.

Sure enough, the book *How to Do Sudoku* was published five weeks later, just in time to ride the wave of the tabloid newspapers joining the rush. Within three months, we'd sold half a million copies and in total over a million copies were sold in this country alone. I travelled to the States, where the book became a bestseller, and more books followed, including what is probably my favourite, *How to Do Extreme Sudoku*. That involved much deeper logic, which I sat at home and happily worked out. There is a lot of maths in Sudoku. There were also DVDs and PSP games and just about everything under the sun. The books have been translated into over 20 languages and I was thrilled to see just how powerful a mathematics puzzle can be. But, then again, perhaps I shouldn't have been surprised, bearing in mind that by then Richard and I had made over 4,000 *Countdown*s together.


## VOWELS AND CONSONANTS

Over the years, *Countdown* gathered an army of followers and, believe me, even the most unexpected of people watched.

When I went to see my friend Claire Sweeney's opening night with Patrick Swayze in the West End musical *Guys and Dolls*, I took Mum along. The party afterwards was packed with stars from both sides of the Atlantic.

Mum and I had only been there a few minutes when Grace Jones came bowling up to us with a very handsome young man in tow. Grace seemed quite excited and, suddenly, as she screeched to a halt in front of us, she spoke in her strong

American accent. 'Oh, it's Caroooool. I watch *Countdown* every day!' As I struggled not to look staggered by this, she added, 'It's fantastic. You've gotta come and talk to me later,' and with that, she turned on her heels and was gone.

So, later on, Mum and I went to find her. She was surrounded by a circle of security men. 'Carol, you've brought your mother!' The bodyguards parted like the Red Sea and Mum and I were ushered into the inner circle. Grace asked what we wanted to drink and Mum asked for a cup of tea—she's never been a wild child. So there we sat very happily for the next hour, with Mum sipping her tea daintily, in a West End bar in the dead of night, with Grace Jones chatting away about *Countdown*. I longed for her to be in Dictionary Corner, but it didn't happen.

Celebrities often asked Whiters and I, 'How do I get into Dictionary Corner? When we first started out, we had our regulars: Ted Moult, Kenneth Williams, Willie Rushton, Richard Stilgoe, Denis Norden and Gyles Brandreth, who with his signature hand-knitted jumpers competed with Richard in the sartorial stakes in the 80s. Gyles's clothes may have mellowed over the years, but not his biting wit.

As time went on, we added to the mix politicians, former pop stars, West End legends and actors. These included Anne Widdecombe, Stephen Fry, Rick Wakeman, Barry Cryer, Lord Attenborough, Sir Tim Rice, Sir Michael Parkinson, Martin Jarvis, Tom O'Connor and Richard's own personal hero, Sir David Frost.

Even the edgier comedians were drawn to *Countdown*, such as our great friend Richard

Digance and the wonderfully caustic Jo Brand. I remember Richard whispering, slightly nervously, when she arrived: 'I do hope she's in teatime mode today, Vorders.'

Slowly, *Countdown* gained a celebrity fan club which included Gordon Brown, Sir Alex Ferguson, Julie Andrews and Sir Anthony Hopkins. When George Clooney was in the UK promoting a new movie, he was asked which TV shows he'd watched and, because he'd been ill in bed during the day (the usual excuse), he said he'd seen *Countdown*, apparently saying, 'Carol is amazing; she's brutal,' which the *Sun* managed to convert into how he wanted to have children with me! It naturally made my day, even if it was faintly ridiculous.

There were many long-running gags on *Countdown*. Richard collected facts, which he would repeat time and time again. We were made for each other as a TV couple, as I can happily listen to the same story many times over, as long as it's told with gusto, which Richard always did.

The classic example of this was with the word 'leotards'. When the word first came up, Richard sat back and—in the manner of a wise schoolmaster imparting crucial knowledge—said, 'Do you know, Carol, that the leotard was actually named after a person called Monsieur Leotard, who was a weightlifter in a French circus?'

The first time Richard told me this, I found it genuinely interesting and told him so. When the word cropped up again some months later and Richard repeated his fact, I said politely, 'I'll remember that.' The third time the word came up, Richard trotted out the same fact and this time I just stared at him blankly. The fourth time, I jumped in and told Richard the anecdote before he had the chance to say anything. And from then on, whenever the word 'leotard' was used, the entire audience would cheer. And so it became 'the *Countdown* word' for every contestant to look out for.

The most important people to us, by far, were our loyal viewers, our Countdowners. They loved the show as much as we did and Richard and I both had the most tremendous respect for them. Students loved *Countdown*, children loved *Countdown* and a lot of our less youthful friends loved it too. We understood entirely that *Countdown* didn't belong to us; it belonged to our viewers.

Every day for nearly 30 years, I have been stopped by kind and smiling faces who tell me of their love for the programme and pass on their stories. Sometimes these tales are about two-year-old children who have learned their alphabet watching the programme, or Aunties who imitate me putting up the letters at home, or a time when they were watching alone, got the conundrum faster than the contestants and couldn't get anyone to believe them. Sometimes these conversations are particularly poignant.

Once, I was on a plane to Manchester and got chatting to the gentleman sitting next to me. After a few minutes, he said, 'Carol, it's so good to meet you today.' I asked him why and he said, 'Well, I've lived in Canada for 30 years. I came home last month to spend the final few weeks with my mum, who was ill in hospital, before she died. Every afternoon she perked up and said, "Don't let anyone talk now. *Countdown*'s on," and she'd get out a pad of paper and a pen. She always said how lovely you and Richard were and she called you "our Carol". I'm going back today for her funeral, so thank you for giving her so much pleasure.' The privilege was ours, always, to be part of something so loved.

Woe betide anyone who messed about with what Countdowners wanted. Particularly the *Countdown* music. I've heard the last ten seconds of the *Countdown* music being sung at me in bars, shops and building sites around the world, and I never tire of it.

But once, our first *Countdown* producer, John Meade, decided to have a new arrangement of the music recorded. Yes, he dared to tinker with it. Was he being brave or foolish? The answer, when it came, was unanimous: Countdowners hated it and the Channel 4 switchboard went into meltdown. It was a worrying time.

Another John Meade idea was to try a new colour scheme on the set. Part of this new design was to remake our magnetic lino letters. They had always been white letters on a royal-blue background, but the new design gave us red letters on a beige background. Lovely? Not quite. We recorded nearly 50 programmes with these new letters and they started to be transmitted a couple of weeks later. Instantly, thousands of people bombarded the bosses, pointing out that red lettering on a beige background is just about the worst selection of colours if you are remotely colour blind. In other words, the letters effectively disappeared before their eyes. We had an emergency situation on our hands. The recorded shows were binned and we were rushed back into the studio to record the programmes afresh, with the old colours.

So, you can imagine how we felt when, in 2003, Richard and I were told that the time slot we had occupied for over 20 years—around 4.15 p.m.—was going to be changed to 3.15 p.m. It was a massive demotion for the programme, even though *Countdown* had just been voted Channel 4's Best Show of All Time by viewers in a poll published in the *Radio Times*.

We were absolutely apoplectic. For all those years we had been the number one show in the afternoon across all channels, sometimes reaching 5 million viewers a day. And we still were. Not surprisingly, we wanted to know why.

Along with our managing director, we went to a meeting at the channel's headquarters with Mark Thompson, then the chief executive of Channel 4 and now the director general of the BBC, and Tim Gardam, who was his second-in-command.

The day turned out to be full of suprises.

At the time, *Countdown* was transmitted at 4.15 p.m. and was followed at 5.00 p.m. by Richard and Judy's hour-long show. Eighteen months earlier, Richard and Judy had been brought over to Channel 4 from ITV and Mark Thompson had two life-size cutouts of them in his office, which didn't please Whiters for a start.

In 2003, *Countdown* was getting an average of up to three million viewers a day, which in the days of multi-channel TV was still phenomenal. When Richard and Judy started at 5 pm they inherited an audience from us and within ten minutes almost a million people changed channels from Channel 4 to another station, which meant that their ratings were much lower than ours. I'd prepared graphs about the ratings and Richard had done research about our viewers and their habits and why our time slot was perfect for us, and so we went into the meeting armed with data, ready to protect our show.

It didn't appear that straightforward to others and our arguments were to no avail, as became immediately obvious.

It seemed to us that the channel didn't see *Countdown* as the huge success we did and that they were putting their faith in Richard and Judy as the future of the channel. Indeed, we had heard whispers that some described *Countdown* as being a programme in a state of 'decline'.

It didn't make any sense to me. As I pointed out, about a million people were switching off when we'd finished and were not watching Richard and Judy, so it was suggested at the meeting that we were 'handing over the wrong kind of audience to them'. Wrong kind of audience? How can millions of *Countdown* viewers be the wrong kind of audience?

But we were beaten. They changed the slot and our ratings fell, as viewers couldn't get home early enough to watch. Richard and I spent many a morning in tears in the make-up room reading the kind and sad messages from viewers who had been with us for decades, but who could no longer share some time with us.

I can't begin to tell you how much we loved to chat to our studio audiences. We had many regulars and they loved coming in to see us as much as we loved to see them. We would chatter and natter and tease all day long.

By the late 80s, there was a huge waiting list for

tickets and some people had to wait as long as two years to get into the studio. We had coaches of Countdowners who would make the long journeys from Devon and Cornwall, as well as trippers from Ireland, the Shetlands and the Edinburgh Countdown Club, who would come to Leeds at their own expense.

In 2003 we had almost 200 students in the studio, the first time that the entire audience was actually younger than the show itself. Fabulous. One row of young men had dressed like Richard and they said to him, 'We asked our dads for their worst jackets and their loudest ties,' which made Richard think what marvellous taste their fathers had.

Whiters was in a league of his own when it came to getting things muddled up. When it came to the 'teatime teaser', a conundrum given to the audience and viewers at home before the commercial break, Richard would often merrily give out the answer to the anagram instead of reading out the clue.

Then there were his monologues, often so funny that the rest of us would be laughing so much that we simply couldn't speak, and so long that Richard would sometimes forget what point he was trying to make. He once confessed to me that he would often start a sentence without knowing how it was going to end, and it was not unusual for him to launch into a five-minute speech, without pausing for breath, before returning to the quiz with the line, 'Now, where were we?'

I nearly couldn't breathe with laughter after one massive error. We were recording the Christmas show one year and Richard had been sent a hand-painted tie by a viewer. 'Isn't this marvellous? Just look at this, the hand-painted Christmas trees and all the letters of the word "Countdown" painted on and running from the top of the tie to the bottom. On silk, no less. I don't wear polyester . . .' And on and on he went, to anyone who would listen. We recorded the show quite happily, without noticing anything out of the ordinary, and it was transmitted a few weeks later. The very next morning, our phones were red hot. On the front pages of the tabloids was: WHITELEY IN EXPLETIVE TIE DISASTER. What no-one in the studio had seen was that some of the letters of the word 'Countdown' had disappeared. When Richard sat on his chair, the letters 'down' were hidden behind the desk. Then he clipped his microphone onto his tie, to perfectly cover the letter 'o' of 'Count'. And there he sat, with the remaining letters shouting out from his tie, all through the transmission of the programme, with a daft grin on his face, none the wiser.

One year, Richard persuaded me to buy a share in a horse called the Mare of Wetwang, a pun on Richard's honorary title of mayor of Wetwang, a beautiful Yorkshire village. She was a pretty little thing, but was never going to challenge Desert Orchid on a racecourse. He would defend her on the show when I said she was racing on Blackpool Beach with the donkeys that Saturday. But I had to eat my words when our pretty mare actually won a race. Well, strictly speaking, she was second and the horse which had originally been declared the winner was disqualified for unladylike behaviour. Hooray for the Mare of Wetwang! We celebrated as if she'd won the Derby.

Richard's weight was, let's say, a fluctuating affair, although mine was too, to be fair. He would often ask me if I thought he'd put on weight since our last studio session, so I became his weight monitor. This is how we'd do it. In front of the studio audience, I'd go close up behind him and put my arms around his tummy. If my fingers touched exactly (the norm), he'd stayed the same weight. If they overlapped a bit, then he'd lost a few pounds and if, God forbid, they couldn't touch at all, it was the cabbage soup diet for another week for him.

I remember trying ice skating once in London. After 20 minutes of not falling over, I obviously thought that I'd morphed into Jayne Torvill, so I tried a little skippity-hop, crashed to the ice, landed on my wrist and it split beautifully. An hour later, I was in St Thomas's Hospital with my arm in a plaster cast up to my elbow. There it remained, so when we went back into the studio a couple of weeks later, I had to perform 'one-armed *Countdown*', pulling letters out of the boxes. I worked out that plaster casts look extremely tatty after a matter of days, so I bought different coloured opaque tights which I cut up into tubes and threaded over the plaster, tucking the ends in. It worked a treat, so much so that when I went to a Pride of Britain reception at Clarence House with Camilla, Duchess of Cornwall, and Prince Charles, His Royal Highness thought that I was wearing long ball gloves. I had to tell the truth—that I was just appalling at ice skating.

I've been asked countless times if I ever got bored of making the programmes (nearly 5,000 in all) and I have to be honest and say no. I was tired sometimes, but never bored. Of course, I loved the numbers game most of all, but I'd play all the word games too. I think I might have made the quarter-finals of a series, if I'd had a lucky streak. Conundrums beat me up, but the numbers and I were friends. There were no calculators, no earpiece, none of that nonsense, just me, my numbers, some sheets of paper and a pen.

I had a little shorthand notebook for each series where I would enter codes for how well I did on each numbers game, and I'd fill it in religiously. My basement is full of them from over the years. I'd put a tick if the contestants also got it right in 30 seconds, an asterisk if I got it and they didn't within the time allowed and a big, nasty cross if I didn't get it spot on in 30 seconds. That way I could keep track of my score. So I know that I got about 60 per cent of them spot on instantaneously, before Richard had even *started* the clock, and 94 per cent of them spot on in the 30 seconds allowed.

We had a great team of people over the years, including more or less the same camera crew—Eric, Ernie, Barry, the Matts, Annie and Bob. I had my special little team—my props boys—who were in charge of taking the letters down in about a nanosecond in between rounds. They were Stan, Harry, Eugene, Vinnie, Treasure, Spike and Little Digit (John Anderton). Then there was our smiley beauty Demi, the stage manager; Lisa, the floor manager; and Dudley and Greg, the audience liaison officers—the warm-up men to you and I.

Lovely Eugene, one of the props boys, was an endless source of love and laughter. I used to say that I wanted to put a clause in my contract to make him wear shorts every day, even in winter, because I had a thing about his knees! So poor Eugene (he loved it really) wore trousers into work and then would have to change into his shorts before I'd let him touch his letters. Well, it made us laugh.

We also had wonderful teams upstairs in sound and lighting and on the main desk. Brenda was our director for many years and there was Norman and Limo-Rick, who'd make up cheeky poems for Richard to read out. So many wonderful people. There was Helen from the costume department and in make-up there was my angel Pam Fox, whom I called Lady Pamela, as well as Martin Maclean, who was lovely, and Amy, who was in charge of Susie Dent's make-up.

We had some great executive producers over the years too, including the wonder who is Arch Dyson and after Arch came Chantal Rutherford Browne, before my old friend Clare Pizey took the reins.

And our contestants? They were incredible. The ultimate *Countdown* champ was probably Harvey Freeman, undefeated after 19 shows. His ability with words was extraordinary and he would sometimes press the bell to answer the conundrum before Richard had even had a chance to start the clock. Then there was Tanmay Dixit, an eight-year-old contestant whose first word was 'farted' and whose second was 'fannies'. Instant national recognition and much laughter from us.

In 1983, Richard and I fell in love with a 16-year-old lad, Mark Nyman, our world Scrabble champion, who eventually became a producer. He would sit in the gallery and send words down to Dictionary Corner through their earpieces with lightning speed. I would sometimes play a letters game with him in the bar, so I could witness first-hand just how fast he was. It was like watching witchcraft with words.

Richard and I loved our little family and would often get on to the bosses to promote someone if they were doing well. So Mark was championed by Richard and Michael Wylie, our runner-up in 1982 and a great numbers man, was championed by yours truly. Susie Dent was championed by both of us.

Up until 2003, there had been a succession of lexicographers in Dictionary Corner. Because they were changed regularly, we found it quite difficult to build up an ongoing screen rapport with them. So Whiters and I hatched a plan to ask for Susie to become our full-time lexicographer. She was very good at getting words herself so we cornered the boss and nagged until Susie became the third full-time member of our onscreen team.

As for our vowels and consonants, well, we had a lot of rude words which came out of the boxes. Probably the most common to come out in order was 'arse'. An 's' followed by an 'h' followed by an 'i' was also common, and the contestant would usually then ask for another consonant, hoping for a 't'. If rude words came out, we generally had to stop the programme and re-record the round if this happened, but you can still find some of the outtakes on the internet, including the infamous 'w******' round. It was great fun, perfectly innocent and kept us on our toes.

Kathryn Apanowicz, Richard's other half, occasionally came on the show to sit in Dictionary Corner and he was never quite sure whether he loved those shows or not, as he was then nagged by

Kathy as well as me. He would introduce her by saying courteously, 'Well, she's back because she's a cheap cab fare,' or some such intro. But, banter aside, mention the word 'marriage' to Richard and he would turn pale. He told me he'd switch his phone off on 29 February in a leap year, just in case anyone proposed to him!

And then, one day early in 2005, totally out of the blue, he told me that he was going to ask Kathy to marry him. I laughed, expecting him to follow up with one of his famous punch lines, but he said, 'No, I mean it. We're going to get married.' He hadn't quite got round to asking Kathy, as he wanted to get it right, so I was sworn to secrecy. I was so happy and already planning which hat I would wear.

Over the years, come rain or shine, we both turned up for the recording of each and every show. Once, I went in with chickenpox and the make-up ladies did a fine job of covering all my spots. Another time, I had such bad tendonitis I couldn't stand and was wheeled around in a wheelchair and tipped into position. Richard, in the meantime, would struggle in after suffering severe asthma attacks. Nothing stopped us and nothing, we believed, ever would.

Richard's birthday fell during the Christmas break, on 28 December. One year, he had a huge birthday cake made in the shape of the *Countdown* clock. He took it to the studio before Christmas and left it, so that he could share it with all the crew when we got back in January.

Three weeks later, he made us all gather round in the studio and sing 'Happy Birthday' and then grandly cut me the first slice. 'This is for you,

Vorders.' I sank my teeth into it—and promptly spat it straight out again.

The cake was full of curdled cream.

He had ordered a fresh cream cake and had promptly left it to curdle for weeks, without realising what he had done. It was such a shame, but funny too.

But there was no disappointment at all when we celebrated Richard's 60th birthday. Yorkshire Television asked what he wanted for a present and he decided on a very posh party to be held at Harewood House, a stately home between Leeds and Harrogate.

No expense was spared. The ground-floor dining room was hired and caterers supplied. Around 40 of his oldest friends were there, all in black tie, awaiting the arrival of the host.

Richard turned up fashionably late. He walked in and his face lit up at the sight of us all. 'Darlings, darlings, darlings . . .' he began to say. He saw me. 'Ah, Vorders, come and give me a birthday hug.'

As I drew close, a pungent smell assaulted my nose. Richard gave me a giant bear hug and I realised the appalling smell was coming from him. It was a sickly odour and it appeared to be emanating from every pore in his body.

Richard, for his part, seemed oblivious to it. I pushed him away, laughing. 'Richard, you stink! What on earth have you got on?'

He looked confused. 'I'm wearing the aftershave you gave me after your summer holidays, darling.'

'What aftershave, Richard? I didn't give you any.'

'Yes, you did. You gave me that lovely scent.' He put on his best French accent. 'Homme Fragrance.

236

I have sprayed it all over in your honour.'

I suddenly twigged that he'd misread the label. 'That wasn't Homme Fragrance, Richard, it was Home Fragrance—room spray—for your dressing room.'

With that, we collapsed laughing. It was the first time, I'm sure, that anyone has worn air freshener to their own black-tie dinner.

We both loved parties, but the heady side of the showbiz world that involves illegal substances never entered our orbits. We both went to a Channel 4 party just after yet another celebrity had been exposed by a national newspaper allegedly snorting cocaine and paying a lady for entertainment. The whole party was buzzing with the news and when we got into a taxi together, Richard hissed at me loudly, 'We're useless at all that, Vorders, aren't we? But I've got some drugs in my pocket. Do you fancy some tonight?' With that, he pulled out a packet of Rennie's, the indigestion tablets—it's the closest we ever got to being rock 'n' roll.

In April 2005, we went to the British Book Awards together. There were a large number of celebrities presenting different awards, and Richard and I sat down at the round table where we were all gathered waiting to be called to present.

He immediately turned to the beautiful and famous woman sitting next to him and flashed her a charming smile. 'Oh, gosh,' he said, 'it really is a pleasure to meet you.' I could see her smile, thinking what a lovely man he was.

Richard continued happily, 'I've read all your novels and they are marvellous—simply marvellous.' By now, she was looking at him slightly strangely, and so was I, as I wasn't aware that this famous actress had written any novels. But Richard had warmed to his theme and he carried on. 'All the passages about cloisters and choristers. Evocative and wonderful. I take your books away on holiday quite often.'

At this point, the lady was pulled away to hand out an award. I said to Richard, 'I didn't know that the actress Patricia Hodge had written any books.'

Richard looked at me aghast, his face registering genuine horror. He groaned loudly and said, 'Oh no! I thought she was the writer Joanna Trollope.'

We didn't see her later so, to make it all better, he sent Patricia a bunch of flowers the next day, by way of apology. On the card, he wrote: 'I'm sorry about last night. You must have been confused. I thought you were a Trollope.'

It was classic Richard. Hilarious. Priceless. Well-meaning. Unforgettable. How happy I was to be sitting beside him, laughing at his error. How honoured I felt that this wonderful man was my friend. I just didn't realise that the laughter and the buffoonery and the shared love was all about to end. It was the very last event we attended together.


## I MISS YOU, WHITERS

On 5 May 2005, as we larked around in the studio together, Richard turned to the camera to rehearse the opening of the final programme of our 53rd series of *Countdown*. We'd made over 4,000 *Countdown*s together and knew exactly what the other would say. We were as one, a pair of idiots really, who just loved being together in our little *Countdown* world. But this time he said something he'd never said before. He beamed his daft smile and said, 'Hello and welcome to the final *Countdown*.'

Then he said quickly, 'I mean the *Countdown* final.' It was a joke, but a shiver had already gone down my spine. From beside the letters board, I said, 'Richard, you mustn't say that.' I hated it, but not for one second did I realise the awful truth: that this show *would* be his final *Countdown*. It was our last hour together on camera and if I could go back to that moment, I would—in a heartbeat. The clock had already started ticking on our life of laughter and love and companionship, and we didn't know that within seven weeks, Richard would have 'left the party'.

By the time we filmed that last programme of the series, something didn't seem quite right with Richard. The change was so subtle that no-one else seemed to notice, but to me, he seemed tired. There were opportunities for quips which he would normally jump on and turn into one of his wonderful, hilarious, rambling monologues that would leave everyone else gasping for breath through their laughter. But he didn't seize the opportunities as he usually did.

In the commercial break, I said to our executive producer Clare Pizey that I didn't think that Richard seemed to be his normal self. She agreed and we decided that he was probably tired. Too much partying. Too many late nights. *Countdown* studio runs could be hard and a final was always extra work, so that we could do justice to the clever contestants who'd battled through to this last stage of a series.

He was obviously already feeling unwell, but he wouldn't have missed a recording because of that. In all the 23 years we had spent together, he had missed only one show. That was the day he discovered that his beautiful mother had died and, even then, he rang me on my mobile with apologies. 'I'm sorry, Vorders, but I can't do it today. I know you're on the train from London already, but would you mind . . .'

Looking back, there were several awful coincidences which occurred during that final programme. The answer to our nine letter conundrum was 'FALSIFIED', but it was presented for our contestants to unravel, in classic *Countdown* tradition, as 'LIFE FAIDS'. I have hated the word 'falsified' since that day.

Afterwards, we had an end-of-series drink. It had been a long week and I wanted to get home to the children, and Richard, the man who usually commanded centre-stage at every opportunity, seemed uncharacteristically preoccupied.

I gave him a hug and a kiss and said, 'See you next time.' We were due to have a break of four weeks in between filming. I didn't look back as I left the room and I wish more than anything that it hadn't been such a casual and breezy goodbye. I wish that some omen had sent me straight back into the room to tell Richard just how much I loved him. But it didn't. I was never to see him again.

Over the next few weeks, I heard from Clare

that Richard had been fighting the flu. Then, one morning, as I was sitting at home, I had a phone call from Kathy. I knew immediately that something was wrong, although Kathy was trying her best to sound calm. Her first words were, 'Dick's not very well.' She told me that he had been suffering from a virus, but had taken a turn for the worse the night before. She had been so alarmed that she rushed him to the local hospital. In doing so, it transpired later, she had temporarily saved his life. Doctors at the small local hospital assessed him, but as his condition rapidly deteriorated, he was transferred by ambulance to Bradford Royal Infirmary.

There, he was put in intensive care, while a battery of medical tests were undertaken. Kathy was obviously worried, but incredibly strong and very optimistic. He was in the best hands. The doctors would treat him. He would be back home in a week or two. He was going to be fine.

But as she spoke, I had a terrible sense of foreboding. When she said that everything was going to be alright, I had such a strong feeling that it wasn't that I felt physically sick. But I wasn't going to tell anyone, particularly not Kathy, this fine woman who would fight with every cell of her body to do right by him.

A few days later, I had a meeting about another programme with some TV executives which I couldn't cancel. In truth, although I managed to somehow get there, I was in such a state that I don't think I took in a single word that was said.

For the first time in my life, I just had to get away. To run away. I didn't want to speak to anyone or see anyone. I just wanted to keep my mobile free in case Kathy rang.

It was a Friday and the children had gone to stay with their dad that particular weekend, so I didn't have to worry about them. I quickly packed a bag and headed straight out of London and down to the West Country, where I booked myself into a hotel.

As soon as the door of the hotel bedroom shut behind me, I didn't go out again. I spent the next days like a total zombie. I was unable to think or to function properly. All that mattered was how Richard was, but I had a gut-wrenching feeling that things were not going to get better.

I sent just one text—to Mum, saying, 'Gone away. Don't worry.' Then I switched the mobile off, only switching it on every so often to check if Kathy had left a message. I spent the next two days just sitting in that room. All I wanted to do was to think about Richard.

Kathy's messages were optimistic, strong and positive. 'He's in the best hands. He'll start to get better soon.' But the truth was, things were not improving.

I didn't sleep in those days. Then, finally, I checked out of the hotel and headed back to London, to face life once more. Richard's illness had made headline news.

My first instinct was to try to get to see him and be by his bedside. But Kathy and I discussed it and decided against it. As soon as news of his illness and dash to the hospital became public knowledge, photographers began camping outside the hospital. Kathy knew that if I turned up the photographers would go into overdrive, especially as some newspapers were suggesting his condition was far more serious than was appreciated at the time. The last thing she wanted was to alarm Richard and make him think that I was coming to say goodbye. So Kathy decided it was best for me to keep away, and I had to respect the wishes of my friend. I sent Richard little teddy bears, daft cards and notes which I hoped would make him laugh.

Kathy kept me updated on his progress, but when it became clear that he wasn't bouncing back to health as quickly as we'd hoped, a decision had to be made about filming the new series of *Countdown*.

Time was running out fast. The new series was due to air in July or August, but a date hadn't been set and this was already now the end of May. The channel bosses called me in and said they felt that filming must continue, but with a guest presenter. I knew instinctively that Richard would worry about just one person taking over his role and the last thing I wanted was for him to be stressed further while he was in hospital. *Countdown* was so important to him and another person sitting in his chair day after day would upset him so much. I immediately said no.

They kindly went back to the drawing board. Richard had been in hospital for about five weeks when it was suggested that we use a number of guest presenters, a different one each week, until Richard was well enough to come back to us. It wasn't great, but it was a compromise and I totally understood that they needed to get *Countdown* filmed, albeit in a temporary manner.

Clare Pizey went to see him and she rang me after her visit. She had been shocked by just how unwell Richard had looked. She said he had lost an awful lot of weight. 'He doesn't look like the Richard we know anymore,' she said. Then she added, 'Carol, don't be surprised if he isn't back until the end of the year. I think it will take him a long time to get over this.'

The thought of filming a whole series without Richard was devastating. I couldn't imagine working without him after 23 years together and yet I knew it was something we had to do. *Countdown* had to come back on air and I knew that I could make it right in the studio by talking about him all the time and making up some long-running gags which he would be a part of—we could have 'diaries from Dick' and jokes about stairlifts and special baths for him and all the usual *Countdown* gentle teasing. But inside I felt torn to shreds.

More than ever before, I wanted to reassure him that he was the best. Absolutely irreplaceable. I wanted to tell him that I would do my utmost to manage the shop while my boss was away.

We were due to begin filming on Monday, 27 June 2005 with a guest presenter, and I arranged to meet station bosses a few days before in London. In truth, Channel 4 had been incredibly supportive while Richard had been ill.

Before I went in for my meeting, I snatched the chance to have a quick cup of tea with John Miles, my manager, in a little outside café. While I was there, my mobile rang. It was Kathy. Instantly, I knew something serious had happened. She said that Richard had been rushed to Leeds General Infirmary to have an operation to replace a valve in his heart, because the wretched virus had damaged it. She insisted that Richard would be fine once he'd had the operation, but I could tell from her voice that this was going to be major surgery and she was very worried indeed.

When I walked into the meeting with Kevin Lygo, the head of Channel 4, and Adam Macdonald, the wonderful head of daytime in those days, I was in pieces. They were both were so kind. But, in truth, there was nothing any of us could do to help.

I can't remember anything about that meeting other than shaking with nerves throughout. The rest of the day was spent waiting, thinking of Richard and the heart surgery he was going through.

We knew that the operation was due to take up to 12 hours, and when Kathy rang in the late afternoon, it was with the first bit of good news that we'd had for weeks. Surgeons had opened Richard up, but found less damage to his heart than they had feared. The heart had been repaired and the operation had been far quicker than anyone had expected. It looked to be a total success.

Kathy and I both whooped with joy over the phone. We knew that his recovery was going to be tough, but at least his fortune appeared to have turned. How wonderful it felt that day to be celebrating instead of sitting in horrible, silent dread.

Richard slept through Saturday and all was calm. My partner Des Kelly was looking after me well and so on Sunday I felt able to go to visit his mum and dad in Mitcham in south London. Chris and Don Kelly are kind and lovely people. That day, they spoiled me.

Kathy had promised to ring me with an update, but I'd heard nothing and I started to panic. I rang Clare Pizey, but she had heard nothing either.

Lunch was served, but now I was so nervous that I couldn't eat. There was a growing sense of unease. Things had been so positive yesterday. Why hadn't I heard anything this morning? I was worried sick.

We drove home from Mitcham in silence. I just wanted to hear Kathy's voice, or anybody's voice, reassuring me that all was well. But the phone didn't ring until the early evening, at about eight o'clock. I saw Clare Pizey's name light up on my mobile and I blurted out, 'How is he?'

There was just the smallest of pauses. A tiny, almost indiscernible hesitation. Then she said, 'Carol, I'm so sorry. He died about twenty minutes ago.'

I can't properly recall that moment, but it seemed as if the entire world had stopped still and then everything suddenly spun around. My own heart felt like it had stopped beating; I felt as if someone had just torn me in two.

I started to cry, and Clare did too. I can't remember what we said to each other, if anything, such was our shock and misery. Through her tears, Clare gently said, 'I've got to go. The press will be on the phone within minutes.' She had her job to do.

She rang off and I staggered into the front room. Des was there and I didn't even have to tell him what had happened. It was obvious. I fell into his arms and he hugged me, but nothing could actually offer me any comfort.

The sense of loss was all encompassing. It filled

every part of my being. I had plenty of friends but Richard, with his laughter and his buffoonery, had joked and belly-laughed beside me for years. Richard was my constant—the one who could read my mind and knew what I would say before I even opened my mouth. Now I couldn't imagine a world without him in it.

And then there was my friend Kathy, who had nursed him and loved him. I knew that her heart would be broken. I couldn't speak to anyone that night. The press got hold of our news within minutes and the phone was ringing off the hook.

The next day had previously been scheduled as a *Countdown* filming day. Richard had died hours before we had been due to start filming with a guest presenter, perhaps another coincidence. The next morning Clare and I were driven up to Leeds. What else could we do? I know it might seem like only a bunch of plywood flats and a clock that goes halfway round and a desk covered in carpet and letters with bits of magnetic strip on the back, but it was our little *Countdown* world and the greatest place of comfort at that time.

We were all stunned, unable to function and looking for comfort. There was such a sense of Richard in the building that morning. It was hard not to half expect him to come through the door, wearing one of his funny jackets.

Together with friends and the *Countdown* crew, I watched some of the tributes which were paid to Richard on TV. The tragedy was that Richard would have been bowled over by the attention and the fuss. He really didn't know how much he was loved. We saw so many famous faces pay moving tributes to him on the news programmes.

I didn't want to talk to anyone, but once I'd seen these tributes I knew that I had to pay my own. I knew that Kathy couldn't and that I only had the strength to do it once, so I agreed to film an interview for that evening's local *Calendar* news programme and then other stations could take their clips from that one interview. I don't remember what I said, but I wore black and Richard's favourite piece of jewellery, a big cross made of rough quartz which Des had bought for me in Italy a few years before.

That night, I went to the warm little cottage on Ilkley Moor that belonged to Richard, nestled down a sweet country lane. Kathy and he lived in North Yorkshire, many miles away, but while he was in Leeds, he would stay there.

His coat was hanging in the hallway and I saw it as soon as I stepped in. The smell of him and the sense of him lingered in the air. Inside, Kathy was sitting with some of Richard's family and friends. There was his brother-in-law Judge James, his sister-in-law Christine Stewart, who had been a rock to Kathy all through Dick's illness, their friend Maggie, Richard's niece Georgina and her fiancé Tim, Kathy and myself. We sat in a daze. We told each other stories of Richard and remembered how he had made us laugh. But mostly we cried.

That's my memory of that day. Nothing more.

On Monday, *Countdown* was taken off air. The channel then asked if they could screen Richard's final week of *Countdown* shows, leading up to the last show Richard had ever recorded, just seven weeks earlier.

It felt so wrong to pull the programmes that

248

week, as if Richard had never existed, as if he should be wiped from everyone's memory. So— with Kathy's blessing—it was decided that the programmes would be screened. I knew that Richard would have wanted the show to go on, particularly with all the fuss and attention. He loved the viewers and he would have wanted them to share his last *Countdown* days. I am absolutely convinced of that.

I was asked if I would give a short introduction as to why we were showing the programmes. I did that, but I hardly made it through my tears. I couldn't look at his chair. It was empty and I was lost. Sitting in the studio to record the short piece was hard because the warmth that had always been there had disappeared. Then, suddenly, I felt as if he was standing by my shoulder. It was such a strong, physical force that I turned around, but no-one was there. To this day, I believe that Richard was standing beside me in the studio, willing me on.

I stumbled through the next two weeks before Richard's funeral. I couldn't eat, couldn't sleep, couldn't function. I had never experienced grief in my life before. I know that so many other people have grieved for their loved ones and that Richard was not my husband, but the grief was, in those early days, a deep, bottomless pit of loss.

Richard was front-page news and whole programmes were devoted to him in Yorkshire, but I couldn't watch them. The only one I watched was our own *Countdown* tribute programme, which aired next to the series final on the Friday after his death. The first half was full of his funny moments, of which there were many, and the second part had the song 'Fields of Gold' by Eva Cassidy playing in the background. The tears flowed. When I hear that song now, tears well up again.

The one comfort came from the tens of thousands of letters and emails which came flooding into the office. There were tributes from students who had watched us throughout their time at university, and messages from older ladies who had laughed alongside us every afternoon and from young families who had loved to see Richard's familiar, smiling face every day while the children learned their sums. Richard was as special to them as he was to us.

The little world which had belonged to Richard and I had stretched out into so many other lives. And it was there to be seen, in every handwritten note piled up in the stacks of post bags in the office. How I wish that Richard could have read some of the lovely things which were said about him. I estimated that about a quarter of a million messages of condolence had been sent in some form or other.

On Wednesday, 6 July at 3.15 p.m., *Countdown* time, Richard's funeral began. It was held in the beautiful St John the Evangelist Church in the village of East Witton, where he and Kathy had lived so happily together. I came up the night before to see Kathy and stayed in a room at the Blue Lion pub, just yards from the church. We'd had many a good night there in the previous years.

Kathy had asked four of us to speak: Bob Warman, one of his oldest broadcasting buddies and a very funny man; Iain Johnstone, probably Richard's longest-standing friend; Geoff Druett, his co-presenter on *Calendar* for decades; and me, his TV wife, as Kathy called me. The funeral was a private service, but the church was standing room only and overflowing. Richard's coffin was in the centre of the altar, covered with a huge tumble of red roses from Kathy as a sign of her love.

I had to do my great friend proud. This is some of what I said.

### Richard Whiteley, the Mayor in the Chair, Deputy Dick, OBE

Richard often said that he was proud of being the first face on Channel 4 when he welcomed everyone to *Countdown* on Tuesday, 2 November 1982. He *was* proud, and he had every right to be.

Over the many years since that first day, Richard was the man who millions of Countdowners welcomed into their homes every afternoon without fail and who they came to love for the fact that he broke all the rules.

They loved Richard because he wasn't slick, because he wore jackets that could outdazzle Elton John, because his ties were loud and his jokes were so bad they were jokes only Richard could tell, but Richard made them funny with his shining eyes and huge grin.

Instead of giving clues to the teatime teaser, he'd give the answers; he'd forget contestants' names and he could hardly understand a word that Scottish people said, which caused no end of problems. He would say ridiculous things and not know why we were laughing in the studio. It's for all of these reasons and many more that we grew to love him.

Beyond the walls of this church and through his parlour game, many others came to love Richard. This last week, Countdowners from across the world have expressed their thoughts for Kathryn, for his son James and for the rest of his family. Countdowners are decent people; they are mourning him in their way and, wherever he is, he knows that. Their respect for him was matched only by his respect for them.

So many messages have been sent by our Countdowners that it's almost as if every one of them wants us all to know how big a part he had played in their lives.

These are some of the messages which have been sent.

**From Helen Hooper in Barnet, London:**
You were my afternoon comfort blanket. You were my sit-down, between work and getting the supper ready. You were my friend, but I never met you. Goodbye and thank you, Richard.

**From Petra Evans in Wales:**
My grandmother never missed a programme until her death; with you another little part of her has passed away.

**From Diana Foster in Market Harborough:**
You gave us so much pleasure; we even laughed at your jokes.

Richard loved every second he was on *Countdown*. Richard was our star and we didn't want him to leave our party.

Kathy said that I could talk for three minutes, but in your honour, Richard, I've over-run.

You never could resist reading a final letter from a viewer, even when Cindy and Damian were shouting in your earpiece for you to stop. So, Richard, here's a bit of banter fodder written by **Ray Cornell in Saffron Walden**, and it says it all:

'I know that Richard would want me to watch the end of the series and laugh at his unfunny but funny jokes and I have tried. I've tried very hard. I would like to make a nine-letter word and get the numbers every time and solve the conundrum, but there must be something wrong with my television screen . . . I can't see the picture clearly anymore.'

When his coffin left the tiny, packed church, he was taken to a picturesque corner of the graveyard where you can look up and see the house where he and Kathy lived together. I stayed behind in the church; I couldn't move.

# WE SHOULDN'T HAVE LEFT
# IT SO LONG

Back in the early 1990s, my father—Tony Vorderman—had written me a letter.

To this day, I don't know what my letter said. I remember picking up the envelope and seeing his writing and the Bedford postmark. On the back, written carefully, was the name and address of the sender. I didn't hesitate; I simply wrote, 'Return to sender' and posted it straight back.

I knew that Tony's second wife had recently passed away and perhaps now that he was on his own, he wanted to make contact. The cynic in me wondered why he had never made an attempt before.

I knew from Trixie that Tony watched *Countdown*. I also knew that he had been planning to write. But nothing he could say, no sudden flow of paternal love, could make up for a whole lifetime of nothing.

When my mother was pregnant with me, he was having an affair with a teenager and then when I was born, it took him just three weeks to say that he didn't want his family anymore. This was the man who had never held me as a baby and had never wanted to take me on the occasional outings he shared with my older brother and sister. He had never spoken to me as a child, never taken my hand in his, never cared.

He had a second family, for whom he had been a loving and devoted father. For their sakes, I was pleased about this, but it only served to highlight his absolute disinterest in me.

He'd created so much hardship and pain for my mother. He had, eventually, after many years, paid my mother a pittance for our upkeep and that was only after a court order, in spite of having the money to do so.

I had, over the years, tried to offer an olive branch. When I was planning my first wedding, I had also planned a reunion. I had felt it was a perfect opportunity to mend bridges, so I invited Tony and his new family.

Karen, my half-sister, had come to my hen party, but Tony didn't want to come to the wedding. It was like he was saying, 'Carol, as far as I'm concerned, you're not my daughter and you never have been.' So when I received his letter, I thought what's the point of letting someone like that into your life?

After I sent his letter back I had no more contact with him for another ten years.

When our half-sister Karen was getting married, she invited us all to her wedding, including Mum. I decided not to go, but Trixie, Anton and Mum said that they would. Anton and Mum had met Karen a few times and they had all got on well. Anton was in two minds whether or not he should go, as he wasn't sure whether he would want to wallop our father or hug him when he saw him, but in the end he decided to go.

It was the first time that Mum and Anton had met our other half-sister, Alberdina, and her family and they all liked each other immediately. Our father's most important moment came when he made his father of the bride speech, which for him and Karen was very special, and rightfully so.

He said that he was very proud that day, as he had not only seen his daughter married, but had gained his true son, because Anton was there. In wonderfully prosaic terms, he described how proud he was to have his son back after so many years. Apparently, there wasn't a dry eye in the house. Apart from Mum and Anton, who remained very stoic!

Following the wedding, Tony and Anton kept in touch and he would sometimes go to stay with Anton in Holland, but for the three of us, Mum has always been and will always be the parent we adore.

And so it started to become a little ridiculous that everyone else in my family saw my father, albeit sporadically, and I didn't.

Des Kelly was giving me counsel. He said, 'One day you won't have a choice about meeting him, Carol. One day it will be too late. Don't look back and regret it.'

In a sense, I didn't mind if I never met my father, but then I realised that it was my own children who were perhaps missing a piece of their jigsaw puzzle, although Katie and Cameron loved my mother completely.

My father was by now an elderly man. He had mellowed over the years, so too had I. At the age of 40, I didn't harbour any bitterness. I simply hadn't thought about him much or wondered what he was like, for quite some time I had just got on with life. Now it was time to put the past aside. It was a big decision and I hoped it would be the right one. My anger towards him had left me years before. I asked Trixie to talk to Karen to arrange a get-together and a few months later we were all ready to meet up at Karen's house in Bedford.

Trixie and I travelled to Bedford together. I was a bit nervous and it made me quite giggly. I was laughing with nerves throughout the journey. I said to Trixie, 'This is a little odd, isn't it? Going to meet your father for the first time when you are in your 40s.' I tried to think what on earth I would say to him, but my mind was blank.

I don't know what I was expecting at our first meeting. Perhaps a strong man, like the figure who had stared back at me from that one black and white photograph I had seen as a child. I somehow hadn't banked on him being frail.

When Karen welcomed me, I stepped into the front room and there he was. I found myself staring into eyes which were exactly the same as mine. I was so like him that it actually took my breath away. His dark eyes and high cheekbones and the shape of his face made me feel as if I was looking in a mirror. He reminded me of the actor Dirk Bogarde.

Once that second of shock had passed, I stepped forward and said simply, 'Hello, Dad,' and with that I put my arms out to my father for the first time. He burst into tears and I put my arms around him and comforted him, as if it was the most natural thing in the world to do. Trixie and Karen were also in tears, overcome by the moment. I could say that I sobbed and that the moment our eyes met, I understood everything, but that would be a lie. I didn't cry. I didn't even need to hold back the tears. It really was too late for all that.

We sat down and, over a cup of tea, we began to chat. I was entranced by his eyes. They danced with mischief. He told amusing stories in his Dutch accent and laughed out loud, and with a pang I realised that he reminded me, in some ways, of Gabriel.

I suddenly saw how my quiet and determined mother had fallen for two similarly charming men. The appeal that my father must have had as a young man was evident. Several hours passed quickly and there was none of the awkwardness or regret that I had feared.

He didn't say sorry for all the lost years and the lost love, but he didn't have to. I felt the most tremendous relief that I had met him at last, before it was too late.

Tony didn't ask about my childhood and I didn't mention it. Instead, he said that he watched *Countdown* and that he was incredibly proud of me. In turn, I told him about the two grandchildren he had never met, Katie and Cameron, and said time and time again how proud I was of them.

When the time came to leave, I hugged him once more. There was no sudden love, no special empathy, but there was a genuine warmth. The only regret I had, as we drove away, was for the wasted years. It had been 15 years since I had invited him to my first wedding and he had refused to come. All that time that we could have got to know each other, and shared so many moments.

Several months later, Karen organised a big party at her house for all the generations of the family. It would be the first time that all the Vordermans would be together. Katie and Cameron would finally meet their granddad.

My children were pleased and he greeted them with genuine delight. This was a full-scale family

258

party. Karen had two children at that time and Alberdina had three; Trixie's two sons were there and my two children, so his nine grandchildren were all together for the first time.

But what made the day even more extraordinary was the fact that Mum came along too. I wouldn't have gone without her. With three generations of one family together under one roof, Mum and my father automatically slipped into the roles of grandparents. They sat together with ease and laughed and talked. I almost had to do a double-take.

This was a couple who had been wrenched apart by his adultery and separated through decades of bitter silence. To see them together, at their first ever family occasion as if nothing had ever happened, was quite bizarre.

If circumstances had been different, they might have stayed together. But nurture shapes you just as much as nature and so I would have been a different person. The fear which had kept pushing me on through my childhood and my adult life may well have been lacking. My father's rejection had, peculiarly, driven me to find success somehow or other.

And yet now he was sitting easily beside my mother, a contented older pair. And that was all down to the gentle and totally forgiving nature of my extraordinary mother, Jean.

After this, I met up with my father again. We chatted, but not once did we have a deep, meaningful conversation. As a father to us, he had behaved atrociously, but that was left unsaid. To remind him of it would have served no purpose now that he was older. We had a couple of lovely meals where he was surrounded by his four daughters at a local pub. He teased a lot and was great company. But, although I didn't realise it, our brief time together was already running out.

It brought back the feelings I had for Gabriel who, as far as I was concerned, was still 'my Dad' and always will be. I had missed Gabriel from the moment we'd stolen away one morning when he had gone to the quarry for a lorryload of stone, back in 1981. I missed his laughter and not knowing what on earth he would get up to next. I even missed his snoring while he pretended to watch the telly in the evenings. He'd had such a huge influence on me.

After Mum left Gabriel that final time, she had wanted a complete break and I believe that he was very upset about it for a long time. But to settle Mum, as she was going through a rough patch, I'd kept away from him for a number of years. After everything had calmed down, I did see him again. Gabriel died on 26 June 1993, 12 years to the day before Richard Whiteley passed away. We all went to his funeral. He was buried in Denbigh in North Wales where he'd made so many people laugh over the years. I miss him now and I wish he could have been part of my telly years—it would have been a riot. I often think of him and, just as when I think of Whiters, it's always with a wide smile.

In 2007 I was invited to take part in the television programme *Who Do You Think You Are?* a series where celebrities are taken back through their family history, with the help of researchers who unearth secrets, and discover something of the lives of their ancestors.

Due to our family separation, we knew so little

about Tony Vorderman's Dutch side of the family and wanted to find out more. So, with the encouragement of Mum, we (as this was very much an adventure for Trixie and Anton as well) went ahead with the programme.

At first, we delved into the Welsh side of my family, my mother's side. My mother had been born on a farm, which had been a bishop's palace centuries before, and was from a long line of farmers. Our great-grandfather, Daniel Davies, was a self-made man. Starting from very humble beginnings, he became a butcher and slaughterer in Prestatyn and exported stock to Liverpool by sea for sale in the markets there. He was a great character and very well known locally. It was Daniel Davies who bought four houses in Palmeira Gardens, including the one where I grew up. He left one to each of his surviving children when he died, which is why I had so many cousins living so closely, decades later.

We learned a great deal about his strength of character. In 1890 his beloved wife died of TB shortly after giving birth to their fifth child, Arthur Llewelyn. The baby died of the same illness just a few days later and Daniel buried both his wife and son within a painfully short space of time. When he died years later, he was buried with them. We were able to find his grave and have since restored the stone.

The TV production company then arranged for Trixie, Anton and me to fly to Holland. Our father was too frail to travel, at the age of 86.

The first extraordinary discovery was that my great-grandfather, Adolphe Vorderman, had been the inspector general and chief medical officer of the Dutch East Indies in the late 1800s. A scientist and a doctor, he had been the first medic on the scene when the volcano erupted at Krakatoa in 1883. The eruption had been so powerful that the island had been virtually destroyed. As well as tending to the wounded, he also taught them how to make presses for their burns from what nature had provided.

At that time, beriberi, a medical condition which caused muscle-wasting, paralysis and ultimately heart failure, was killing millions of people in the Far East, but no-one knew if this was because it was contagious or whether there was some other cause. All signs pointed to contagion, as beriberi occurred in clusters. Certain regiments of Dutch soldiers or inmates at particular prisons would get it, but others in different regiments or prisons wouldn't be affected at all.

After meeting with Dutch scientist Christiaan Eijkman, Adolphe conducted an extensive and scrupulous scientific study, which he published. He discovered for the first time that people who ate brown rice didn't fall victim to the disease, whereas those who ate polished rice (white rice) suffered from the condition. In the days before scientists knew about vitamins, he concluded that something which existed in brown rice was missing from white rice and this resulted often in beriberi. Today, we know the vitamin B1 is found in the husks of unpolished rice and prevents the fatal disease.

Adolphe died in 1905, but his evidence led directly to the first research into vitamins and although his work eventually saved millions of lives, it was Christiaan Eijkman who was awarded the Nobel Prize for medicine for his work on beriberi in 1929. The prize was shared with Sir Frederick Hopkins, the great British scientist who officially 'discovered' vitamins.

On the TV programme, the director of the Eijkman Institute in Holland said that my great-grandfather would also have shared the prize, but that Nobel Prizes are not awarded post-humously. It was incredible to have found so much out about a man who was the person I would have wanted to be, in another time. He was my great-grandfather and I had known so little about him before.

But what of our more immediate bloodline?

For the first time outside the UK, we met other Vordermans: our cousin Peter and his wife Yvonne. Peter is the son of Dolf, one of my father's brothers. He told us that during the war, Dolf had been captured and locked up in a camp by the Nazis. Our father, as cheeky as ever, had written a letter to the commandant of the camp, pleading that their father had died and that Dolf needed to come home for the funeral. Their father hadn't died, of course. Tony said that Dolf would be returned as soon as the funeral was over. Astonishingly, he was released and went immediately into hiding, never to return to the Nazi camp.

And what of Tony in his earlier days?

We were now reconciled, but Tony Vorderman refused to talk about his time during the war to anyone. None of his five children actually knew what had happened before he turned up in North Wales just after the war, a somewhat mysterious figure. And so the researchers turned their attention to my father. We knew that he had been involved with the Dutch Resistance movement as a

263

young man, but beyond that, we didn't have a clue about what he had done or how he had managed it.

Old newspaper records were dug up and surviving members of the Dutch Resistance were tracked down. Over the few days that we were there, the true story of my father's youth began to emerge.

At the start of the war, Tony Vorderman had joined the Dutch army. But Holland had fallen within days and the German army tore through the country. At the time, Tony lived in an area which was close to the German border and the German industrial heartland, near to the River Maas.

He joined the Dutch Resistance as a 'radio man' at a time when the Nazis had outlawed owning radios, a ban that was brutally enforced. That particular group of the resistance movement would illegally tune into the BBC World Service station, to get news reports of how the war was progressing. They would then print counter-propaganda news pamphlets and distribute them throughout the neighbourhood.

This was truthful information at a time when the Nazis were telling a wholly different story. But it came at a huge cost. Any resistance worker found with leaflets or with one of the few radios which could receive the World Service would be shot immediately.

My father, it seemed, had his own brushes with death. The researchers introduced Anton, Trixie and me to an elderly Dutch lady who told us how Tony had been listening to World Service radio reports in the back of her house when Nazi troops had burst in through the front door.

Tony escaped back and fled into the streets,

finally finding a safe house in which to hide. If he had hesitated for just a couple of seconds, he would have been captured and shot, but this close shave wasn't enough to deter him from his job.

Towards the end of the war, English and American soldiers had captured the land on the other side of the River Maas. The German side was fortified with watch towers and land mines, to stop anyone from attempting to cross. On 19 December 1944 the Germans learned about the printing press, perhaps from a local quisling. A whole group of resistance workers fled, including Tony, or Tonny, as he was known to his Dutch friends.

Their only chance of escape was to cross the river. Thirteen men, including the very young Tony, reached the bank under cover of darkness. A canoe lay bobbing on the water and some of them jumped in it and began to paddle. Just then, Tony stepped back—and triggered off a landmine. It exploded, causing him injuries down one arm and alerting the German guards.

Their flashlights started searching the water and two of the men in the boat were machine-gunned to death. One escaped to freedom and the rest, including my father, ran back for cover to safe houses, where they remained until the end of the war months later.

While we were filming in 2007, we didn't discover the whole story at once. We learned first that our father had been in the resistance. Then, on a gloriously sunny day, we all went for lunch before filming started again to hear the second part of our father's tale.

It was a wonderful day and our moods were all

as sunny as the weather. Then, as we ate, Trixie's mobile phone rang. Almost immediately, we could see that something was wrong. It was a call from our half-sister Alberdina, to say that our father had collapsed at home after he'd returned from a walk and rushed to hospital. Alberdina said she'd let us know the report from the hospital later in the day.

We carried on filming that afternoon on the banks of the River Maas and it was there that we were shown a police report which told of the horrific events which unfolded that night. To stand in the place where my father, as a young man, had defined his role as a member of the Dutch Resistance was incredibly moving. For all of my life, I had known him only as an absent father, a man who had avoided all his responsibilities to his three eldest children. Now I saw him as somebody different. A young man who had been seconds away from death. A boy who had done his bit during a terrible period in history.

It was while I was digesting this news that Trixie's phone rang once more. Karen and Alberdina had been told that our father's condition was very serious. More than 60 years after he had escaped death at the hands of the Nazis, he was a dying man.

We decided between us that Trixie would go to Bedford on the next flight, which was early the following morning. When she got there, very sadly, she was told that he was not expected to live another day, so the day after his collapse, we cancelled the filming and Anton and I got on the evening flight back to the UK.

We knew that there was nothing we could do for our father, but our half-sisters Karen and

266

Alberdina adored him and we felt that it was our duty to help support them.

We flew back into Luton airport and raced straight to the hospital in Bedford. Tony was unconscious. His five children were sitting around his bed, which felt right.

And while he wasn't always there for us in life, we were all there for him in death. Sitting by his bed, holding his unmoving hand, I saw his wounds from the landmine for the first time. We tried to comfort the girls who were naturally distraught. We said prayers and I read from the Bible.

We stayed for two nights, but I had to return to my children, 200 miles away. Anton and I said a private goodbye before we left. Trixie had to go to London to be with Mum as she was moving house to be with us in Bristol two days later. On the Monday evening, our father died, with his beloved daughters Karen and Alberdina by his side. Days later, I read at his funeral and we had the wake at the pub where we had shared happy times together.

When Tony died, we were a family united. I didn't feel the desperate grief that Karen and Alberdina felt, but I was sorry to see their sorrow and I remembered just how physically painful that can be.

I felt saddened that those final clues to my father's early days had come too late for me to talk to him candidly. We had made our peace at the end of his life, but so much had remained unsaid.

In our brief time together, Tony had said time and time again that he was very proud of me. How ironic that after discovering that he had been so brave during the war, I never had the chance to tell him that I was proud of what he'd done at that time too. I dedicated the *Who do You think You Are?* show to his memory.

I shouldn't have left it so long.


## THE FINAL COUNTDOWN

Perhaps, when I shakily left the church on the day of Richard's funeral, I thought that the worst was over. How wrong I was. Over the next few months, the sense of appalling loss deepened. Grief overwhelmed me and I found myself drowning in its wake.

It was the first time, in a lifetime of coping, that I came close to a breakdown. I found it almost impossible to sleep. Then, in the middle of the night, when I had finally fallen into a fitful slumber, I would wake suddenly and sit bolt upright, covered in sweat and yet shivering with cold.

For the first time in many years, I didn't really care about everyday things. It became an effort just to get up each morning and to get through each day; some days I could act as though life was normal and I was bubbly, but the pretence would leave me exhaused and only highlighted the darkness. If it was like that for me, then for Kathy and Richard's family it must have been a hundred times worse.

Little things set me off. Once, at a supermarket, a lovely lady said sympathetically, 'I am so sorry about what happened to Richard.' Within minutes, I was in floods of tears in the middle of the aisle.

It would take just one trigger—however small, however insignificant—to bring me to my knees. And it was so very public. The only escape was at home, and yet I wanted to escape that too.

People were so, so kind. Not just the people who had known Richard or had worked with us, but wonderful Countdowners who would come over and tell me just how much his death had affected them. It did help. It made things slightly better to see what much he had meant to so many people. I always passed on these comments to Kathy and they made it better for her too.

Of course, many people have lost parents, husbands, wives and—God forbid—children. I understand now how their grief can easily become overwhelming. Mine could not compare to theirs, so why did it hit me so hard?

Well, Richard had been so many things to me over our 23 years together. He had been friend, mentor and companion. He had seen me through two marriages, two divorces and the arrival of two children. Every day of my adult life, if I wasn't with him, I was having conversations about him. He was an ever-present feature in my world. And, quite simply, I loved him.

I read books about bereavement, to try to help myself move on. In those first few weeks, I dreaded going out, because I was only just holding it together. But after many months, I realised that I had to start to function normally for the sake of my family. The children had seen me so sad and I didn't want their lives to be affected by this. As their mother, I owed it to them to force a smile and carry on.

And to carry on meant to face the question of

the very future of *Countdown*.

The bosses at Channel 4 in 2005 were quite wonderful and it was some weeks before they spoke to me about what would be next, giving me time over the summer weeks to steady myself. They were very kind and for that I will always be grateful.

When the future of *Countdown* was raised, Kevin Lygo, the overall controller of the channel, together with Adam Macdonald, the head of daytime programming, asked me outright if I would like to take Richard's old job and host the programme.

I said no immediately. I didn't even consider it for one second. I knew that I couldn't sit in Richard's chair and do the job that he had loved. I wouldn't do it. So a question mark was raised over whether the programme would return at all.

I didn't particularly want to go back into the studio where we had shared so much together over the years. The pain of being in our little world without him was palpable. But if I didn't return, there was a strong chance that the channel would simply rest the show indefinitely.

At the time, *Countdown* was the only regular programme being made at the Leeds studio. If I didn't walk back into the studio, there was a grave possibility that dozens of other people would lose their jobs, from the sound men to the props boys and the make-up ladies. Too many livelihoods were at stake for me not to return, no matter how I felt. Not only that, the Countdowners, the many millions of viewers who had loyally been part of our family for decades, would feel let down too.

So I agreed to go back—provided they found a

new host. The search was on, and what a difficult task it was. After Richard's death, many top names put themselves forward to replace him. We just had to find someone with the right personality, who would enter into the unique spirit of the show.

One of the names interested was Des Lynam, who had for many years hosted *Grandstand* and *Match of the Day*. He was a public face, a veteran broadcaster and, crucially, he had a great sense of humour. I had met Des many times over the years and had always got on with him. He was very cheeky and I've always liked that.

I remember saying at the time that I would really like Des to get the job, because I thought that Countdowners would be able to fall in love with him, just as we all had with Richard. I really hoped that would be the case, but, in truth, I was utterly terrified. It could never be the same with Des as it had been with Richard. That came from years of sticking together through thick and thin. We all knew that but when Des got the job there was no question that I would give it my best shot and work as hard as I knew how.

On Des's first day in the studio, Kathy sent him a card and a little pressie, wishing him good luck, which was dignified of her. She is a 'quality bird', as Richard would call Kathy, Christa Ackroyd and myself. His three QBs.

I hadn't appreciated how difficult it would be on the first day of recording and to see someone else in Richard's chair. The sight of Des Lynam sitting there actually took my breath away. I had to force a smile on my face and just go into 'work mode'.

In production meetings, Clare Pizey, who was then in charge, agreed that we should speak about

Richard a lot during the show, to keep his memory going. I wanted some sort of lasting tribute to him too, so we also agreed also that the champion of each series would be given 'Richard's memorial trophy'. The office immediately went searching through websites to find a trophy for us to buy and engrave and suggested one which was medium-sized and tasteful. When I saw a photo of it, I rang and said, 'That's not big enough, not nearly big enough. He'd be very disappointed with that. This is King Dick we are talking about here.' So back on the internet we went and they ordered something more over-the-top and extravagant that we knew Richard would have loved.

As we made our first shows, it became obvious that Des didn't really like the scripted puns which were used to introduce each programme. He didn't find them funny (well, he had a point) and felt uncomfortable saying them. So Clare suggested that I should introduce the celebrities instead, just as Richard used to do.

For the first time in all my years at *Countdown*, I had to wear an earpiece, which I absolutely hated. They wanted me to hear all of Des's instructions, as well as feed me my own, but, frankly, I didn't want to know what was going on in the studio gallery. I didn't want to hear any words being fed to Dictionary Corner (although Susie also got a lot of them herself as she's very clever.) I wanted to concentrate on the contestants and the audience. So I dumped the earpiece after a few weeks.

Nothing felt the same. Just hearing the music again made me physically shake. The old magic, the Richard touch, had gone forever. Nobody's fault, it was just how it was.

Des and I worked hard to get the chemistry between us right and I think we did an okay job of it. After each day of recording, we would sit down together and work out how we could make it better. It took us many weeks to relax and I know that it must have been difficult for Des, stepping into Richard's shoes.

Meanwhile, there were moments which would turn me inside out.

Once, a gentleman from the audience innocently came up and asked me to sign something and when I looked at it I saw it was Richard's photo handout, which he had signed when the man had been a member of our studio audience years before. I burst into tears. I'd counter-signed so many thousands of them before, but his handwriting brought it all back again.

I did feel alone for a long time. Whenever I left my dressing room to start filming, I would pause at the large photograph of Richard and I on the wall in the corridor, kiss my fingers and plant the kiss on his face. It was my little comfort blanket while the grief subsided.

On 10 November 2005, five months after his death, thousands of Richard's friends and Countdowners gathered at York Minster for a memorial service to celebrate his life. Kathy asked some of us to speak. I said that he'd loved nothing better than a big party and that if he'd been here, he would have welcomed everyone one-by-one and would have wanted a photograph taken with every person to remember it by.

Gyles Brandreth described him as 'a love god, but he was the most innocent love god you could imagine. He was like a ray of sunshine and, like sunshine, we all warmed to him.'

His amazing niece Georgina spoke so beautifully of the uncle she'd loved dearly. One of our favourite ever guests in Dictionary Corner, Barry Cryer, wrote a poem, which was perfect. And Rick Wakeman played one of Richard's favourite pieces on the piano exquisitely. As I sat next to Kathy, I could see Matt—Richard's cameraman— up high with his camera, looking down across the congregation, and we were a family again for another day. I went home on the train from York that night and we drank the buffet car dry along with some complete strangers, including a group of young ladies who were going to London for a hen party. I made them promise that they would drink a toast to him on the big day of the wedding. They'd never met him but, bless them, they did have a toast and contacted me to tell me so. It made me so happy.

About a year after his death, when things had settled down and I thought we had stabilized, in August 2006, press reports claimed that the filming of *Countdown* was going to be moved from Leeds to London. I was utterly distraught. This would mean the closure of the studios in Leeds and the loss of all the jobs I had tried so hard to protect in the months after Richard's death.

I was called to emergency meetings with TV bosses. It was said at the time that Des Lynam was tiring of the long commute from his home in the south of England up to Yorkshire. The TV bosses suggested that we should compromise, with half of the programmes being filmed in London and the other half in Leeds.

The crew was horrified, and so was I. In the

274

past, Richard and I would have joined forces to fight such a move. Now I was on my own, and I struggled even more. Petitions were signed and another round of unhappiness ensued.

A month later, in September, Des resigned, saying that he hadn't realised jobs would be lost if such a switch was made. He was quoted as saying: 'I didn't want to be responsible for that disruption ... I've decided that, after a year and a half, that'll do nicely. I'm going to withdraw and save the wear and tear.'

Now I was asked once again if I would take over as the *Countdown* host for the new series, due to start in January 2007. It was a big decision. Should I give up the letters and numbers and host the show I loved? I'm not sure I made the right decision but once again, I said no. I was exhausted and too frightened, so I clung on to what I thought I knew best.

The search for another familiar face was launched and possible hosts were screen-tested. And then along came Des O'Connor, our second Des.

Des particularly enjoyed chatting to the audience beforehand, just like Richard and I had done, he felt the same way about them as we had. He came alive in front of an audience, and we hit it off.

During 2007, with Des in the chair, we settled nicely. The shows were looking good and we were all happy. Ratings were steady at around 1.5 million viewers (*without* the addition of repeated shows or those played an hour later, a trick often used by many today); things were definitely looking up. Then several things

275

happened at once which were to send us crashing.

The first was that as we were building up to our 25th anniversary programme, to be shown on 2 November 2007, Des fell ill. He was unwell for many weeks and during that time we were worried whether or not he would be fit enough to host the anniversary show. I was asked once more if I would host the programme and this time I said yes, as long as it was only for the one special programme, as that would have made sense to our audience, given the circumstances—after all, I had been there since 1982 and this was our Silver anniversary. So the plans were put into place. But, thankfully, and I was very relieved, Des recovered just enough to record the show.

But his illness coincided with several changes in the top management at Channel 4, most particularly the departure to ITV of the inspirational head of daytime, Adam Macdonald, who had commissioned three huge hits—*Deal or No Deal, Come Dine With Me* and *The New Paul O'Grady Show*—during his time at Channel 4. In September 2007, his deputy, Helen Warner, a woman I had helped in the past and regarded as a friend, took over the position. There was also a new executive producer on the programme when Clare Pizey left to go to a bigger job at the BBC. They had no history with the show.

It was decreed that we had to film around 80 shows very speedily to make up for lost time. I felt it was an appalling decision and I was quite vocal about it, but was overruled. These very long days of non-stop filming were draining. I had been on *Countdown* since it began and knew its natural ebb and flow. I was struggling myself and Des was still recovering. If an error was made or the show was generally under par and not thought through, we just had to keep ploughing on. All production meetings were cancelled, so we went into studio 'blind'. *Countdown*, in my view, was now in freefall as it had never been before.

My confidence in how *Countdown* was progressing was very low and the production team told me they felt the same way, but the show still meant as much to me as it always had. It was Febuary 2008 and I knew the time for renewing my contract was approaching. But as spring drew nearer, we hadn't heard a word. There were no reassurances about *Countdown*'s future.

Just as we were wondering what was going to happen next, we suddenly found ourselves in the thick of negotiating a contract. We were told that, due to the recession, production budgets had to be slashed by a third. I completely understood the position and, without any hesitation, I told John Miles that I would offer to cut my salary by a third to be exactly in line with the budget. In private, we were prepared to cut it by half, because I couldn't imagine not making *Countdown* and I had a feeling that the future of the Leeds studio was in question too, which worried me immensely, just as it had after Richard's death, and also when the move to London had been considered a year earlier.

Filming continued as the negotiations were going on. I had an uneasy sense that things may not be quite right and this anxiety started to make an impact on me physically.

One night, stressed, I woke to find that I couldn't move. The whole of my right side had gone completely numb, the same sensation I had felt years before. My skin was cold and I couldn't raise my arm. I thought that, this time, I really had suffered a stroke.

I couldn't get out of bed. I kept thinking, 'I'm on my own with the children. They depend on me. What am I going to do?' I couldn't move until the morning, when I remained numb but had regained some movement down one side. I rang the doctor straight away. He ordered me to go to the hospital and there they ran a whole battery of tests, including an MRI scan.

It was utterly terrifying, but in the end the doctors determined that I hadn't suffered a stroke. It was simply an extreme physical reaction to all the stress.

It is worth explaining here the workings of the TV industry and why the negotiation wasn't straightforward. Very few programmes aired on Channel 4 are made by the channel itself; most are commissioned from independent production companies and bought as a package by the channel.

In the case of *Countdown*, the production company who owned the licence was ITV Productions. So, put simply, Channel 4 would give ITV Productions a budget to make *Countdown* and anything left over after costs would be taken as profit by ITV. So when John did the negotiations for my contract, it was actually with ITV Productions. Historically, negotiations had always been really straightforward.

The channel confirmed that they wanted me for another two years. Over the years I'd had numerous opportunities to defect to other channels, but I had always remained completely loyal to *Countdown* and I wanted to stay, in spite of the problems.

So we went back to the studio while everything was up in the air, not expecting the shock that was to come within days.

We were recording five shows a day at the time and on the first day in the studio, a Wednesday, I had come up to Leeds, unpacked my suitcase, chatted to my friends in make-up and went into the studio with Des. After the first two shows had been recorded, I went into my dressing room for a cup of tea. The phone rang. It was John Miles. The first thing he said was, 'It's not good.'

Then he said, 'They want you to take a 90 per cent pay cut, and you have until noon on Friday to take it or leave it. I told them that we would cut by a third, in line with the overall budget, but they say 90 per cent or leave.'

For a few seconds, everything just swam around me. Then I felt physically sick. There was only one thing that this ultimatum would mean: I would be out. My instant reaction was that this was not just about the money. I immediately felt that all they wanted to do was to get me out of the show. In my mind, they knew that there was simply no way I would accept a 90 per cent reduction in my salary—I felt this was power-play and nothing more.

Also, they knew what it would mean to me, they knew I'd grieved for Richard, they knew that I was in the middle of recording programmes and that I would have to carry on in the studio for the next two days while I was still reeling. To my mind, there was no need to create that deadline, no need to have the conversation this particular week and certainly no need to do it while I was in the studio. Surely it could have waited a week until we broke for the summer?

I was alone in my dressing room, knowing that back outside in the studio, the crew would not have a clue what was going on. I was in shock. If Whiters had been there, this would have been so very different.

I stood up and, almost robotically, walked back into the studio. The lights were on, the audience was sitting and chatting in pleasant anticipation and they turned and smiled when they saw me.

My heart was thudding so loudly that I was convinced they would hear it. I forced a smile on my face, but I felt like running from the building as fast as I could. I just knew that I had to survive this show, then another two in the evening, and within six hours this awful day would be over.

Thoughts of Richard swam in my head; all the fun we shared together and the hurt of his death. It took all my effort and strength just to pull the letters out and attempt some sums. All the time, my mind was racing, churning over the facts.

I deliberately tried not to catch the eye of any of my friends: the cameramen, the props boys, 'Lady' Pamela Fox and Martin in make-up.

It had become something I loved, part of me. Countdowners had shared my mistakes, my triumphs, my pregnancies and any muck-ups that I'd made along the way. Together, we had all laughed with Richard and then grieved for him. And none of those faces smiling at me that day knew what was going on behind the scenes.

I did my job that day, and nothing more. I felt exhausted and tearful and I wanted to escape back to my hotel room. It must have shown, because after recording the first part of the programme immediately after the fateful phone call, one of the crew came up and asked me if everything was okay. I forced a bright smile on my face. 'It's fine, everything is fine,' I lied.

I couldn't understand why the ultimatum had to be delivered right in the middle of filming. We had 15 shows to record from the Wednesday to the Friday. The news had broken when I had made just two programmes, giving me an unlucky 13 still to record.

When we finished filming on that first day, I left immediately. I went straight back to my hotel room and shut the door. I longed to be with the children, to hear Katie's laughter and see Cameron's lovely smile and talk to Mum, the woman who'd applied for the job on my behalf 26 years before. It was impossible to tell Mum though, as I knew how upset and stressed it would make her. So instead, I sat alone, feeling sick with everything that had happened that day. I couldn't sleep. When I arrived for work the next morning, I had to force a smile back on my face and carry on as if nothing had happened.

We were still recording programmes when, on the Friday morning, I spoke to Helen Warner, the new head of daytime at Channel 4. She was being told that if *Countdown* could survive without Richard, it could survive without me. I was appalled that they could seem so utterly cynical about Richard. There would have been no *Countdown* at all had it not been for Whiters. It would have been killed off years before and consigned to the TV dustbin.

*Countdown* had become one of the longest-running programmes in the world. And with me, Richard had nurtured it and protected it for the 23 years he was on it.

John managed to speak to one of the big bosses at Channel 4, who was on holiday at the time, who assured him to 'take no notice. They're taking the p***. Tell Carol I definitely want her on *Countdown* in the future, so not to worry.' Even within the channel, there were conflicting messages.

When the deadline of Friday noon came, John refused to give our answer. John spoke to the person he was negotiating with and said, 'Well, if *your* boss said to you that you'd done a fantastic job for the last 26 years and he wanted you to continue for another two years, but was cutting your wage by 90 per cent, what would you say to him? And that's what we are saying to you.' So it wasn't an answer.

I was still recording in the studio. I knew that my time on *Countdown* was soon to end, but it took another week of turbulence before the final blow was delivered. Another week of phone calls and new deadlines.

Then, on Wednesday, 23 July 2008, Des announced that he was going to leave the show. I felt they had allowed him to leave with dignity, but not me.

On Friday, 25 July 2008, John spoke to ITV for the final time and we knew that it was all over. John and I agreed that we should issue a statement. But I didn't want the *Countdown* crew to find out from a news broadcast, so before we issued our statement, at about 5 p.m. on Friday afternoon, I went into the garden in the sunshine and wrote a text to all my friends on *Countdown*. It said, 'Vorders here. This is a really hard text to write, but I wanted to tell you before I tell anyone at the channel or at ITV, as you are far more important to me than they are. In an hour, I'm going to announce that I'm going to leave *Countdown* and I want to thank you with all my heart for everything, all the joy we've shared and the years of messing around with our lovely studio audience. We've laughed more in our little *Countdown* world than most ever will in a lifetime. And I can't thank you enough for all your kindness when our Richard left us. You know how much I love you and the highest regard I hold for you. I'm heartbroken. Please forgive me.'

John issued a brief statement and within seconds the phone lines were lit up like Christmas trees, it was running as breaking news on Sky and the other news channels and every news crew known to man was after the story. I hated it all. I was a wreck and felt like I had no fight left in me. Not even anger at the way that I had been treated could take over. I was saying goodbye to Richard all over again, saying goodbye to something I loved, and I was broken.

I could have coped eventually with leaving a show I loved if I, like Des, had been able to depart with dignity. If I'd had the chance to say goodbye on good terms. If ITV Productions had simply said that they could no longer afford me, much as they would love to keep me. However, within an hour, the rumours had started circulating. It was even being said that I had demanded a *pay rise* of half a million pounds. As if. On Saturday morning that story was printed in the national newspapers.

I couldn't let those unfounded rumours gain momentum, so I had no option but to give my story to a major newspaper. By Sunday morning, we were front page again. This time in the *News of the World*, where I set out what had really happened. I genuinely hadn't wanted to do this, but felt like I had been pushed into a corner—it was all so unnecessary. All I had wanted to do was to walk away with my head held high and with good memories, but it all turned bad and I had to defend myself.

Again, the phone lines went into meltdown in the *Countdown* office and thousands of letters and polls and support of all kinds flooded in from viewers who were disgusted by what had happened. Channel 4 cancelled the transmission of the programme for four weeks and my own phone was red hot with text messages and emails, all saying the same thing.

*Countdown* transmissions started again in late August, completely unannounced, and as most viewers thought I'd already left, the ratings plummeted to below 1 million viewers, in seeming protest. It took months for them to grow again, as slowly it dawned on us all that the game was not yet over. How I wish it had been. The thought of going back in and making another 60 *Countdowns* was awful.

I headed back to the studio with a truly heavy heart. Most of the crew were terribly upset and we were all dreading the final goodbye. Those last few months of filming were like a long, lingering farewell, painful and drawn out.

Only once, in all that time, did I actually lose my

composure. And that was when I just couldn't get my numbers right. I was so frustrated with myself and so upset with everything that was happening that I just ended up in floods of tears. The lovely floor manager, Lisa, came over immediately and put her arms around me.

The entire crew did everything they could to make those weeks easier. The girls from the canteen, Lorraine and Jackie, left bowls of lovely things to eat in my dressing room. Other people left little cards and messages. But the silliness with the powers that be continued for a long time. I won't bore you with the details.

I tried to be dignified for my last ever show, so I rang up the specific people involved in the saga, even though by now we weren't on speaking terms, and invited them. Someone had to be a grown-up.

A week later, we were back in the studio to record my last *Countdown*, which would transmit on 12 December 2008. I was absolutely dreading it. I knew that it would be so hard to film. As I was putting up the letters for the conundrum, I saw some of the crew start crying. I glanced at the board and the conundrum which was the nine letter word 'CASSEROLE' jumbled up to read: 'ERA CLOSES'. I remember thinking, 'Don't look, Carol, don't look.' The last thing I wanted to do was to break down in tears myself, but I did.

After recording the last *Countdown*, it had been arranged for us to film a special tribute show. This I was really dreading. I asked for all my favourite viewers to be in the audience, the Countdowners who had been with the show through thick and thin over the years. I wanted Gyles Brandreth to host it for two very simple reasons: he is cheeky and he was one of the first celebrities ever to appear in Dictionary Corner and has been there more often than anybody else.

My mum came up and told her story and Katie and Cameron were there as they, of course, had both appeared on the show for many months during my pregnancies. They wanted to take care of their mum. Cathy Hytner, our first hostess, was there too, along with Richard's Kathy. It was her first time in the studio since Richard had died and even though it was hard for her, she did it to show her support, and it meant a lot to me. We relived some of the moments and I would have enjoyed it had the circumstances been different.

Immediately after the recording there was a drinks reception in the bar, where we'd all shared so many good times in the past, and speeches were made by all and sundry. They were all lovely except one: where I was thanked for sowing the seeds of what would *become* a great programme. I couldn't believe what I was hearing.

I'd been asked many weeks before what I'd like as a present and I'd said a great big party in a good restaurant for me and the crew. So that's what I got and we had a cracking night. I wanted to say goodbye to the people I'd known and loved and to have the chance to laugh with them one last time. And I did.

For my leaving present, they bought me a silver friendship bracelet, which I often wear. Somehow, during that night of partying, where we swapped our raucous Richard stories and shared our favourite *Countdown* moments, I started laughing once again.

Everyone was there, including my Prince of

Numbers, Michael Wylie, the contestant from our first series in 1982 who had eventually become a producer and who had been asked to leave the programme himself a year earlier.

Our lovely Michael had stopped calling me a "Welsh witch" by this time (mind you, it had taken 25 years for this to come to pass) and I actually have a text from him sent during 2008 where he calls me 'an angel'. I'm keeping that one for posterity. He hadn't wanted to come back to the building, as he hadn't been able to say goodbye properly, so I'd had to bully him into coming to my last programme and I'm so glad that he did. A matter of days after the party, in November 2008, Michael Wylie had a heart attack and died.

His funeral was held two days before my last *Countdown* was aired on 12 December 2008. It got ratings of over two million viewers. No-one called from the channel or the production company. I guess they wanted it to go unnoticed, but my friends in the press helped me out.

When I was told that a new series of *Countdown* was to be recorded, I sent flowers and cards to both Jeff Stelling, the new host, and Rachel Riley and wished them well for the future. After all, the furore had had absolutely nothing to do with them.

People still stop me every day to talk about *Countdown* and they are always tremendously generous with their words, and it's always lovely to chat.

According to a newpaper report, one man was so incensed by my departure that he threw an ice bucket full of water over Helen Warner at a TV bash in January 2009.

A matter of months after I left, in April 2009, it

was announced that *Countdown* would be moving from the Leeds studios where it had been made since 1982 to the Granada studios in Manchester. Just as I had suspected.

I have never been invited back to the *Countdown* studio again.

I was not even invited to the recording of the 5,000th show, in spite of making 4,800 shows myself. I found out that the 5,000th show with Des Lynam as the guest in Dictionary Corner was to be shown by reading about it in the newspapers.

*     *     *

*Countdown* was, and still is, a huge part of my life. I loved it from the first moment I went for my maths test on a Sunday afternoon with the fantastic Yorkshire producer John Meade and I carried on loving it until my 'TV husband' Richard Whiteley died 23 years later.

It's hard to write these things and during the process the tears have flowed again many times. But I've never stopped feeling thankful for what life—and *Countdown* especially—has brought me. I have been so lucky.

## ALL CHANGE

When I first told the children that I was going to be leaving *Countdown*, I didn't know what their reactions would be. In fact, they were both delighted: 'Mum, you won't have to go away anymore. Hooray. Let's bake a cake and have a party.' I was so relieved. The guilt of being a working mum was something which had never gone away. Now it was time to break the cycle.

In the week of the transmission of my final *Countdown* many messages of kindness were sent to my home, including one letter from the then prime minister Gordon Brown and a beautiful handwritten letter from Prince Charles. That seemed like a good start to whatever was to come next.

But the truth was, I didn't know what to do. The previous three years hadn't been easy and I'd already made many changes to our lives.

Richard's death had knocked me sideways. He was only 61 and the shock made me review every aspect of my life. I thought, 'Why am I doing this and why am I living here?' At that time, home for the children, Des and I was a large penthouse on the banks of the River Thames, overlooking the Houses of Parliament. A place of privilege and it was easy to live the celebrity lifestyle. Lunch at the Ivy. Showbiz parties. But the truth was, I didn't really do much of that anyway. It was fun in small doses, but it has never been a motivation for me, which is why I've lived in the North or outside of London for the vast majority of my life, away from that world. It's fantastic in small packages of time, but I'm a home bird at heart.

While we were in London the children were both in good schools they liked, but Katie was about to become a teenager and in central London there were few places for her to safely hang out with her friends. Meanwhile, Cameron was eight and I wanted him to have the freedom of wandering home from school on his own or just play out with his friends freely as he grew older.

With all this in mind, it was in 2006 that I started to think about our options. I knew Bristol quite well, as my agent John Miles lived there and had always loved it. I knew that if I moved out of London it would mean dropping a lot of my television work, but at least I would be doing this for the children and Richard's death had made me realise that time with the people you love is so precious.

So the children and I moved to Bristol in January 2007 and rented a small flat in Clifton. It had a little galley kitchen, one reception room, three tiny bedrooms and the few clothes that weren't in storage sat in two canvas wardrobes from Argos in my cramped bedroom. Inside this small flat, we were happier than we had been for years, as the kids had proper freedom. They were able to walk to school down leafy, safe avenues and have friends round for tea and sleepovers without endless organisation.

Having turned my back on London, I became much more of a mother. In London, I had been there for my children at both ends of the day, many days of the week, but here in Bristol, I could be with them all the time.

But just as we were making a fresh start, life dealt us another blow. In March 2007, Mum was making plans to move to be with us in Bristol and went to hospital for an ultrasound check for a hernia which she believed she'd developed after her ovarian cancer operations. We assumed something relatively minor to be recommended, but it wasn't to be. At the top of the scan, a highly observant medic spotted a tumour on her right kidney. Her second cancer.

It was a terrible shock. We simply hadn't expected it. We knew that the chances of her developing a secondary tumour from her ovarian cancer in this short time were absolutely minimal and this new tumour on her kidney was unrelated. Luckily, the cancer was calculated to be less than 4 cm long, which meant that it was a stage one cancer.

Advice varied from removal of the whole kidney to leaving it and monitoring its growth, as Mum was almost 79 by then. I was adamant that she shouldn't just leave it and I wanted her to have the less invasive keyhole surgery. Trixie and I had been Googling treatments and found that the difference in recovery time between the two treatment options was huge, particularly for older patients. Obviously, we were worried sick about her and wanted the best treatment possible.

In the end, she had the keyhole surgery in London. She needed one quarter of her right kidney removed, which is a much more difficult operation than the removal of a whole one apparently, but it meant that her kidneys could then function more efficiently if the operation was successful. Her surgeon was Mr David Hrouda at the Charing Cross Hospital and Trixie, Anton and I watched over her like hawks, just as we had before. She stayed in hospital for about a week and recovered incredibly quickly. It was such a relief for her, and for us too. The children were old enough to realise what was going on and their concern for Nana was palpable. After all, they'd been with her almost every day of their lives.

And so she now has a nickname. After having

two cancers and various bits taken away, she's now known as 'the incredible shrinking woman'. I managed to buy Mum a flat in the same block as us and she was able to move down to Bristol in early July 2007, the day after our father Tony Vorderman died in hospital in Bedford.

Living between two flats, upstairs and downstairs, it was not unusual to have seven teenage bodies crammed into our tiny lounge, with Cameron and his friends racing up and down the stairs between the apartments. It felt liberating and the happiness echoed that of Prestatyn, where I had lived as a child. Nothing makes Mum happier than being surrounded by her children and grand-children. Some of Katie's friends call her Nana now too. It's lovely to see her so full of life and she deserves it, after everything she's done for all of us.

Bristol has become a proper home, just as Leeds had been 25 years earlier. It's a great city; it has everything you could ever want. Nobody who lives here wants to leave and I know why. It's one of Britain's best-kept secrets.

We have many streets of bohemian shops and places to eat, all charging far less than those in central London so in 2007, I decided to drive as little as possible and bought a pair of MBTs and a pink wheelie trolley, said goodbye to a lot of work and walked around the city every day. I must have walked about five miles a day and the weight dropped off me so much that I could actually sit down in my faithful weight-judging 'trying-on trousers' for the first time since I bought them. In Bristol, the weight fell off. I was skipping with that much happiness.

I was so lucky to have a life with many

highlights, one of which was a trip with the Red Arrows.

Kathy and I met the Red Arrows and their wives and partners in 2006 after we'd staggered around the Great North Run in Newcastle in honour of Whiters, wearing some of his less tasteful jackets, to raise money for Marie Curie Cancer Care. We were physical wrecks, dressed in tangerine, with rained-on hair and wearing glasses without lenses, when the red-overalled boys took pity on us and bought us a drink.

They became good friends and we have helped various charity events together since then. People to be proud of. For one piece of work, I went up in a famous red Hawk jet with Red Leader, Jas Hawker, for a little spin. I screamed and laughed my way round one of the greatest experiences ever. We were followed very closely (about 8 feet behind), going at over 400 mph in a loop the loop, by a second Arrow. Then out of the loop the loop into the barrel rolls and all the time I'm screaming 'Jas, he's still there' as I looked out of the window and felt as though I could touch the Arrow at our wingtip. Unbelievable. As we flew over Leads Bradford airport Jas gave his identifying call sign to air traffic control.

'Red One, this is Red One.' It doesn't get cooler than that.

Fantabutastic. And I have relived the thrill a thousand times telling friends and audiences about it!!

In 2007, seven years after I'd gone to Buckingham Palace to get my MBE, I received a wonderful letter inviting me back, this time to a private lunch with the Queen and Prince Philip.

What a complete honour! Even though she wasn't coming with me, Mum was bursting with pride.

This time I thought I'd better get the outfit right and take a handbag and not my rucksack, so I chose a pretty tea dress. The children were very excited. Cameron was ten and had been saving up his pocket money. His favourite shop is Argos—or 'Our Goss', as he calls it—and, unknown to me, he bought me a special present for the event: a beautiful 'diamond' on a thin chain. I put it on and it complemented the dress perfectly.

The day was wonderful. There was a private reception for the dozen or so guests before lunch and then we all sat around a huge, polished table and were served delicious courses by liveried footmen. After a lively lunch, everyone gathered once again in the outer room for about an hour to talk some more. The Queen and Prince Philip were fantastic; they flirted with and teased each other endlessly. Prince Phillip said, 'I don't understand why she watches horses going around in circles,' and she teased him back and giggled. I never thought I'd hear the Queen giggling. It was so touching. At one point, Prince Philip commented on my necklace and said how beautiful it was, so I told him, much to Cameron's delight later that evening, how Cameron had bought the chain and stone for me as a special gift from Argos with his pocket money and how it was my prized possession. Not quite the crown jewels, perhaps, but it is priceless to me.

But the beginning of 2009 was a time for change again. After *Countdown* was well and truly over at the end of 2008, I was exhausted and low and trying to keep on smiling, so things seemed normal to the outside world. But, inside I was quite broken. There were many days when I wanted to wander off into another life entirely. I needed a year off, but I couldn't allow myself to take it. Vacuums aren't a natural state and the great hole that *Countdown* had filled for me, with not only work but spirit too, had become an empty chasm. I needed something else to fill it.

I had plenty of new TV offers from many old friends, especially to do game shows, but I didn't want to take on something as a knee-jerk reaction, as a kind of 'see, I can still be on the telly' statement to the world. And I felt so battered, I wasn't even sure that I wanted to be on the telly much.

I did know one thing without any doubt at all, and that was that I wanted to be with the children more. So I made the very conscious decision to just appear as a guest on other people's TV shows and only present the Pride of Britain Awards. It turned out to be the right thing to do.

I had a great time on lots of the panel shows: *Never Mind the Buzzcocks*, *8 Out of 10 Cats*, *The One Show*. One of the funniest times was making a *Celebrity Apprentice* programme for Comic Relief.

We were split into a boys' team and a girls' team. We had Fiona Philips, Michelle Mone (the uber boss of Ultimo Bra Company), Ruby Wax and Patsy Palmer and I. It was about four days of intense work. The boys' team was made up of Alan Carr, Jonathan Ross, Gok Wan, Jack Dee and Gerald Ratner (the official businessman of the bunch). Jonathan was right in the middle of his Andrew Sachsgate affair and so the paparazzi were out in force, but not to see the girls, which was just as well, as Ruby and I ended up clad in Velcro-covered leotards most of the time, not looking our best.

We had to design a toy and then present it to a room full of toy industry people, as well as friends and family. After a few days everyone was getting very tired (oh poor, poor showbiz types, eh?) and tempers had started to fray. We came up with a concept of two Velcro suits, one with the smooth Velcro on it and one with the hooks. So every time one player touched the other, they were stuck together in that position. We called our genius creation Stick Stuck.

The suits were the best fun ever. Ruby and I will take one secret to our graves, but I can tell you that it involved her kneeling on her hands and knees with me Velcroed to her back, completely stuck and totally unable to move for laughing. It was an interesting experience and 'Suralan'—as he still was in those days before he was uplifted to the heavenly House of Lords—was in full-on grumpy mode, which is what he's best at.

On our final day, one member of our team had an explosion of rage. Let's just say that I've never witnessed anything like it in nearly 30 years of telly. Many there were shocked. I went outside for some air and burst into tears, even though the tirade wasn't aimed at me. It all calmed down, thanks to the efforts of the producers, and eventually the girls' team went on to win the contest. The boys then had to fight it out to see which one of them would be fired. It was Chatty Man Alan, but he carried on smiling anyway.

And so, for the first time in my life, many of my days were free and clear, but the demon inside me that doesn't let me rest meant that something else had to take over—and it did.

Education has been an unerring passion of mine during my adult years. Going to Cambridge University all those years ago from a small comprehensive school and having the very good fortune to be taught by a brilliant maths teacher in my teenage years made an incalculable difference to my life.

Over the years, I have been a school governor, and a trustee of NESTA: together with the President of the Royal Society Lord Martin Rees and Dame Bridget Ogilvie; a wondrous woman, all three of us were under the leadership of Lord Puttnam. I've also published many maths books, been involved in schemes to encourage children, particularly in the areas of maths, science and engineering, worked with institutions of all persuasions in these areas and sung times tables songs endlessly with lots of lovely classes. In recent years, I have been most privileged to receive a number of honorary doctorates from the University of Bath, the University of Cardiff, Leeds Metropolitan University and Bangor University in North Wales, where I went to see maths lectures as a child. And when I sat back and thought about what I wanted to do, this passion for education kept raising its head.

It will come as no surprise that I love sums and numbers are my friends. Maths actually gives me one of the greatest buzzes I can get. Quite simply, I adore it—always have and always will.

And so I'd been talking to people since 1999 about how I wanted to set up my own maths school on the internet.

I wanted it to be a fantastic, fun place for children to learn maths. As well as writing books, I'd obviously taught my own children over the years and could see for myself the incredible difference constant practice of simple sums makes. When young children are learning English, they practise it outside the classroom—reading comics, books, web pages and so on—and all the while they are getting more and more fluent with their reading and writing. But, since the advent of calculators, the same can't be said for sums. It just doesn't crop up throughout a normal day in the same manner, which makes it doubly important for a bit of maths, maybe just 15 minutes, to be done nearly every day, but in a fun way. Every child has to know their additions and times tables automatically if they are to go on to do anything more complicated. It isn't rocket science, it isn't difficult to learn, as long as they are taught well and practise. Done in the right way, it becomes an adventure.

So in 2007 I started to build my internet maths school: the Maths Factor. Simon Cowell has his *X Factor*; I have my Maths Factor at *www.themathsfactor.com*.

By 2009, once *Countdown* was out of my life and I had more time, the online maths school was well on track. It was very exciting. I put together a vibrant team of teachers, computer programmers, graphic artists and children, of course, to try it all out on.

I built my own little TV studio to record the video lessons which would teach every pattern, trick and concept in a fun and clear way. I made thousands of teaching videos, including those showing people how to avoid the easy errors.

We have also made exciting, cartoon-style computer maths games, games to print out and play and a million sums, all ordered and categorised properly. We have systems whereby parents can reward the children for the number of lessons they've completed and times tables have been set to videos featuring rap and rock 'n' roll. Always good to have rewards.

And while we were creating this maths school for 4- to 12-year-olds, my confidence was returning. Maybe it was standing in front of an interactive board in my maths TV studio for days and days, which was so like answering the numbers games on *Countdown*. Maybe it was working with a team again. Maybe it was being at home so much more and being able to just walk down to the office once the children had gone to school. Maybe it was my new friends in Bristol, who made me laugh a lot, especially Mandy Prowse, and my lovely right-hand woman Karen 'Babs' Cleverley. But something changed that year. Something happened which made me forget *Countdown* and the hurt.

It took us many months to build the most enormous website, but finally The Maths Factor internet school was launched on 4 March 2010. I was overwhelmed with the support we had from people who said what a difference it was making to their children. Thousands of children who were once struggling seemed to now be excited about sums.

The team who have built the school with me are as committed as I am. Amanda Bell, Jason Woodford and Mark Ralph have slaved over it as much as I have. The results have been tremendous and it lifts my heart. All the time we are growing; we're starting to work with children from deprived areas now.

The great thing is that I have just as much time with my children and my Mum as ever. I don't have to leave them and we all love that.

In August 2008, I was asked by the shadow secretary for education, Michael Gove, to set up a task force to look at maths education in primary and secondary schools. Gordon Brown had also asked me to get involved in this area with the Labour government. I decided to work with Michael instead, not for party political reasons, but because I felt his motivation was for a better education for all.

I found the members of the task force after talking to various people about who they would recommend in maths education. Our compact team is made up of Professor Chris Budd from the University of Bath, an absolutely brilliant and enthusiastic mathematician; Roger Porkess, the man who has, with a small team, turned around the fortunes of A level maths and further maths; Richard Dunne, a highly experienced secondary maths teacher and now a man devoted to teaching the teachers; and Pepe Rahman Hart, the most ebullient headteacher I've ever met. Pepe won the Pride of Britain Teacher of the Year Award in 2008.

On a voluntary basis, we've spent about a year putting the report together. We've visited schools and talked with children, teachers, employers and parents about what they want and don't want.

Before this project was announced to the press,

I met David Cameron, then leader of the opposition, in December 2008 in his private office. He was absolutely charming and obviously intensely interested in, and concerned about, education. It was decided that we should announce the plan in early February 2009 and a huge press conference was called at a school in south London.

That morning, the capital city was thrown into chaos as the snow came down by the bucket load. The event had to be cancelled, as no-one could get to the school, but it was hastily reconvened at the Conservative party headquarters in Millbank, very close to the Houses of Parliament. And so David Cameron and I had a surreal photocall, flinging snowballs at each other in the gardens of Westminster. I found that he was a much better shot than me, which could have been painful, but my coat was quite padded, so there were no bruises from the man who was to become our prime minister a year later.

Life has been busy but strangely, leaving *Countdown* hasn't meant that *Countdown* has left me. Since Richard died, Kathy and I have become very good friends. We chat all the time and have some raucous nights and weekends, in his honour, of course. On 2 November, the anniversary of the first transmission of *Countdown*, I like to take a big wreath to his grave which is made up of 23 white roses, one for each of the years we shared together, and then yellow roses for the years he's been missed. Afterwards, Kathy and I usually throw a bit of a do, which always includes Christa Ackroyd— Richard's three 'quality birds' together again.

One night in Leeds, we had a quick supper together—as if we could ever have anything 'quick'—and seven hours later we poured out of the restaurant, which was about 100 yards from our hotel. It was taking us quite a bit of time to stagger back, giggling and larking around. Suddenly, a young woman appeared in front of us, jabbed me in the chest and said, 'Hey, love, can you and your mates move on—this is my patch.' Yep, we were in the middle of the red-light area and not welcome. We laughed so much, we couldn't walk at all.

In the last few years there have been great holidays, seeing wonderful things. We have larked around in boats, visited the Kennedy Space Centre in Florida, where the first peek of a Saturn V rocket made me cry in awe, and danced fully clothed in the fountains of the Space Centre rocket garden to celebrate.

We've spent quite a bit of time in New York with my good friend Merrill Powell and have tried out some new sports. Even though I broke my wrist ice skating, I do love it. So I've been on the rink in Central Park when it was snowing, and it was magical.

But I still have to remind myself that 'having it all' is not an option. I don't feel in competition with myself anymore. Although, I was chuffed to bits when the best-seller lists for the decade were published at the end of 2009. I was the second best-selling non-fiction female author behind Delia Smith. Who says that maths isn't loved? It made my decade.

Speaking of decades, on 24 December 2010 I will be 50. It's another big milestone in my life. My early 40s were fantastic but my late 40s have not been so great. I suppose, if I've learned anything at all, it's that life is not a dress rehearsal. Time itself is a gift. I want adventures now; they will be my treasures. As a woman who puts a lid on everything and gets on with the next part of life without looking back, writing this book has been a rollercoaster. Sometimes it felt as though I was opening Pandora's box and I wasn't sure I wanted to do it. I've realised the many errors I've made in life, a few of them have been colossal, and I wish I could go back to those times, unpick the moments and do it differently . . . but I can't.

Would I change anything if I had the chance to do it all again? Most definitely: I have done it 'my way', but that wasn't necessarily the best way.

Yet I know without question now, just how lucky I've been.

Lucky to have my family, lucky to have been given the opportunities I've been given, lucky to have shared years with some big characters in my life and oh-so-lucky to be here to tell the tale.

And so, in the manner of a movie, when they tell you what happened next, this is what the main players are doing now.

Katie is 18. She's just taken four A levels in maths, further maths, physics and chemistry and will be going to university.

Cameron is 13 and growing about an inch every six weeks, so I'm in a race to find clothes that don't ride up above his ankles. He makes me laugh out loud every day and he sees his purpose in life as to entertain.

And, importantly, my mother is still by my side. Mum, who is now 82, has been there through it all, no matter what. She has often said to me when we've come back from wonderful events, or when we've just been sitting around at home having a cup of tea, 'My life has been like something from *Arabian Nights*—Carol, thank you.'

No, Mum. Thank *you*. You are the greatest.

# PICTURE CREDITS

All images courtesy of Carol Vorderman.